A GIFT FOR:

_____

COMPLIMENTS OF
BUD'S BEST COOKIES

_____

BILLY GRAHAM

WISDOM
for Each Day

THOMAS NELSON
Since 1798

PREFACE

Christianity is more than a system of beliefs or a series of moral guidelines. Christianity is a relationship—a personal relationship with God through faith in Jesus Christ. When we commit our lives to Him, the barriers are torn down . . . the gap between us is bridged . . . and we become members of God's family forever. We no longer face life alone, for Christ's promise is true: "I am with you always, to the very end of the age" (Matthew 28:20).

But like any other personal relationship, our relationship with God must be nurtured and strengthened. If it isn't, our faith will grow weak and we will become increasingly vulnerable to Satan's deceptions and temptations. Nor will we experience the joy and peace that Christ promised us, even in the midst of life's worst storms.

How do we grow in our relationship with Christ? The most important step we can take is to set aside time each day to be alone with God—reading His Word, meditating on its truth, and coming to Him in prayer. Even a few minutes alone with God will help you keep your priorities straight, and focus your heart and mind on God's love and God's will for your life.

This book isn't a substitute for reading the Bible more extensively—but my prayer is that God will use it to strengthen you and give you the wisdom you need to live for Christ each day.

— BILLY GRAHAM

JANUARY

NEW YEAR, NEW WAYS

"Give careful thought to your ways."
HAGGAI 1:5

Making New Year's resolutions and not keeping them is a universal experience. We may be sincere when we make them, but then we find them too hard to keep, or perhaps we forget all about them.

Let me give you two reasons why it can be good to make resolutions at the beginning of a new year. First, it forces us to look at ourselves—to be honest about our failures and our need to change. Many New Year's resolutions are unrealistic or only wishful thinking, but the exercise of examining ourselves—with God's help—and seeing where we fall short is important.

Second, making a list of resolutions can turn us to God. If we are honest, we know we fall far short of being what we ought to be—and because of that, we need God's forgiveness. We'll also realize that we can't live the way we should in our own strength. We need God's help.

Begin this year by making resolutions—especially the resolution to open your heart and life to Jesus Christ more than you ever have before.

WISDOM FOR TODAY

Open our eyes, Lord, to areas of our lives that need to be refreshed, refined, or redirected. Please give us the strength to make whatever changes will make our lives more pleasing to You.

HOPE FOR THE FUTURE

*If anyone is in Christ, he is a new creation; old things have
passed away; behold, all things have become new.*

2 CORINTHIANS 5:17 NKJV

As we start a new year, the Bible tells us there can be hope for the future.
First, there is hope of a changed person. No matter how hard we try,
we are incapable of ridding ourselves of the selfishness and greed that cause
conflict and strife and war. Our only hope is a changed heart—and Jesus is in the
business of changing hearts.

Second, there is hope of a changed world. When we know Christ, He gives
us by His Spirit a new love and concern for others. We can no longer be indifferent to their sufferings, and we'll want to do something about them. Changed by
Christ, we can begin to change our world.

Third, there is hope of an unchanging eternity in heaven. This world is not
all there is. Someday all its pain and heartache will come to an end for those who
know Christ (Revelation 21:4). Evil and death will be abolished, and we will be
safely in God's presence forever.

As you read the headlines or look at your own life, you may be wondering if
there is any hope. The answer from the Bible is a resounding yes.

WISDOM FOR TODAY

Thank You, Father, for the fresh hope that a new year brings. Because of
Christ, we can experience new birth within ourselves, encourage those hurting around us, and eagerly anticipate the heavenly joys to come.

3

YOUR PURPOSE IN LIFE

Teach me your way, O Lord;
lead me in a straight path.
Psalm 27:11

God has a plan or purpose for every person, although many people go through life without ever thinking about it. But their lack of awareness doesn't change the fact that God put each of us here for a purpose.

We aren't here by accident. We are here because God put us here. And He put us here for a reason: so we could come to know Him in a personal way and then live in a way that brings glory to His name.

This is the greatest discovery you will ever make: you were created to know God and to be His friend forever. When I was young, my mother taught me from our church's catechism that "the chief end [or purpose] of man is to glorify God and enjoy Him forever."

But God not only has a general purpose for each of us; He also has a specific plan for each of our lives. Don't wander through life without any purpose or direction, but pray and seek God's will, and learn to follow Him.

WISDOM FOR TODAY

A life without purpose is an empty existence, Lord, and You didn't create anyone to live that way. Teach us to use the gifts You've placed within us to fulfill Your plan for us and, ultimately, to bring You glory.

REVIVAL BEGINS WITH YOU

"Repent, for the kingdom of heaven is near."

MATTHEW 4:17

If Christianity is important at all, then it is all-important. If it is anything at all, then it is everything. It is either the most vital thing in your life, or it isn't worth bothering with.

So don't give the lie to the Christian faith by professing Christ without possessing Him. Don't lock the church door with the key of inconsistency and keep the lost from coming to Christ. Don't hinder revival by your unbelief and prayerlessness. Don't cheat yourself out of spiritual victory by allowing sin to imprison you. Seek God's face and turn from your wicked ways. Then you will hear from heaven and true revival will begin—starting with you.

The Church holds the key to revival. It is within our grasp. Will we rise to the challenge? Will we dare pay the price? The supply of heaven is adequate for the demands of our spiritually starved world. Will we offer that supply to the hungry masses?

May the revival that the world needs begin in you—starting today.

WISDOM FOR TODAY

Forgive us, Lord, for the times we've been fickle followers of Christ. May we never be the reason someone does not come to You. Please fan into flame the faith within us.

Tending to Our Earthly Tent

We know that if the earthly tent we live in is destroyed, we have a building from God, an eternal house in heaven.

2 Corinthians 5:1

Her uncle had some very bad health habits that would kill him if he didn't stop them. But when she shared her concern, he laughed and said he'd rather enjoy his life, even if it shortened his days. Why, she asked me, would anyone act like this?

I was first struck by his self-centeredness. Deliberately doing something that will cut short his life revealed that he was thinking only about himself, and ignoring all the hurt and sorrow his premature death would bring to his family. Perhaps, I suggested, she could remind him of this—as well as urge him to give his life to Christ.

But his situation got me to thinking: In what ways might we be like him? What health rules are we violating? In what ways are we not taking care of the body God has given us?

Someday each one of us who follows Jesus as our Savior and Lord will leave behind our earthly tent—our flesh-and-bone body—and join Him in heaven for eternity. But until that day—as the Bible says—"Honor God with your body" (1 Corinthians 6:20).

Wisdom for Today

Everything we are is Yours, Father, including these earthly bodies we inhabit. We will honor You by caring for them to the best of our abilities. Please give us the wisdom to make healthy choices in this new year.

VISION, INTEGRITY, PRESENCE

*Do not conform any longer to the pattern of this world, but
be transformed by the renewing of your mind.*

ROMANS 12:2

I n many contexts, VIP means "Very Important Person." But the acronym also offers us a character test.

The *V* stands for VISION, for "where there is no vision, the people perish" (Proverbs 29:18 KJV). Having a vision means seeing what can be done, what ought to be done, and how to get it done. The highest vision we can have is to glorify God by discovering God's will for our lives—and then doing it.

The letter *I* stands for INTEGRITY, meaning that a person is the same on the inside as he or she appears on the outside. There must be no discrepancy between what we say and what we do between our walk and our talk.

The *P* stands for PRESENCE—God's presence in our lives. Without God's help we are doomed. Only in Christ do we find out who we are, why we are here, and where we are going—and only in Him do we find the power to fulfill our God-given vision.

So be steadfast in your commitment to Christ, and be a real VIP—a person with vision, integrity, and God's presence.

WISDOM FOR TODAY

Lord, we have wasted time seeking earthly praise. We choose, now, to be a better steward of our days. We will be busy with things that matter to You, knowing that it may not make sense to those striving for worldly glory.

HOW WILL WE LEARN?

The unfolding of your words gives light;
it gives understanding to the simple.
PSALM 119:130

We know we ought to know more about the Bible—but perhaps you're like many Christians: it's so overwhelming you've never really gotten into it. The first step is to realize what it is: God's "love letter" to you.

From one end to the other it tells of God's love for us—a love so great that He sent His Son into the world to redeem us. You wouldn't ignore a letter from someone who loved you; don't ignore God's love letter either.

Then think of ways you can learn about the Bible from others—gifted teachers on the radio, your pastor's sermons, group Bible studies, even books like this. Some people have a special God-given gift for teaching His Word, and they can help you learn more about it.

Finally, get acquainted with the Bible on your own. Set aside a few quiet minutes and begin reading through one of the Gospels (such as John)—perhaps only a paragraph or two at first. Ask God to help you understand it and to apply it to your life every day.

WISDOM FOR TODAY

Within the pages of Scripture, Lord, is everything we need to navigate the world around us. Thank You for continually calling us back to Your Word so that, within its pages, we are reminded of who we are in Christ.

EYES THAT REFUSE TO SEE

"They have eyes to see but do not see and ears to hear but do not hear, for they are a rebellious people."

EZEKIEL 12:2

The Bible tells us that we have two sets of eyes. We have physical eyes— but we also have spiritual "eyes." With one set we see the physical world around us, while with the other we discern the spiritual truths God has set forth for us in His Word. Tragically, some who are able to see physically do not see spiritually—and spiritual blindness keeps us from knowing God.

Sometimes physical blindness can be prevented or cured. Spiritual blindness, however, is caused by sin—and only the Lord Jesus Christ can cure spiritual blindness because only He can take away our sin.

When we come to Christ, He comes to live within us by His Holy Spirit—and He then opens our spiritual "eyes" to God's truth. This is one reason why the Bible is important, because God uses it to help us discern His truth.

May you turn to God and receive from Him the cure for your spiritual blindness. May He open your eyes to His love so you learn to trust Him no matter what troubles you. And may He guide you as He opens your eyes to His will every day.

WISDOM FOR TODAY

Remove the scales from our eyes, Lord, that we may see You more clearly. Help us to recognize Your presence and to behold the wonderful truths found in Your Word.

GOD'S DESIRE FOR YOU

We . . . are being transformed into [Christ's] likeness with ever-increasing glory.
2 CORINTHIANS 3:18

God can seem near to us when we walk in the woods or are surrounded by the grandeur of a starry night, and that is a wonderful experience. But it shouldn't become a substitute for going to church.

Never forget: God doesn't want us to just feel His presence. He wants to change our lives. He wants to take away our self-centeredness and make us more like Christ. He also wants to teach us His truth and prepare us to become His servants.

How does this happen? How does God change us into the people He wants us to be? Not just by a walk in the woods, as pleasant as that may be. No, God mainly changes us by His Word, the Bible, as we listen to its truth and allow it to shape our lives. That is one reason I urge you to become active in a church where God's Word is taught and lived. You will become more like Christ as you hear and obey His Word.

WISDOM FOR TODAY

Lord, we come to the pages of Scripture not to be entertained but changed. May every moment spent within its pages cause us to be more and more like You.

NEW HEARTS, NEW WORLD

"I will give you a new heart and put a new spirit in you; I will remove
from you your heart of stone and give you a heart of flesh."

EZEKIEL 36:26

Today we have more knowledge than at any other time in history. In seconds our laptops or personal computers can call up information about a topic that would have taken years to collect formerly. Young people graduate from high schools, colleges, and universities with more knowledge than ever before—but they are not always acquiring the wisdom to use it. In spite of their knowledge, they are confused, bewildered, frustrated, and without moral moorings.

Why is there so little peace in a world of unprecedented knowledge and unlimited potential? The problem, Jesus said, is the human heart: "Out of the heart proceed evil thoughts, murders, adulteries." (Matthew 15:19 NKJV). The new world will come about only when Jesus Christ, the King of kings and the Lord of lords, reigns supreme in people's hearts. At the end of the present age God will act, and Scripture promises that He will act dramatically and decisively. But before that time comes, God wants to rule in our hearts.

Is He ruling in yours?

WISDOM FOR TODAY
We were created for Your glory alone, Lord. Let us spend our time and energy building Your kingdom and not kingdoms for ourselves that have no eternal value and are destined to crumble.

WHAT ARE YOU PURSUING?

I denied myself nothing. . . .
Yet when I surveyed all that my hands had done
and what I had toiled to achieve, everything was meaningless.
ECCLESIASTES 2:10–11

King Solomon was convinced he knew how to find happiness—and because he had vast resources at his command, he was able to pursue it. Wealth, fame, pleasure, power, lavish houses, a reputation for wisdom—you name it, King Solomon achieved it. And yet after gaining everything he had ever wanted, he reluctantly concluded that his life was still empty and without meaning. His search for lasting happiness had failed, and his soul was still empty.

Are you in danger of making the same mistake King Solomon made—convinced that the things of this world will bring you happiness and peace, and pursuing them with all your might? Don't be deceived; they never will. And the reason is because you were made to know God.

Later, King Solomon realized this. He should have known it sooner; after all, his father, David, was a man after God's own heart, and Solomon himself had vowed to live according to God's wisdom. Don't be misled (as he was), but make Christ the center and foundation of your life—beginning today.

WISDOM FOR TODAY

The world makes a lot of empty promises concerning happiness—what it looks like and how to obtain it. We will choose the happiness that comes to those who delight in and meditate on God's Word.

TRUE WORSHIP

Come, let us bow down in worship, let us kneel before the Lord our Maker; for
he is our God and we are the people of his pasture, the flock under his care.

PSALM 95:6–7

When was the last time you truly worshiped God? What is worship anyway? Worship in the truest sense takes place only when our full attention is on God—on His glory, His power, His majesty, His love, His compassion. And if we're honest, this doesn't happen very often, because even in church or in our times of quiet devotion, we get distracted and fail to see God as He truly is.

Notice in these verses what prompted the Psalmist's worship. First, he recognized that God was the Lord—the sovereign, all-powerful God of the universe. He recognized, too, that God had made him; he wasn't here by accident but by God's perfect plan. Finally, he worshiped God because God had made him part of His flock, constantly watching over him and providing for his every need.

Learn to shut out the distractions that keep you from truly worshiping God. Then turn your mind and heart to Him every day, praising Him for who He is and thanking Him for His love for you in Christ.

WISDOM FOR TODAY

You are worthy, Father, of the first fruits of our time, energy, and focus. We will commit to giving You all the praise You deserve. Please open our eyes to things that distract us from a sincere and pure devotion to You.

GOD'S LIFE-CHANGING WORD

They asked each other, "Were not our hearts burning within us while
he talked with us on the road and opened the Scriptures to us?"
LUKE 24:32

Can an ancient book that was written by many people over the course of many centuries have anything to say to us today? Is the Bible's message honestly relevant?

Yes, it is—as millions of believers around the world would attest. If anything, in fact, it's more relevant today than ever before, as we see the storm clouds gathering and events taking place that herald the Second Coming of Jesus Christ. As the Bible says, "Our salvation is nearer than when we first believed" (Romans 13:11).

But the Bible is as up-to-date as tomorrow for another reason: it alone answers the deepest questions of the human heart—questions that have not changed over the centuries. Who am I? Why am I here? Where did I come from? Where am I going when I die? How should I live? Only the Bible gives us firm answers to these questions—and the reason is because it is God's Word, given by Him to guide us and point us to Christ. Is the Bible the foundation of your life?

WISDOM FOR TODAY
Father, You speak to our souls in a way only You, the Creator of them, can do. Though the world attempts to woo us with its version of truth, we know only You hold the words of eternal life.

LOVE IN ACTION

"Since God so loved us, we also ought to love one another.
No one has ever seen God; but if we love one another, God
lives in us and his love is made complete in us."

1 JOHN 4:11–12

Jesus said, "All men will know that you are my disciples, if you love one another" (John 13:35). But how do we put that love into action?

Serve one another. The Lord modeled this when He washed His disciples' feet. Be patient with one another. This is possible because of the Spirit's presence in us. Be courteous to one another. Even if someone is difficult or disagreeable, treat them with gentleness and love. Set an example for one another "in speech, in life, in love, in faith and in purity" (1 Timothy 4:12). Forgive one another, because God forgave us. If we do not extend forgiveness, God "will not forgive your sins" (Matthew 6:15).

We are not to judge one another. That is the Lord's job. We may be called to rebuke or reprove in love, but we are not to judge. Be subject one to another. That will mean not always having things our way. Edify one another. We are to encourage and build up our brothers and sisters in Christ. Pray for one another. What a privilege to come before the Lord on another's behalf.

WISDOM FOR TODAY

Lord, help us to love as You love. Create in us hearts that seek to serve others even when it's inconvenient, uncomfortable, or unappreciated. May others who look at us know that we are disciples of Christ.

SEEKING THE TRUTH

While Paul was . . . in Athens . . . he reasoned in the synagogue
with the Jews and the God-fearing Greeks, as well as in the
marketplace day by day with those who happened to be there.
ACTS 17:16–17

When the apostle Paul came to Athens, Greece, he saw people who were like many in our world today: they were trying to put together the puzzle of life.

The average Athenian of that day was a religious person who had numerous gods and followed numerous philosophies in their search for truth.

One group of philosophers, the Epicureans, thought that happiness and pleasure were the goals of life. They sought an absence of pain and a maximum of pleasure.

Another group, the Stoics, believed that the world was governed by reason or logic, and the goal of life was to accept whatever life sent to them.

Those philosophers argued with Paul—but some were serious searchers after truth. And they heard the truth as they listened to Paul tell them about Jesus and the hope we can have because of Him.

Are you searching for the truth? Don't let anything—or anyone—keep you from Jesus, who alone is "the way and the truth and the life" (John 14:6).

WISDOM FOR TODAY
We are so grateful, Lord, that You have chosen to reveal Yourself to us through Your Word. Please place within us an insatiable hunger for Your truth and teachable spirits that continually seek to know You more.

ASK . . . AND RECEIVE

"Ask and it will be given to you; seek and you will find;
knock and the door will be opened to you."

LUKE 11:9

How can you know you'll go to heaven when you die?

Suppose a friend comes by your house and offers you a gift. What would you do? Would you refuse to take it until you had paid him for it? Would you decline it because you felt you weren't worthy of it? No, of course not. Your friend wants you to have it and has already paid for it; all you must do is accept it.

In a far greater way, this is what Jesus Christ did for you. By His death on the cross He paid the price for your salvation—completely and fully. Now He offers it to you as a free gift—and all you have to do is receive it. The Bible says, "The wages of sin is death, but the gift of God is eternal life in Christ Jesus our Lord" (Romans 6:23).

Have you received this gift? You can, by confessing to God your sins and your need of Christ, and then asking Him to come into your life. Salvation is God's free gift; why not receive it today?

WISDOM FOR TODAY

What a price You paid, Father, to bring to us the gift of eternal life! May we never take for granted that precious gift that was paid for with the blood of Christ.

PROBLEMS—AND PEACE

Present your requests to God. And the peace of God, which transcends all understanding, will guard your hearts and your minds in Christ Jesus.
PHILIPPIANS 4:6–7

God doesn't necessarily remove all our problems when we become followers of Christ. But He has promised to be with us and help us and encourage us in the midst of those problems. Jesus' promise to His disciples is still true: "Peace I leave with you; my peace I give you. . . . Do not let your hearts be troubled and do not be afraid" (John 14:27).

How is it possible to experience this kind of peace? It's possible first of all because we are never alone if we know Christ. He loves us and is with us, and nothing we will ever face takes Him by surprise. This peace is also possible because the Holy Spirit gives us patience and joy even in the midst of life's difficulties. And peace is possible because we know our problems are only temporary; someday they will all come to an end.

Which is better: facing life's problems and hurts without God—or facing them with Him? Which are you choosing today?

WISDOM FOR TODAY

When troubles come our way, Lord, we will choose to pray instead of panic. It's comforting to know that, by turning our concerns over to You, we can experience peace in the midst of life's problems.

PUTTING THE PIECES BACK TOGETHER

Though I walk in the midst of trouble,
you preserve my life.
PSALM 138:7

Do you feel as if you've let God down? Let me reassure you that He loves you no matter what you've done. The last thing God wants you to do is to spend your life filled with guilt and shame and remorse.

May that truth give you hope, because it means that God wants to help you. He wants to put back together the pieces of your life and make you whole.

Think about the apostle Peter. After Jesus' arrest, Peter denied three times that he was a follower of Jesus, or that he even knew Him (Matthew 26:69–75). But God forgave Peter, and he went on to help build the early church. He's still ministering to believers today through his New Testament letters.

So if you feel as if you've failed God, ask for His forgiveness—and ask Him also to help you forgive yourself for what you have done. Then commit your future to Him. God will be with you, and you can trust Him to help you.

WISDOM FOR TODAY

Guilt and shame have been the enemy's game from the beginning in the garden, but it is not so with You, Lord. We are grateful that You extend grace, mercy, and restoration to Your children.

WORDS FOR THE CROSSROADS

I will instruct you and teach you in the way you should go;
I will counsel you and watch over you.
PSALM 32:8

Sometimes we face a major crossroad in life, and when we do, we find ourselves wondering what God's will is for the decision we must make. Maybe that's where you are right now.

The most important advice for life's crossroads is this: seek God's will. He knows what's best for you, and He doesn't want you to wander aimlessly through life.

Never forget: God made you, and He knows all about you—including the gifts and abilities He gave you. More than that, He loves you and wants what is best for you. Maybe you've been living for yourself and for the moment rather than for Him and for things eternal. But don't stay on that path; you will only end up at a blank wall if you ignore God's plan for your life.

Ask God to guide you as you make decisions about your future. He may not show you everything at once, but with Christ in your heart, you can face the future with confidence, knowing He will lead you in His perfect way.

WISDOM FOR TODAY

Too often we look to the world for direction and guidance. May we always remember, Lord, that Your will for our lives is found in Your Word. We will seek Your face, study Your Word, and stay on the right path.

GOOD REASON

He had no beauty or majesty to attract us to him,
nothing in his appearance that we should desire him.

ISAIAH 53:2

I t has always been interesting to me that—outside of the hints given in Isaiah 53—the Bible does not tell us what Jesus looked like, nor were paintings or drawings made of Him during His lifetime. Artists throughout the centuries have tried to imagine what He must have looked like, but the truth is, we don't know.

And I believe there is a very good reason for this: God knew that if we had an accurate portrait of Jesus, we would be tempted to worship it instead of worshiping Jesus Himself. We could even lapse into a type of idolatry, and that would be wrong.

But someday we will know what the risen Christ looks like, for someday we will enter into His presence forever. And when we do, the Bible says, "we shall be like him, for we shall see him as he is" (1 John 3:2). Then we will share in His resurrection glory, and we will share in His sinless perfection.

Are you ready for that glorious day? You can be, by committing yourself to Christ and opening your heart and life to Him.

WISDOM FOR TODAY

We long for the day, Father, when we find ourselves face to face with Your glory. Though our finite minds cannot begin to comprehend Your beauty, we live with anticipation of one day being in Your presence.

Choosing the Minority

"If the world hates you, keep in mind that it hated me first."
JOHN 15:18

People often have one of three reactions to the message of the Gospel.

First, some people will deny the Gospel is true. They laugh and scoff and say, "This talk about sin and resurrection is foolish and ridiculous." Pride may prompt this scorn. Others fear what people would think, so they don't give credence to God's truth. Other fears also can keep us from committing our lives to Christ and following Him closely.

Second, some people delay. They say, "I'll think about it and maybe make a commitment to follow Jesus some other time." But it's dangerous to delay making a decision, because you may never hear the Gospel again. Or your attitude toward God may be different, or you may not see another tomorrow.

Third, some people will make a decision for Christ, even though they know that being a believer may place them in a minority. It's tough to be a Christian in our world. We need to be willing to take on Jesus' unpopularity and the scorn that is often heaped on Him.

What is your response to Jesus? Denial . . . delay . . . or decision?

Wisdom for Today

Father, may we not be counted among those who deny or delay. Give us hearts that seek to follow Christ. Fill us with boldness to share the Gospel. Please mold us into the image of Your Son.

PHYSICAL AND SPIRITUAL HEALTH

Physical training is of some value, but godliness has value for all things,
holding promise for both the present life and the life to come.

1 TIMOTHY 4:8

Eating right, exercising regularly, and sleeping adequately—these are some of the components of a physically healthy life. And God wants us to take care of the body He has given us. The Bible says, "Your body is a temple of the Holy Spirit. . . . Therefore honor God with your body" (1 Corinthians 6:19–20).

But we can give too much attention to our bodies and almost worship them by giving them the amount of attention that only God deserves. We can focus on our physical health so much that we ignore the health of our soul.

Has this happened to you? Only you can answer that question, and I hope you will face it honestly. Only God should have first place in your life, for only He is worthy of your worship.

Someday your life will be over, no matter how much attention you give to your health. Will you look back with regret because you nourished your body but starved your soul?

WISDOM FOR TODAY

It's a common error to focus on the urgent at the expense of the eternal; this is true for our health as well. Forgive us, Father, for becoming caught up in the appearance of this temporary flesh and neglecting the state of our souls.

HOPE FOR THE HOPELESS

As a father has compassion on his children,
so the LORD has compassion on those who fear him;
for he knows how we are formed.
PSALM 103:13–14

Discouragement, hopelessness, despair—so many situations in this fallen world can make us feel this way. Problems and struggles can wear us down physically, emotionally, and mentally—and can even erode our faith.

But God, our loving heavenly Father, understands our feelings at times like these, and He wants to encourage and help us. After all, His Son, Jesus Christ, went through the same experiences we do—although without sinning (see Hebrews 4:15). We are never alone when we know Christ, and we can trust Him to lead us and point the way out of our dilemma.

Life sometimes takes us through hard places. But even in the midst of them, God is with us, and nothing can happen to us that is beyond His ability to help.

The Bible says we can "rejoice in our sufferings, because we know that suffering produces perseverance; perseverance, character; and character, hope" (Romans 5:3–4). Being joyful may seem hard to you right now, but put your hope in Christ, and thank Him that He will never abandon you.

WISDOM FOR TODAY

In a world where friends can prove fickle and loved ones sometimes leave, we have a Savior who promises never to forsake us. We are precious to You, Father, and nothing can separate us from the love of Christ.

ONLY . . .

We have only five loaves of bread and two fish.

LUKE 9:13

"We have only . . ." Little did the disciples know what Jesus would do with only five loaves and two fish. The Bible tells us that everyone in the crowd ate—and there were twelve basketfuls of leftovers. And the men alone numbered five thousand.

Perhaps when you give to your church or some other ministry, your thinking is like that of the disciples: "I can give only. . . ." But let me challenge you to do just that! Give what you can give—and give in faith.

After all, Jesus had only a few loaves of bread and a couple of fish, but in His hands God multiplied it, and it became a huge feast for the crowd. In the same way God is able to take even a very small amount of money and use it to accomplish His purposes—if we dedicate it to Him.

Jesus gave everything for your salvation, even His life. Have you given everything back to Him in return—including your finances? Make it your goal to serve Christ in every way you can, including with your money.

WISDOM FOR TODAY

We will hold every earthly gift in open palms, Lord, allowing You to use them as You see fit. Every good and perfect gift comes from You, and to trust You with them is an act of worship on our part.

LOOKING INTO THE MIRROR

No one will be declared righteous in [God's] sight by observing the
law; rather, through the law we become conscious of sin.
ROMANS 3:20

Why did God give us the Ten Commandments when He knew we would break them?

He gave them in order to show us that we are sinful and weak, and that we need His mercy. When I look into the "mirror" of the Ten Commandments, I see that I am a sinner. Then I cry out, "God, be merciful to me!"

It's significant that after the giving of the commandments is the story of the building of the sacrificial altar. The Ten Commandments were given first, but the law and the altar go together. The law reveals that we are sinners and that we need forgiveness. But the law also reveals that the only path to forgiveness is through sacrifice. The law enables us to see ourselves as morally dirty and in need of cleansing. But it also points us to the place of cleansing: the cross of Christ.

God's law shows us what we really are: sinners who need God's grace and mercy. May the law continue to be the schoolmaster that leads us to Christ and His forgiveness.

WISDOM FOR TODAY

Thank You, Father, for the law that reminds us how desperately we need Jesus. We have no righteousness of our own, but, like Abraham, our faith is counted as righteousness. May our sinfulness not bring us shame but, instead bring us closer to You.

TALKING TO GOD

Oh that men would praise the LORD for his goodness, and
for his wonderful works to the children of men!

PSALM 107:8 KJV

When you were very young and first started speaking, did you talk to your parents in long sentences and for great lengths of time? I doubt it. And yet they weren't disappointed in you; they were delighted by your first attempts to speak.

In the same way, when we truly understand that God is our loving heavenly Father and we are His children, then we won't worry so much about disappointing Him by our prayers. Don't worry about your lack of eloquence; no matter how simple they are, God delights in our prayers when they truly express the feelings and desires of our heart.

If prayer feels uncomfortable to you, begin by thanking God for all He has done for you, and praising Him for His love and goodness. Then confess your sins and ask for His forgiveness. Finally, bring your concerns to Him. You may even find it helpful to keep a list of people for whom you are praying.

Remember: Jesus Christ opened heaven's door for us by His death on the cross. When we know Him, we can be sure God hears our prayers.

WISDOM FOR TODAY

Father, You don't need our many words or our list of requests. Thank You for Jesus' example in Scripture on what prayer should entail. May the words of our mouths and the meditations of our hearts be acceptable in Your sight.

No Secrets from God

You alone know the hearts of all men.

1 Kings 8:39

Do these words frighten you? They well might, because they remind us of a truth we often forget: God knows everything about us, even our deepest thoughts and motives. We can hide them from other people; we may even hide them from ourselves. But we can't hide them from God.

This shouldn't surprise us; after all, God knows everything. The Bible says, "Nothing in all creation is hidden from God's sight. Everything is uncovered and laid bare before the eyes of him to whom we must give account" (Hebrews 4:13). Think back over just the last twenty-four hours at all the thoughts you didn't want anyone else to know. But God knew them—every one of them.

But something should surprise us: in spite of all He knows about us, God still loves us. In fact, the verse above occurs in a prayer by King Solomon, thanking God for His love and forgiveness. Thank God for His grace, and thank Him that in spite of all He knows about us, in Christ "He forgave us all our sins" (Colossians 2:13).

Wisdom for Today

Thank You, God, for Your indescribable love for us. That You would send Your Son to die for us is more than we can comprehend. We are forever grateful that Your love for us is based on Your goodness and not our own.

Letting Go of the Past

Get rid of all bitterness, rage and anger, brawling and
slander, along with every form of malice.

Ephesians 4:31

Have you ever noticed that if you continue to hate someone, whatever they did will continue to hurt you? Our anger and hatred just keep reopening the emotional wounds of the past.

This is one reason we need to let go of the past and—with God's help—release our anger and hatred and replace them with His love. If we don't, our souls will be poisoned the rest of our lives by bitterness and resentment instead of reflecting the love and mercy of Christ. Remember Jesus' command: "Love your enemies and pray for those who persecute you" (Matthew 5:44).

Admittedly this isn't easy to do. That is why I urge you to turn to Christ and seek His forgiveness for all the ways you have hurt Him. When we realize how much we have hurt God, the hurts we have received from others will begin to fade.

Wisdom for Today

Forgive us, Father, for the times we've held a grudge against or attempted to heap guilt on someone. Open our eyes to just how much grace we've been given, and soften our hearts so we desire to extend grace to others.

USING OUR GIFTS

We have different gifts. . . . If it is serving, let him serve; if it is
teaching, let him teach; if it is encouraging, let him encourage . . .
if it is showing mercy, let him do it cheerfully.
ROMANS 12:6–8

One of Satan's oldest tricks is to make us think we aren't worth anything and that God can't use us. But it simply isn't true. From one end to the other, the Bible tells us that God loves us. If He didn't, Christ never would have left heaven's glory and come down to this earth to die for our sins. But He did—because God loves us.

But God also wants to use us—and as the verses printed above make it clear, He has equipped every one of us with the gifts we need to serve Him.

What spiritual gifts has God given you? They won't be the same as someone else's gifts—but they are the ones God knew you needed. Don't say your gifts are insignificant or don't matter; God didn't make a mistake when He gave them to you. You may have a special gift for welcoming visitors to your church, or helping the church's nursery, or praying for others, or becoming part of a team that does errands for sick people. It may be helping in a homeless shelter or packing boxes of clothing to ship overseas.

Ask God to show you your gifts—and then ask Him to help you use them for His glory.

WISDOM FOR TODAY
Thank You, Father, for creating us with purpose. Help us recognize our gifts and to use them for Your glory.

HE CAN BE TRUSTED

God is not a man, that he should lie,
nor a son of man, that he should change his mind.
NUMBERS 23:19

Can God's promises be trusted? Take, for example, His promise to be with us in every situation: "Never will I leave you; never will I forsake you" (Hebrews 13:5). Is it really true? When life turns against us and we can't see any way out of our problems, is He still with us—even if it looks as if He has abandoned us? Can His promises really be trusted?

Yes, we can trust His promises—because God does not lie, nor does He change His mind. What if He did? Then we wouldn't have any reason to depend on Him; His Word could not be trusted. But He doesn't lie, and He doesn't change His mind—because He is perfect and holy, and He loves us.

Perhaps this is a discouraging time for you. But God knows your problems, and He can be trusted to be with you. God hasn't promised that our way will always be smooth and problem-free, but He has promised to be with us—and that should give us great comfort.

WISDOM FOR TODAY

In a world where promises are broken (accidentally and sometimes on purpose) every day, God, You are a promise keeper. You are good, and all of Your ways are good. We trust that Your goodness will be with us all the days of our lives.

THE TRAP OF LAZINESS

Be diligent in these matters; give yourself wholly to them,
so that everyone may see your progress.
1 TIMOTHY 4:15

Let me suggest a little exercise, the results of which may surprise you. Take a piece of paper and write down all the things you do in an average twenty-four-hour day—sleeping, eating, working, shopping, watching television, surfing the Internet, and so on. Then put beside each item how much time you spend on it in an average day.

Now look at your list. How much of your time is used for things that really aren't important, or may even be morally or spiritually harmful? Take television or the Internet, for example. We all need to relax, and I'm not suggesting all entertainment is harmful or bad—not at all. But how much of your spare time is simply wasted?

One last question: how much time did you give to God? Remember: Satan doesn't need for us to fall into gross sin in order to defeat us; a large dose of laziness will do the trick just as well. Put Christ first in your life, and then commit every hour of the day to Him.

WISDOM FOR TODAY

Help us, Father, to use all our activities, obligations, and interactions as opportunities to bring You glory. May we use discernment as we create our schedules so we are making the best use of our days.

FEBRUARY

RIGHT AND FAIR

Masters, provide your slaves with what is right and fair, because
you know that you also have a Master in heaven.
COLOSSIANS 4:1

Thankfully slavery is a thing of the past for us—but the underlying principle the apostle Paul gives us here still stands: if we are employers or supervisors, we are to do "what is right and fair" to those who work under us. After all, he reminds us, we, too, have a Master, and someday we'll give an account of our lives to Him—including how we treated others.

Admittedly this isn't always easy to put into action. In some situations it's not always clear what is right and fair, and sometimes people react negatively even when we do treat them fairly. Human beings can be very difficult to deal with—as you've probably discovered! But the principle still holds, and we should seek God's wisdom to carry it out.

This is true for all of us—for it is just another way of expressing Jesus' words to His disciples: "In everything, do to others what you would have them do to you" (Matthew 7:12). Write this principle on your heart—and put it into action every day.

WISDOM FOR TODAY

Open our eyes, Father, to times we've been overly harsh toward or critical of others. Help us see people through Your eyes so we may be quick to listen, extend grace, exhibit compassion, and humbly serve.

GOD'S LOVE AND JUDGMENT

The LORD is gracious and compassionate,
slow to anger and rich in love.
PSALM 145:8

I magine what the world would be like if God were only a God of love, who never judged evil or tried to stop it. Evil men could carry out their plans without fear. They would never have to worry that God would judge them or try to stop them.

Now imagine what the world would be like if God were only a God of judgment, who punished us every time we did wrong. If God were like that, none of us would ever have a chance, for we sin every day. Sometimes, however, God does correct and discipline us—not because He hates us but because He loves us and wants us to turn from the destructive path we are on.

If you are a parent, you love your children, but at times you need to discipline them for their good. In a far greater way, God loves us, so He also disciplines us when we need it for our good. The Bible says, "Do not lose heart when he rebukes you, because the Lord disciplines those he loves" (Hebrews 12:5–6).

WISDOM FOR TODAY

Give us humble and teachable spirits, Lord, so we may rightly receive the correction You give and learn the intended lesson from it.

WHO'S TO BLAME?

"God did not send his Son into the world to condemn the world, but to save the world through him."
JOHN 3:17

Why would a loving God send anyone to hell? Let me answer that question with a question.

If someone deliberately commits a crime and is caught, who is to blame if that person is found guilty and sentenced to jail? Is the judge to blame—or is the criminal?

The lawbreaker is to blame for what has happened to him, not the judge. Yes, the judge sentenced him, but he alone broke the law, and he alone is to blame for the penalty he received. The judge was only following the law. The lawbreaker can't blame the judge; he can only blame himself.

Likewise, when we break God's law, we stand condemned, and we ourselves are to blame for what happens to us, not God. We can only blame ourselves for the consequences.

But we don't have to pay the penalty for our sins, because Christ has already paid it for us. By His death on the cross, Jesus took the punishment you and I deserve. Jesus suffered judgment and hell for us. Praise God for His love!

WISDOM FOR TODAY

We live in a world that often demands fairness while being ignorant of what it would entail. Christ, knowing exactly what would be fair, never sought fairness. He willingly bore the burden of all our guilt and gave us His righteousness in sin's place.

God's Sovereign Power and Constant Presence

The Lord reigns forever.
PSALM 146:10

If we looked only at the headlines every day, we would have good reason to be pessimistic about the future. But don't forget two important truths.

First, the future is in God's hands, and nothing takes Him by surprise. He is sovereign over the history of the world as well as our own personal histories, and behind the scenes He is at work to accomplish His purposes. Even when the future seems dark, we can turn to God—who "reigns forever"—and entrust the future into His hands.

Second, never forget that even when the future is unclear, God is with those of us who are trusting Christ as our Savior and Lord, and He helps us. The apostle Paul faced great danger and uncertainty, but he could still say, "I can do everything through him who gives me strength" (Philippians 4:13). No matter what the future holds for you—no matter what today holds for you—you do not face it alone if you know Christ.

Wisdom for Today

Father, perhaps we sang about You holding the whole world in Your hands, but we live as if we don't believe it. Remind us that, no matter what awaits us, You *still* have the whole world in Your hands.

PERFECTION DESTROYED

Now the LORD God had planted a garden in the east, in
Eden; and there he put the man he had formed.
GENESIS 2:8

The garden of Eden is not just a symbol. It was a real place—just as real as Adam and Eve themselves. The garden's exact location is not known, although it was apparently somewhere in the Middle East.

The opening chapters of the Bible tell us that the garden of Eden was perfect—a place given by God to Adam and Eve so that every need would be met. The reason the garden was perfect was because sin had not yet entered the world. But when Adam and Eve listened to Satan and turned against God—when Adam and Eve sinned—that perfect garden was no longer perfect. God banished them from the garden, and they would never return.

Since that time the human race has been searching for the peace and perfection Eden once provided—but without success, because sin has ravaged our world and our hearts.

But that is not the end of the story. Christ came to conquer sin and death—and He has! In Him there is hope!

WISDOM FOR TODAY

We were created to live in Your presence, Father, and nothing will be right until we are there once again. Our hearts long for the day when we will experience and enjoy the peace and perfection found in heaven.

MEET ME IN HEAVEN

At the name of Jesus every knee should bow,
in heaven and on earth and under the earth,
and every tongue confess that Jesus Christ is Lord,
to the glory of God the Father.
PHILIPPIANS 2:10–11

Once I read a biography of Queen Victoria, and I learned that she would sometimes go into the slums of London. One day she went into a home to have tea with an older woman.

When she rose to leave, the queen asked, "Is there anything I can do for you?"

The woman said, "Yes, Your Majesty. You can meet me in heaven."

The queen turned to her and said softly, "Yes. I'll be there, but only because of the blood that was shed on the cross for you and for me."

Queen Victoria, in her day the most powerful woman in the world, had to depend on the blood of Christ for her salvation. And so do we. God provided the way of salvation: He accepted as a covering for your sin and mine Jesus' blood, shed on the cross for us. The war that exists between holy God and us sinful human beings can be over! The peace treaty was signed more than two thousand years ago in the blood of His Son, Jesus Christ.

WISDOM FOR TODAY

None of us arrives at the foot of the cross any more or less deserving of grace than another. Lord, may we always remember and live with an awareness of what an extravagant price You paid for our salvation.

THE DECEIVER AT WORK

"Watch out for false prophets. They come to you in sheep's clothing, but inwardly they are ferocious wolves."
MATTHEW 7:15

Sometimes it is extremely difficult for us to recognize a false prophet—someone who claims to speak for God but in reality does not.

The underlying principle of all of Satan's tactics is deception, and no Christian, however spiritual, is beyond the seductive assaults of this crafty and clever enemy. He began his work of deception in the garden of Eden, and it continues to this day. Satan does not build a church and call it the First Church of Satan—he is far too clever for that. Instead, he tries to infiltrate the theological seminary and the pulpit, invading the Church under the cover of an orthodox vocabulary—but emptying sacred terms of their true biblical meaning or denying their truth.

The sword of the Spirit—the Bible—is the weapon God has provided for us to use in this battle between truth and deception. Make it a priority to wield that sword skillfully. God's followers need to know the truth He sets forth in His Word so that we can confidently discern between His truth and Satan's lies.

WISDOM FOR TODAY

The enemy's deception is discreet, and his seduction is subtle. Many have fallen prey to his ways. Lord, help us to be so immersed in Your Word that any false teaching is glaringly obvious.

CHILDREN OF GOD

How great is the love the Father has lavished on us, that we should be called children of God! And that is what we are!

1 JOHN 3:1

When we commit our lives to Jesus as our Savior and Lord, we become His sons and daughters. At one time we were alienated from God, with no rights and privileges. But in Christ we were adopted into His family.

Because God is responsible for our welfare, we are told to cast all our cares and anxieties upon Him (1 Peter 5:7). Because we are depending on God, Jesus said, "Do not let your hearts be troubled" (John 14:1).

Children are not shy about asking for things. They would not be normal if they didn't boldly make their desires known. God is keenly aware that we are dependent on Him for life's necessities, so we can freely ask Him for those things. God loves us, and He knows our needs and wants to grant them to us. The Bible says, "No good thing will He withhold from those who walk uprightly" (Psalm 84:11 NKJV).

But as God's children we are not meant just to sit back and selfishly enjoy our privileges. Instead, God wants us to serve Him and to help others.

Are you trusting your heavenly Father to provide for you? Are you boldly asking Him for what you need? And are you serving Him and helping others?

WISDOM FOR TODAY

You are a good Father to us, Lord. You provide and protect in more ways than we can comprehend. May we seek opportunities to use the gifts You've lavished on us in ways that bring glory to Your name.

How's Your Heart?

"Man looks at the outward appearance, but the Lord looks at the heart."
1 Samuel 16:7

Your heart beats about 100,000 strokes every twenty-four hours. It contracts about 4,000 times an hour. Our entire blood supply circulates through our hearts every four minutes. No wonder doctors urge us to take care of our hearts!

As amazing as it is, when Scripture talks about the heart, it's not talking about that life-sustaining muscle. It's talking about our entire inner being. The heart is the seat of our emotions, the seat of decisive action, and the seat of belief (as well as doubt). The heart symbolizes the center of our moral, spiritual, and intellectual life. It is the seat of our conscience and life.

And God knows our hearts well. The Almighty God searches our hearts, weighs our hearts by the teaching of Scripture, opens our hearts to His truth, and gives us new hearts when we come to Christ—hearts of flesh sensitive to His presence, His leading, and His love. Don't ever hesitate to take to Him whatever is on your heart. He already knows it anyway, but He doesn't want you to bear its pain or celebrate its joy alone.

Wisdom for Today

It is so easy, Father, to misunderstand and make assumptions about people. We can take comfort in the knowledge that You, Lord, know us from the inside out. You are aware of every heartache and happiness.

REPROGRAMMING OUR HEARTS

"You are precious and honored in my sight,
and . . . I love you."
ISAIAH 43:4

One thing a computer manufacturer does is program each machine. At the factory a set of instructions is inserted into the computer's memory, and those instructions tell the computer what to do.

In a sense, you and I get programmed. When we are young, our minds are constantly being programmed by the experiences we have. Later on, those instructions that have been inserted into our brains will try to tell us what to do and think. This programming happens to all of us. But when the things that have been put into our memories are bad or untrue, we will have problems later in life.

In that case, we need to reprogram our minds and hearts; we need to replace the bad things that have taken root there with good and true things. And that is where God can help. In His Word, He provides truths to replace the lies you've believed about yourself.

Open your heart to Christ and ask Him to help you see yourself the way He sees you—as His beloved child, "precious and honored in my sight."

WISDOM FOR TODAY

It's easy to sink into despair and believe wrongly about ourselves when we stray from Your Word, Father. Help us immerse ourselves in Scripture so we are reminded of what You have to say to our hearts.

RULING IN YOUR HEART

"The kingdom of God is within you."
LUKE 17:21

Too many people think God is to be found by looking within our own minds and souls, and they often cite these words of Jesus in support of their claim.

Jesus, however, wasn't teaching that God is within us and that all we need to do is look inward to find God. Instead, Jesus was talking to people who believed that the Messiah would establish an earthly, political kingdom—and Jesus said that wasn't His goal. "My kingdom is not of this world," Jesus told Pilate (John 18:36). His goal instead was to rule in the hearts of men and women.

And that is exactly what happens when we give our lives to Christ. When we turn to Him in repentance and faith, He cleanses us of our sins, and He comes to live within us by His Holy Spirit. Once that happens, He begins to rule in our lives. In other words, He sets up His kingdom—His rule—within us.

More and more each day, may your life clearly reflect Christ's kingship over every area of your life!

WISDOM FOR TODAY

In our flesh, Father, we desire to be the rulers of our own lives. We foolishly attempt to build our own little kingdoms, and our efforts are in vain. Rule in our hearts, Lord, and have Your way in our lives.

THE POWER OF TOUCH

Filled with compassion, Jesus reached out his hand and touched the man.

MARK 1:41

As was the custom of the day, the man afflicted with leprosy had called out, "Unclean! Unclean!" to warn people of his presence so they could avoid him. Who knows how long it had been since he had experienced a human touch—a warm embrace, an encouraging pat on the back, a friendly handshake? Had it been months, or even years?

Jesus knew the man needed relief from this disease, but before Jesus dealt with his skin, He healed the man's emotional pain. Jesus reached out and touched him. Can you imagine how that leper felt when someone actually touched him? Then Jesus freed him from his leprosy.

Jesus was teaching us by example that often the best way to help the oppressed, the sick, and the poor is to touch them with our compassion. Jesus had compassion on people; we should have compassion too.

Today, whom will you touch—literally as well as figuratively—in the name of Christ?

WISDOM FOR TODAY

Lord, You could have healed the leper's physical ailment with a word, but You knew the hurt went all the way to his heart. Help us also see beyond the surface and seek to touch the hearts of others.

REBUILDING RELATIONSHIPS

Make every effort to live in peace with all men and to be holy.
HEBREWS 12:14

Is there a relationship you need to rebuild?

Too often people are filled with regret and guilt because they failed to reach out to someone with whom they were at odds—and then death intervenes and it's too late. Don't let this happen to you.

If a broken relationship comes to mind, know that the place to begin is within yourself. Are you convinced that rebuilding this relationship is something God wants you to do?

Then let the person know that you care and that you want your relationship to be different. Don't use words alone; back up your words with action. A small gift or an invitation to dinner can show that you mean what you say.

Most of all, seek God's forgiveness for anything you did to harm the relationship, and trust Him to help you both set aside the past. Don't argue about the past or who was at fault; that only reopens old wounds. Instead, focus on your hopes for the future. Change may take time, but with God's help it can happen.

WISDOM FOR TODAY

Give us the humility and wisdom, Lord, to recognize the part we've played in any broken relationships and to seek reconciliation when appropriate. Help us choose grace over grudges so we are not left with regret at the end of our days.

LOVE ONE ANOTHER

Let no debt remain outstanding, except the continuing debt to love one another, for he who loves his fellowman has fulfilled the law.

ROMANS 13:8

Prejudice or hatred of any person because of their racial, ethnic, or religious background is wrong. God labels it sin.

After all, God created every one of us, and when we hate someone who is different from us, we are hating someone whom God has made and who is valuable in His sight. Every human being is created in God's image, and although sin has blurred that image in all of us, every single one of us still bears the mark of our Creator.

We also must never hate people who are different from us, because Jesus Christ died for them. Jesus didn't die to save just one race or one group of people; Jesus died for all. The Bible says that "God so loved the world that he gave his one and only Son" (John 3:16). Heaven will include individuals "from every tribe and language and people and nation" (Revelation 5:9).

Ask God to free you from any prejudice that lurks in your heart. Ask Christ to fill you with His love. Prejudice flees when we see others through Jesus' eyes.

WISDOM FOR TODAY

We are all fearfully and wonderfully made by Your loving hand, Father. Help us to appreciate the beauty of our diversity and to understand that, even in our differences, we are all made in Your image.

WITH GOD'S HELP

Bear with each other and forgive whatever grievances you may
have against one another. Forgive as the Lord forgave you.
COLOSSIANS 3:13

The command to forgive as we have been forgiven is difficult to obey, but we need to forgive people who have wronged us—even if we don't think they deserve it. If we don't, the poisons of anger and bitterness will eat away at our souls—but with God's help we can deal with them in a way that honors Him.

First, if we were at fault in any way, we need to face it honestly and seek God's forgiveness. Then we need to ask the person to forgive us as well—even if they may refuse.

The next step is to ask God to help you forgive them for hurting you. The only way to do this, I believe, is to realize how fully God has forgiven us in Christ. We don't deserve His forgiveness, yet we "are justified freely by his grace" (Romans 3:24). Open your heart to Christ, and then ask Him to replace your hurt and anger with His love—and He will.

WISDOM FOR TODAY

Thank You, Lord, for the freedom found in being forgiven and in forgiving others. By following Your example, we can set ourselves and others free from the bondage of bitterness and unresolved offenses. It is for freedom that You've set us free.

"I'm Sorry"

Be completely humble and gentle.

EPHESIANS 4:2

Apologizing doesn't come easily to most of us. The Bible, however, offers us instances of people who apologized when they acted wrongly, and we can learn from their example.

On one occasion, for instance, the apostle Paul was arrested and taken before an assembly of religious leaders. He spoke very bluntly to the high priest, not realizing who he was, and was rebuked for speaking disrespectfully to such an important official. Paul immediately apologized for his action, enabling him to continue with his defense.

Have you ever asked yourself why it's so hard to apologize? One reason is pride: we hate to admit we were wrong. But the Bible says that pride is sin: "I hate pride and arrogance" (Proverbs 8:13).

So if apologizing is difficult for you, ask God to help you overcome your pride—or whatever else is holding you back. Seek out one person you may have hurt and say very simply, "I'm sorry." Next time, apologizing will be even easier.

WISDOM FOR TODAY

Asking for forgiveness doesn't come naturally, Lord. Please grant us the humility and gentleness necessary to make amends when we have wronged another person. Help us set aside our pride and pursue peace.

A Picture of Forgiveness

You have been set free from sin.

ROMANS 6:22

I magine for a minute that you committed a crime, were arrested, and were put in jail. The day has now come for you to appear in court.

As you stand before the judge, there is absolutely no doubt: you are guilty of the charges against you. According to the law, you must pay for this crime, and in this case the penalty is a year in jail. The judge issues his verdict and pronounces your sentence. At once the bailiff comes over to lead you away to prison.

But then something almost beyond belief happens. The judge steps down from the bench, stops the bailiff, and takes your place. He is innocent—but he goes to prison and pays the penalty for the crime you committed. You, on the other hand, are free!

This is a picture of what Jesus Christ did for you and me. We are guilty before God and deserve nothing less than death. But the judge—Jesus Christ—took our place. By His death on the cross, He took the penalty we deserve, and we are free. Sin's penalty has been fully paid. Believe it!

WISDOM FOR TODAY

What a price You paid, Lord, so we could be free! Thank You for Your example of extravagant love and sacrifice. May we live with an appreciation and awareness of the freedom we've been given.

OUR HARDEST TASK

"You have heard that it was said, 'Love your neighbor and hate your enemy.'
But I tell you: Love your enemies, and pray for those who persecute you."
MATTHEW 5:43–44

You've heard the expression "Forgive and forget"—but is it really possible? Perhaps someone once hurt you very deeply—and the emotional scars still ache in your memory. The last thing you think you could ever do is forgive and forget.

And yet Jesus goes even further: He tells us not only to forgive and forget but to love the one who hurt us and pray for their welfare. We aren't to erase them from our memories; we are to keep them in our prayers!

Impossible? Yes—apart from God's help. What must we do? First, remember how generously Christ forgave you. You hurt God far more than anyone ever hurt you—and yet He willingly sent His Son to die in your place so you could be forgiven. Never forget how much it cost Christ to forgive you.

Second, begin seeing the other person through God's eyes. He loves them, just as He loves you. Don't hold on to your hurts any longer, but turn them over to Christ and ask Him to help you forgive others—and then love them just as He does.

WISDOM FOR TODAY

You've promised us, Lord, that what is impossible with man is possible with You. We know You can give us a heart that loves even those who have hurt us. Help us follow Your example by loving our enemies.

WE NEED EACH OTHER

Pity the man who falls
and has no one to help him up!
ECCLESIASTES 4:10

Have you ever met someone who was known as a rugged individualist? You probably have; you may even consider yourself to be one. And even if you aren't, you probably secretly admire them, with their drive and their independent attitude and their lack of concern about what others think of them.

Anyone who has made a commitment to Jesus Christ is something of a rugged individualist. He or she isn't going to live the same way everyone else lives; the goal now is to follow Christ. This may mean being scorned by family or friends, or taking stands for what is right instead of what is popular.

But in other ways the Christian must not be a rugged, independent individualist. Instead, when we come to Christ we become part of a family—the body of Christ, the Church. Instead of being concerned only about ourselves, we become concerned about others in the family of Christ and their needs. We become concerned, too, about those who do not yet know Christ. Is this concern becoming a reality in your life?

WISDOM FOR TODAY
Father, give us eyes that truly see the people around us and hearts that are concerned with their eternal destinations. Each individual is infinitely precious to You, Lord. Make them precious to us as well.

THE TRAP OF BUSYNESS

Then, because so many people were coming and going that they did not even have a chance to eat, he said to [His disciples], "Come with me by yourselves to a quiet place and get some rest."

MARK 6:31

Do you have days like this one in Jesus' ministry—days when you have so many demands on you that you don't see how you'll ever get everything done?

Why, in the midst of such a busy day, did Jesus insist His disciples leave the crowds to rest and be alone with Him? He knew that the busier they were, the more they needed to make time to rest and be alone with Him. If they didn't, eventually they would hurt both themselves and those they were seeking to help. The same is true of us.

God knows the demands and responsibilities you face—at home, on the job, even in your church. But God also knows you need His wisdom to keep those things in perspective, and you need His strength to get them done rightly. Begin each day with a brief prayer, committing the day to Him and asking Him to guide you. Then set aside time—even just a few minutes at first—to be alone with God in His Word and in prayer. If Jesus found it important, shouldn't you?

WISDOM FOR TODAY

From the very beginning, God, You taught us to incorporate regular periods of rest into our lives. Teach us to pause long before exhaustion sets in so You can rejuvenate our bodies and refresh our spirits.

TAKE AIM!

Set your minds on things above, not on earthly things.

COLOSSIANS 3:2

During the Second World War, the words of General Douglas MacArthur echoed in the hearts of the people of the Philippines while they were under enemy occupation. He promised, "I shall return"—and he kept that promise. Jesus Christ has also promised, "I shall return"—and He, too, will keep that promise.

A continual looking forward to the eternal world Jesus will usher in is not a form of escapism or wishful thinking. We Christians look forward with anticipation to Christ's return and spending eternity with Him.

The promise of that new world, however, does not mean we are to leave the present world as it is. If you read history, you will find that the Christians who did the most for the present world were those who thought the most of the next. Only Christians who cease thinking of the next world become ineffective in this one.

"Aim at heaven," said C. S. Lewis, "and you will get earth thrown in. Aim at earth, and you will get neither." At what are you aiming?

WISDOM FOR TODAY

This world is full of distractions, Lord, that seek to gain our attention, energy, and devotion. Help us fix our gaze on You so we can keep the things of earth in proper perspective.

LIFE-GIVING FAITH

To all who did accept him and believe in him he gave
the right to become children of God.

JOHN 1:12 NCV

The ugly larva in its cocoon spends sometimes many months in almost unnoticeable growth and change. But no matter how great that growth may be, there comes a moment when the little creature passes through a crisis and emerges a beautiful butterfly. The weeks of silent growth are important, but they cannot take the place of that event when the old and the ugly are left behind, and the new and the beautiful come into being.

Many Christians whose faith and lives testify that they have been converted to Christ do not know the exact day or hour that they left behind the old and the ugly and came to know Him. Whether or not they can remember the specific time, however, they can be sure there was a moment when they crossed over the line from death to life.

That moment comes when we put our faith in certain objective facts—in the work of Christ, His cross, His tomb, and His resurrection. Praise God for calling you to this life-giving faith!

WISDOM FOR TODAY

Thank You, Lord, for making a way for us to step out of the darkness and into Your light. Because of Your love for us, we no longer need to live in fear of death and the grave.

FULLY TRUSTWORTHY

Righteous are you, O LORD, and your laws are right. The statutes
you have laid down are righteous; they are fully trustworthy.
PSALM 119:137–138

It took sixteen hundred years to write. More than thirty authors acting as secretaries for God wrote its sixty-six books. Over those sixteen hundred years, these individual authors wrote the same message, and so unified is the message that the sixty-six books actually comprise one Book.

In the pages of the Bible, the sins of small and great are frankly addressed, the weaknesses of human nature are admitted, and life is presented as it actually is found. The message in every book is straightforward: that message is Jesus Christ. The Bible is primarily concerned with the story of God's redemption of sinful humanity through Jesus Christ.

And the truth in its pages is eminently practical. General Robert E. Lee observed, "The Bible is a book in comparison with which all others in my eyes are of minor importance, and which in all my complexities and distresses has never failed to give me light and strength." Find in its pages the light and strength you need for today and every day of your life.

WISDOM FOR TODAY

We're so grateful, Lord, for the pages of Scripture. In them, You offer words of wisdom for every decision we must make, words of comfort for every pain we experience, and words of encouragement for every step of this earthly journey.

THE FOCAL POINT

I am the Alpha and the Omega, the First and the Last, the Beginning and the End.

REVELATION 22:13

The central message of the Bible is Jesus Christ.

In Genesis, Jesus is the Seed of the Woman. In Exodus, He is the Passover Lamb. In Leviticus, He is the atoning Sacrifice. In Numbers, the Smitten Rock. In Deuteronomy, the Prophet. In Joshua, the Captain of the Lord's hosts. In Judges, the Deliverer. In Ruth, the Heavenly Kinsman. In the six books of Kings, the Promised King. In Nehemiah, the Restorer of the nation. In Esther, the Advocate. In Job, my Redeemer. In Psalms, my Strength. In Proverbs, my Pattern. In Ecclesiastes, my Goal. In the Song of Solomon, my Satisfier. In the prophets, the Coming Prince of Peace. In the Gospels, He is the Christ who came to seek and to save. In Acts, He is Christ risen. In the epistles, He is Christ exalted. In Revelation, He is Christ returning and reigning.

The message of the Bible is the story of salvation through Jesus—and the whole world needs to know this story. Whom will you tell today?

WISDOM FOR TODAY

Lord, please give us minds that see You in the pages of Scripture. Give us eyes that see You at work around us. Give us mouths that are quick to speak of You to others. May our lives always and only be about You.

Now!

"As long as it is day, we must do the work of him who sent me. Night is coming, when no one can work."
JOHN 9:4

Dr. Samuel Johnson wore engraved on his watch the words "The night cometh," from John 9:4. Likewise, we Christians ought to carry written on our hearts the solemn truth of how short a time we have to witness for God. Whatever we are going to do for Christ, we had better do now.

A dying Christian, who had been very reticent about sharing his testimony all his life, said to the man who sat beside him, "If I had the power, I'd shout, 'Glory to God.'" The companion answered, "It's a pity you didn't shout 'Glory' when you had the power."

We had better be sharing our testimony while we have the power. If we are ever to study the Scriptures, if we are ever to spend time in prayer, if we are ever to win souls for Christ, if we are ever to invest our finances for His kingdom, it must be now.

You may not have tomorrow—but you do have today. What will you do for the Lord?

WISDOM FOR TODAY

Teach us, Father, not to take a single moment for granted. Let's live passionately pursuing You, intentionally loving others, and continually sharing the story of Your grace.

STANDING AGAINST SATAN

Be self-controlled and alert. Your enemy the devil prowls around like a roaring lion looking for someone to devour. Resist him, standing firm in the faith.

1 PETER 5:8–9

No Christian is exempt from the attacks of Satan. Our adversary is personal, aggressive, intelligent, cunning, and destructive, and every day Satan must be resisted.

Just as the bows and arrows used in warfare centuries ago are useless against today's highly sophisticated weapons, so the carnal weapons that we try to use in spiritual warfare against the devil have no power against his cunning schemes and fierce attacks. Instead, the greatest hindrance to Satan's destructive efforts is our standing strong in the knowledge and fear of the Lord. The greatest roadblock to Satan's work is the Christian who, above all else, lives for God, walks with integrity, is filled with the Spirit, and is obedient to God's truth.

Your greatest contribution to God's kingdom work—and to defeating the enemy's efforts against this kingdom—is to keep up your daily devotions; live a clean, honest, humble, Spirit-filled life; trust God to guard and protect you morally, physically, and spiritually; and openly witness for Jesus Christ. Don't be a pawn of the devil, but a servant of Christ.

WISDOM FOR TODAY

Help us, Father, not to grow lazy in our study of Your Word so we can wield the sword of the Spirit in battle when the enemy attacks. Remind us daily that, while we do not need to fear Satan, we do need to fight him.

59

WHO WILL GO?

How can they believe in the one of whom they have not heard? And how can they hear without someone preaching to them?
ROMANS 10:14

The risen Christ commands His followers to "go into all the world and preach the good news" (Mark 16:15).

God doesn't promise that obedience will be easy or glamorous or romantic. Oh, I know it's exciting to get on a plane and travel to another land. And perhaps while we're flying God will fill us with His Spirit so that when we reach our destination, we will be prepared to serve Him. But if we are not winning people to Christ here, if we are not witnessing here, if we are not serving Christ here, God can't use us there. We must be faithful here first.

God is calling us to consider His call and wrestle in prayer over the mission He has for us in life. Will you go into the world for Him? There are a thousand things you can do with your life, a thousand ways you can spend it—but how many of them will enable you to have no regrets at the end? Obedience to Jesus is the only path of no regrets.

WISDOM FOR TODAY

We often desire to accomplish big things for You, God, thinking that bigger is better. Instill in us a passion for faithfully doing the small things first. May we seek to be obedient right where You have us today.

THE FIERY FURNACE

"Be faithful, even to the point of death, and I will give you the crown of life."

REVELATION 2:10

Shadrach, Meshach, and Abednego were Jewish captives in Babylon—and they refused to worship the golden image set up by King Nebuchadnezzar.

They could have bowed down and avoided trouble, but that would have compromised all that they believed and stood for.

They could have rationalized and said, "It is our duty to obey the king." But they had a higher law: God's law.

They could have said, "It's just a matter of form. God knows that inwardly we are true to Him." Or they could have stayed indoors that day.

Instead, they risked the tyrant's rage and refused to bow before the idol. They proclaimed, "We take our stand for the living God, even if it means death." Then, calm, self-possessed, joyful, they were condemned and thrown into the fiery furnace, but God was with them and delivered them.

God is with His people in the fiery furnaces of life—our times of temptation, trouble, and trial. And people notice the difference His presence makes. The Bible says that nothing—absolutely nothing—"will be able to separate us from the love of God that is in Christ Jesus our Lord" (Romans 8:39).

WISDOM FOR TODAY

Thank You, Lord, that You go before us in times of triumph and tragedy. We are never without Your presence, power, and peace. We can walk boldly through fire or flood knowing we are not alone.

MERCY BEYOND COMPREHENSION

The LORD your God is gracious and compassionate. He will
not turn his face from you if you turn to him.
2 CHRONICLES 30:9

Of all the people in the Bible, Manasseh may have been the most wicked. Living centuries before Christ, this king of Judah was an idolater who turned against God and worshiped every kind of pagan deity. Manasseh was guilty of immorality; he practiced every conceivable evil and perversion; he devoted himself to sorcery and witchcraft. He also was a murderer and a cruel tyrant, even sacrificing his sons to a pagan god.

So God's judgment fell: the Assyrians captured Jerusalem, and Manasseh was bound in chains and taken hundreds of miles away to Babylon. In prison he had time to think, and he began to pray. In that dungeon this wicked man who only deserved hell cried out to God for forgiveness—and God answered.

The Bible teaches that God is a God of mercy. His mercy is so vast and beyond our comprehension that no matter what sin we have committed, if we truly repent, God will forgive. Be assured that there is no sin you have ever committed that the blood of Jesus Christ cannot cleanse.

WISDOM FOR TODAY

Praise You, Father, for Your infinite mercy that reaches to the deepest pit, brings light to the secret places of shame, and is a salve to our broken spirits. Thank You for Your mercy that is available to us no matter what we've done or where we've run.

MARCH

GOD'S PERFECTION

As for God, his way is perfect;
the word of the LORD is flawless.
PSALM 18:30

Has it ever struck you how important it is that God is perfect? We know God is all-powerful, all-knowing, all-loving, and absolutely pure and holy and just. But He is also absolutely perfect.

What if He weren't perfect? What if He made mistakes . . . or failed to keep His promises . . . or did things only halfway . . . or occasionally told a lie . . . or slipped up and forgot to do what He said He would—all the things, in other words, that we often do (or fail to do)? If God were this way, why bother to trust Him? Why bother to worship Him?

But God isn't like this! God is perfect—absolutely, totally perfect in all He is and all He does. And because He is perfect, you can trust Him. You can trust His love, and you can trust His promises. You can trust Him to guide you, and you can trust Him to be with you even in life's darkest times. Most of all you can trust Him to save you through Christ—because His way of salvation is perfect.

WISDOM FOR TODAY

Help us to view all of life, Father, through the lens of Your perfection. Every trial, temptation, distress, or disappointment is an opportunity to see Your perfect wisdom, love, and strength in action in our lives.

GROWING STRONGER

Grow in the grace and knowledge of our Lord and Savior Jesus Christ.

2 PETER 3:18

So how do we grow spiritually? We grow through the study of God's Word. We will never grow in grace and in the knowledge of God until the Bible becomes part of our lives every day.

We grow through prayer. We should be in an attitude of prayer every minute of the day; we are to be praying constantly. In every choice we make, we should ask our heavenly Father which way we should go and listen for Him to say, "This is the way, walk ye in it" (Isaiah 30:21 KJV).

We grow as well through our fellowship with other believers. Through worship, through hearing His Word preached and taught, through interaction with more mature believers—we need each other in order to grow.

Finally, we grow by witnessing. Just as exercise makes us physically stronger, exercising our faith by sharing it with others makes us spiritually stronger. Are you sharing the story of His love with others?

Make it your goal—beginning today—to grow closer to Christ.

WISDOM FOR TODAY

Lord, we don't want to be satisfied with yesterday's filling of the Spirit. We want our faith to continually grow and our desire for you to always be increasing. Help us to make You the focus of all we do and say throughout our days.

THE YOUNG JESUS

Jesus grew in wisdom and stature, and in favor with God and men.
LUKE 2:52

The Bible doesn't tell us much about Jesus' childhood, but the one incident it does record reveals that He was already aware of His unique status as God's Son, sent from heaven to save us from our sins.

The incident occurred when Jesus was twelve. As was their custom every year, Mary and Joseph took Him on the long trip to Jerusalem for Passover, one of the most important Jewish feasts. Afterward they became separated from Him, and when they finally found Him several days later, He was in the Temple listening to those who were teachers of the Old Testament and asking them questions. When Mary and Joseph rebuked Him, he replied, "Why were you searching for me? Didn't you know I had to be in my Father's house?"

If Jesus found it important to be in God's House learning more about God's Word, shouldn't we as well? And shouldn't we ask God to help us instill the same priorities in our children?

WISDOM FOR TODAY

What a great example you set for us, Lord. Thank You for modeling that gathering with other believers and having a deep understanding of Scripture can begin at an early age.

WHICH IS HARDEST?

As God's chosen people, holy and dearly loved, clothe yourselves
with compassion, kindness, humility, gentleness and patience.

COLOSSIANS 3:12

With a twinkle in his eyes, my friend says that his favorite prayer is the following: "Lord, give me patience—and give it to me right now!" Patience, he admits, has been the hardest virtue for him to acquire.

Look at the five things Paul lists here that should be part of our character as Christians: compassion, kindness, humility, gentleness, patience. Which is hardest for you? "They're all hard for me," you might be tempted to say—and you're probably right. Every one of them strikes a blow at our natural selfishness. No one exhibited them more completely than our Lord, who was completely self-giving.

But for many of us, patience is the hardest. For one thing, our patience is probably tested every day—even every hour. But patience is also critical, for without it the other four—compassion, kindness, humility, and gentleness—are impossible.

When impatience threatens to overwhelm you, ask God to take it away and replace it with His patience. Remember: His patience with you has been beyond measure.

WISDOM FOR TODAY

Lord, every day that You do not return is an example of Your perfect patience. May we strive to have that same kind of patience in our interactions with others, as we await events in our own lives.

THE LAMB'S BOOK OF LIFE

Only those whose names are written in the Lamb's
book of life [will enter the glory of heaven].
REVELATION 21:27

You and I will never be good enough to get into heaven on our own. The reason is because God is pure and holy, and even one sin—just one—would be enough to keep us out of heaven. Any and every sin is an offense to God. He does not take our good deeds and bad deeds and weigh them against each other. Instead, the Bible says, "whoever keeps the whole law and yet stumbles at just one point is guilty of breaking all of it" (James 2:10).

That is why we need Christ, for He came into the world to take away our sins. We cannot remove our sins and guilt—but Christ can, because He was the sinless Son of God. When we come by faith to Him, all our sins are transferred to Him, and we are forgiven. Our names are written in God's book because of Christ.

We can't trust in our own goodness—but we can trust Christ and what He has done for us. Are you trusting Him alone for your salvation?

WISDOM FOR TODAY
Thank You, God, that our salvation is based on Christ's righteousness and not our own and that You do not judge us as we deserve. Only through trusting in the work of the cross can we spend eternity in Your presence.

SINCERE—OR GENUINE?

"Not everyone who says to me, 'Lord, Lord,' will enter the kingdom of heaven, but only he who does the will of my Father who is in heaven."

MATTHEW 7:21

D id you know that the word *Christian* actually means "a partisan for Christ"? It means that you have chosen Christ and are following Him. Partisans are not neutral—they are committed.

Now I want to ask you: "Are you a Christian?" I mean a true Christian, a real Christian. Many people have a wrong idea of what a Christian is. They say, "A Christian is a person who prays" or "A Christian lives by the Golden Rule." But praying or living by the Golden Rule doesn't make someone a Christian. A person may be sincere, but that doesn't make him a Christian.

When I was a little boy, my mother was sincere when she gave me what she thought was cough syrup for my cold. Instead she gave me iodine. She quickly called the doctor, and he said, "Give him some cream." She almost filled me up with cream to neutralize the iodine. Sincerity doesn't necessarily accomplish what you want it to!

Are you a Christian? Have you confessed your sins and your need for forgiveness to Christ, and have you committed yourself to Him as your Lord and Savior?

WISDOM FOR TODAY

Examine us, Lord, and reveal any areas of our lives where we've been offering only lip service to Christ. May we be found, upon Your return, passionately pursuing the things of Christ and dedicated to doing the will of the Father.

A SOLID FOUNDATION

This is what the Sovereign LORD *says: "I am against your*
magic charms with which you ensnare people."
EZEKIEL 13:20

It was a very difficult time to be a prophet of God. The Jewish nation was on the brink of an invasion that would soon destroy it and send most of its inhabitants into exile. And yet few wanted to hear what Ezekiel had to say, for his message warned of God's impending judgment.

Instead, they wanted to listen to prophets who declared soothing words, telling them that Ezekiel was wrong and that soon the nation would experience peace. They also flocked to magicians and astrologers and fortune-tellers who claimed to know the future and promised them better days. They, too, told people that Ezekiel's message was a lie.

Walk into any bookstore and you'll find hundreds of books telling you how to live. Turn on the television or radio and a multitude of talk show gurus promise the same thing. Some may have value—but many are like the false prophets and charm merchants of Ezekiel's day. Don't be misled, and don't be deceived! Instead, build your life on the truth God has given us in His Word.

WISDOM FOR TODAY

Help us, Father, to know and accept truth from Your Word and not to look to the world for direction on how to live. We do not wish to be counted among those who exchange sound doctrine for ear-tickling falsehoods that lead people astray.

WORDS THAT HELP

Do not let any unwholesome talk come out of your mouths, but only
what is helpful for building others up according to their needs.

EPHESIANS 4:29

We've all met people who seem to enjoy correcting others and telling them what is wrong with them. Sometimes it's done with an arrogant attitude—the kind that says, "I'm better than you, and I know what's wrong with you." Sometimes it's done with an attitude of false humility: "I humbly hope I can help you become a better person."

If you're like most of us, however, you probably don't care much for people like this, and (rightly or wrongly) you probably don't listen to their advice. You sense that their real motive is pride, and their main goal is to impress you with how wise and perfect they are.

This is the opposite of what the Bible says here about the way we should speak to others. Instead of pride, our motive should be love. Instead of criticism, our goal should be to encourage and uplift. Instead of impressing others with ourselves, we want them to be impressed with Christ. Learn to avoid hurtful and useless words, and ask God to help you to encourage and help someone for Christ's sake today.

WISDOM FOR TODAY

Remind us, Father, that our words have the power to harm and the power to heal. Help us heed the warning to be slow to speak so we choose words that are uplifting to the hearer, appropriate for the situation, and honoring to You.

POOR IN SPIRIT, PART I

"Blessed are the poor in spirit."
MATTHEW 5:3

At first these words of Jesus sound like a contradiction. What did He mean by being "poor in spirit"—and how could it lead to blessing?

If we are to be poor in spirit, we must be aware of our spiritual poverty. (No one is more pathetic than the person who is in great need and is not aware of it!) Only God can satisfy our soul's emptiness—its deepest longings, desires, and appetites—but not everyone recognizes that truth and turns to Him.

The soul requires as much attention as the body. It demands fellowship and communion with God. It demands worship, quietness, and meditation. Unless the soul is fed and exercised daily, it becomes weak and shriveled.

Wise, then, is the person who openly confesses their lack of spiritual wealth and in humility cries out, "God, be merciful to me a sinner!" (Luke 18:13 NKJV). In God's economy, spiritual emptiness comes before filling, and, spiritual poverty before riches. Happiness, Jesus said, comes from admitting our spiritual poverty and then asking Him to come into our lives. Has this happened to you?

WISDOM FOR TODAY

Lord, we desperately need Your mercy and grace in our lives. We humbly declare that need to You today, knowing You will not turn us away. We, Your people, are blessed by Your willingness to fill the hungry with good things.

POOR IN SPIRIT, PART II

You are all children of God through faith in Christ Jesus.

GALATIANS 3:26 NLT

Being poor in spirit means being aware of our spiritual poverty. Being poor in spirit also means being conscious of our constant dependence on God.

Children depend upon their parents for protection and care. Because of that relationship, children are not poor; but if it weren't for their relationship with their parents, they would be helpless and poor indeed.

Dependent children spend little time worrying about meals, clothing, and shelter. They assume—and they have a right to—that all will be provided by their parents.

When we come to Christ, we become children of God, and we can trust our heavenly Father to provide for us. Jesus said, "What man is there among you who, if his son asks for bread, will give him a stone? . . . How much more will your Father who is in heaven give good things to those who ask Him!" (Matthew 7:9, 11 NKJV).

We must admit we are poor before we can be made rich. We must admit we are destitute before we can become children of God through faith in Jesus Christ. C. H. Spurgeon said, "The first link between my soul and Christ is . . . not my riches but my need."

WISDOM FOR TODAY

We confess our needs to You, Father, knowing that You are willing and able to provide what we lack, strengthen our weak places, and keep us close to Your side. You are a good, good Father to us.

TRUSTING HIS WORD

All your words are true;
all your righteous laws are eternal.
PSALM 119:160

When you were young, your parents probably warned you not to believe everything you read. Their advice was sound; just because something is in print doesn't necessarily make it true. But why, then, should you believe the Bible? Why trust what it says?

One reason is because it tells about real people and real events. It doesn't consist of stories someone made up (unlike many other ancient books); they have the ring of truth about them, because they actually happened.

Another reason we can trust the Bible is because it was written by people who actually witnessed what happened and wrote it down so future generations would have an accurate record of them. As Peter wrote (who was himself an eyewitness to Jesus' ministry), "We did not follow cleverly invented stories . . . but we were eyewitnesses" (2 Peter 1:16).

Most of all, however, we can trust the Bible because it points us to the most important event in human history: the life, death, and resurrection of Jesus Christ. Through the written Word we discover the Living Word—Jesus Christ.

WISDOM FOR TODAY

Thank You, Lord, for the Bible. We believe every word written was inspired by the Holy Spirit and breathed out by You and that it is just as true and relevant today. Help us stand firm against those who stand against Scripture.

HEALING OR HARM?

Reckless words pierce like a sword,
but the tongue of the wise brings healing.
PROVERBS 12:18

How often have you had to apologize for something you said, just because you didn't stop to think? You weren't trying to hurt someone; you didn't intend to be malicious; you may not even have been engaged in a serious conversation. But the reckless word slipped out—and once it was spoken, the damage was done. Jesus warned that people "will have to give account on the day of judgment for every careless word they have spoken" (Matthew 12:36). Those are sobering words.

But the answer to reckless words isn't to try to keep silent! Instead, the Bible says, we should seek to do good with our speech: "The tongue of the wise brings healing." Think back over the people who have encouraged or helped you over the years. Weren't they examples of this proverb?

Remember: Jesus Christ wants to be ruler over every part of your life—including your tongue. Commit it to Him, and ask Him for the wisdom to know when to speak and when to keep silent, and to use your tongue to encourage and help others.

WISDOM FOR TODAY

May we be known, Father, as people of encouragement who speak words of healing. Help us restrain our tongues when we are tempted to use them carelessly, so the words of our mouths would be pleasing in Your sight.

TESTIFYING TO THE TRUTH

*"Always be prepared to give an answer to everyone who asks
you to give the reason for the hope that you have."*
1 PETER 3:15

One night my wife and I were guests at a dinner with one of America's most brilliant scientists. He told us that he had been an agnostic, but through his study of science he had come to believe that there must be a personal God. So he got a Bible and began to read it—and by reading the Bible he came to know Jesus Christ as his personal Lord and Savior.

Another time I received a letter from a man who was reared in a good family. He wrote, "I always thought I was a Christian. But my first weeks at the university showed to me that my religion was more external than internal, and I set it aside. I was successful on my chosen path. Then I received a glimmer of revelation: if Jesus Christ is the Son of God, as He claims, I'm a fool not to follow Him."

What is your story? Be ready to share it when the Lord gives you the opportunity.

God can use it to point others to Christ's transforming power.

WISDOM FOR TODAY

Give us a passion, Lord, for sharing our stories of redemption with others. Help us identify and take advantage of opportunities to tell people about the change You've made in us and can make in them as well.

HEAD BACK HOME!

You may be sure that your sin will find you out.

NUMBERS 32:23

The Bible tells us that there can be pleasure in sin. We know this from our own experience. But the Bible also says that sin's pleasure is only for a season (Hebrews 11:25). Then it's over, leaving us bitter, and finally destroying us. A day of reckoning always comes. No one has ever committed a sin that he or she did not have to pay for.

In Luke 15 we read of a loving father and his son who learned this lesson the hard way. The boy had been reared in a wonderful home, with a father and mother who worshiped God. They loved their children and tried to raise them right. But this young man left home and wasted his inheritance on foolish and sinful living—and he paid the price. Eventually he found himself living in a pigpen and eating with the pigs. That is how low he sank . . . before he headed back home.

What sin do you need to leave behind? Repent and return to your Father today. He wants to welcome you home!

WISDOM FOR TODAY

Thank You, Lord, for being a Father who welcomes home the prodigal child. No matter how far we have wandered or what embarrassment we have brought on ourselves, You readily receive us with open arms and restore us to fellowship with You.

STANDING STRONG AGAINST TEMPTATION

[Take up] the sword of the Spirit, which is the word of God.
EPHESIANS 6:17

Temptation is exactly the same for us as it was for Adam and Eve in the garden of Eden. And Satan also tempts us in the same way as he tempted Jesus—through "the lust of the flesh, and the lust of the eyes, and the pride of life" (1 John 2:16 KJV).

It is not a sin to be tempted, for everyone is tempted. The devil tempts, but he can tempt you only so far as God permits—and God always provides a way to escape (1 Corinthians 10:13). The sin is in yielding to temptation instead of seeking God's power to escape.

When you face temptation, follow Jesus' example. Satan will say, "For a moment's bowing of your head to me, the money, the fame, the business, the success and power will be yours." But do what Jesus did. Jesus didn't argue with Satan; Jesus didn't debate with him; Jesus didn't rationalize. Instead, He replied, "It is written . . ." Jesus responded to the enemy's temptation with the simple but strong truth of God's Word, Scripture.

Do the same today—and always.

WISDOM FOR TODAY
Your Word, Lord, is more than sufficient to provide an escape for every temptation we face. May we spend time daily in its pages so that we are adequately armed when the enemy shows up to do battle.

By Birth, by Choice, by Practice

*Who will rescue me from this body of death? Thanks
be to God—through Jesus Christ our Lord!*

ROMANS 7:24–25

As much as we hate to admit it, we are sinners by birth. The Bible is clear: "Surely I was sinful at birth, sinful from the time my mother conceived me" (Psalm 51:5).

We are also sinners by choice. There comes a time—actually, it happens several times a day—when we deliberately choose to tell a lie, to steal, to covet, to gossip, to rage. Or we deliberately choose not to be kind, not to serve, or not to help. Sins of commission, sins of omission—we choose both.

We are also sinners by practice. The more we do it, the easier it is to practice lust, greed, hate, lying, stealing, or whatever it may be—pride, jealousy, anger. These things beset all of us. And the more we yield to the pressure, the more easily we will yield next time.

So we join with Paul: "What a wretched man I am! Who will rescue me?" And then with the apostle we thank God for sending His Son, our Savior and Deliverer!

Wisdom for Today

Thank You, Father, for opening our eyes to our areas of sinfulness so that we may choose repentance and receive Your forgiveness. We are so grateful for Your generous grace toward us that covers our every sin.

O LORD, MAKE ME PURE . . .

If we confess our sins, he is faithful and just and will forgive
us our sins and purify us from all unrighteousness.
1 JOHN 1:9

Saint Augustine was one of the greatest theologians who ever lived. But before he surrendered his heart and his life to Christ, he was a wicked young man, and his besetting sin was lust.

When he was first convicted of his sin, Augustine prayed, "O Lord, make me pure—but not yet." Only when he prayed, "Now, Lord, now. Do it now, Lord," was he forgiven and cleansed.

Augustine was converted to Christ, and God made him pure. Sixteen hundred years ago Augustine started following Jesus, and he changed the direction of Christianity as he called on people to rediscover the Scriptures and focus on Christ.

What besetting sin do you struggle with? Sin is often, if not always, the perversion of something good. In the midst of all our sinning, though, God is willing to forgive us, change us, and give us a new power to overcome that sin.

Are you praying, "Make me pure—but not yet"? Maybe today is the day to say, "Do it now, Lord. Now."

WISDOM FOR TODAY

Let today be the day, Lord, that we finally turn from our fleshly desires and draw near to You instead. Give us the discipline and devotion to choose You and Your ways each and every day.

FEAR—AND FEAR NOT!

*Now, O Israel, what does the Lord your God ask of you but to fear
the Lord your God, to walk in all his ways, to love him?*

DEUTERONOMY 10:12

The Bible says, "Fear not"—"Fear not, for I am with thee" (Genesis 26:24
KJV). But the Bible also says, "Fear the Lord." If God's Word says, "Fear not,"
and yet it also says, "Fear," which does it mean? The answer is: both.

Fear is a twofold word. It refers to an emotion marked by dread and anxious
concern. But it also means awe and wonder and profound reverence. This latter
is the fear that inspires trust and confidence. The Bible calls us to have the latter
kind of fear.

When we fear God, we don't cringe before Him like a prisoner robbed of
freedom by a ruthless dictator. Our fear causes us to treat God with respect
and trust. It is a reverence that comes from seeing the majesty and holiness and
power of our loving heavenly Father.

There is no shame in being afraid. We're all afraid from time to time. But
there's an interesting paradox here, in that if we truly fear God with all our
heart, then we have nothing to fear.

WISDOM FOR TODAY

Praise You, Lord, that those who live in reverence of You have no reason for
earthly dread. We need not fear the enemy or his schemes, evil people, or
uncertain days, because we trust that You are in control of it all.

LOVE BY YOUR ACTIONS

"Love the Lord your God with all your heart and with all your soul and with all your strength and with all your mind"; and, "Love your neighbor as yourself."
LUKE 10:27

Did you know that the religious leaders of Jesus' day had more than six hundred man-made laws they were required to obey? The people couldn't keep all those laws; it was impossible. Yet the rulers believed that those laws had to be obeyed in order to win God's favor.

But Jesus summed up God's Law with only two commands: "Love the Lord your God" and "Love your neighbor." And He used a special, all-encompassing word for love, a word that includes everyone. We are to love our neighbors, He said, even though they may have a different color skin, ethnic background, or language; even though they look different, walk differently, or act differently. We are also to help our neighbors who are poor. The Gospel of Christ has no meaning unless it is applied to those who are in need.

The Greek word for love that Jesus used implies action. It is not a passive word; it is an action word. We are to love by our actions. What will you do today to show God's love by your actions?

WISDOM FOR TODAY

Lord, You gave us a perfect example of love in action when You came to earth to die on the behalf of all who would believe. Help us to love You and others with the same selflessness, passion, commitment, and obedience to You.

RESPONDING TO GOD'S CALL

There are different kinds of gifts, but the same Spirit. There are different kinds of service, but the same Lord. There are different kinds of working, but the same God works all of them in all men.

1 CORINTHIANS 12:4–6

I can remember when God first called me into His ministry. I thought of all the things I would have to give up or change. I wept, and I fought, and I battled. But ultimately I answered the Lord's call and began to serve Jesus Christ in a new way. I promised God then that I would never do anything as long as I lived except preach the Gospel.

God's call on your life may not be as dramatic as mine was, and the ministry that results from your obedience may not be the same as mine. But none of that takes away from the significance of what you are doing with your life in the service of your King.

William Borden, heir to a large fortune and graduate of Yale, sacrificed everything to go to China as a missionary. He got as far as Egypt and died of cerebral meningitis in Cairo. Later it was written of him that he had "no reserve, no retreat, no regrets." May you and I also live for Christ with no reserve, no retreat, and no regrets.

WISDOM FOR TODAY

God, give us the boldness to go wherever You send us, do whatever You call us to do, and to serve You until our dying breath. A life lived for You is a life well lived.

THE BOTTOM LINE

I resolved to know nothing while I was with you
except Jesus Christ and him crucified.

1 CORINTHIANS 2:2

I remember preaching in Dallas, Texas, early in our ministry. It was 1953. Many thousands attended each night, but one evening only a few people responded to the appeal to receive Jesus Christ. Discouraged, I left the platform.

A German businessman was there, a devout man of God. He put his arm around me and said, "Billy, do you know what was wrong tonight? You didn't preach the cross." He was right.

The next night I preached on Christ and His sacrificial death for us, and a great host of people received Christ as Savior. When we preach Christ crucified and risen, that message has a built-in spiritual power. The Holy Spirit takes the simple message of the cross, with its theme of redemptive love and grace, and infuses it with authority. This supernatural act of God's Spirit breaks down barriers in people's hearts.

So whether you're preaching with actions or words—in your home, neighborhood, or workplace—be sure that you're preaching the cross. The Spirit will be at work.

WISDOM FOR TODAY

Remind us, Lord, as we share our stories, serve our neighbors, and go about our days, to always point others to You. May we live in such a way that Your presence in our lives is obvious.

TEARS OF LOVE

Dear children, let us not love with words or tongue but with actions and in truth.

1 JOHN 3:18

One of our associate evangelists was preaching at a university. He yearned to win the students to Christ, but their reaction was hostile. One young woman was especially antagonistic. After the lecture she came to him and said, "I don't believe anything you said."

He replied, "I'm sorry that you don't agree, but do you mind if I pray for you?"

She answered, "Nobody has ever prayed for me before. I guess it won't do any harm."

He bowed his head and began to pray. She stood looking straight ahead. But suddenly she noticed that while he was praying, tears were coming down his cheeks. When he opened his eyes, she herself was in tears. She said, "No one in my entire life has ever shed a tear for me." They sat on a bench, and that woman accepted Christ as her Savior.

May the Lord use you today to help bring someone into His kingdom by your love and your witness.

WISDOM FOR TODAY

Give us a genuine love, Lord, for the people You've placed in our lives. Make it a love that is evident in the way we live and interact with others so that there would be no doubt that we are Your disciples.

READ THE LABEL

*For the wages of sin is death, but the gift of God is
eternal life in Christ Jesus our Lord.*
ROMANS 6:23

After a minister had spoken strongly against sin one morning, one of his members said, "We don't want you to talk so plainly about sin, because if our children hear you mention it, they will more easily become sinners. Call it a mistake, if you will, but do not speak so bluntly about sin."

The minister went to his medicine shelf and brought back a bottle of strychnine marked "Poison." He said, "I understand what you want me to do. You want me to change the label. Suppose I take this 'Poison' label off the bottle and put on a label like 'Peppermint Candy.' Can't you see the problem? The milder you make the label, the more dangerous the poison's presence."

It is high time we put a "Poison" label back on the poison of sin. The Bible does not sugarcoat the tragedy of sin's consequences. The antidote for sin's poison is the blood of Christ.

WISDOM FOR TODAY
In Your love for us, Father, You speak truth to us through Your Word. Thank You for telling us what we must know and not what we think we want to hear. Help us to do the same for others.

CAVING IN TO THE CROWD

Then Pilate announced . . . "I find no basis for a charge against this man." . . . But with loud shouts they insistently demanded that he be crucified, and their shouts prevailed.

LUKE 23:4, 23

The name of Pontius Pilate will be forever linked to the death of Jesus Christ, for it was he, as Roman governor, who gave the final order condemning Jesus to death by crucifixion.

But the name of Pontius Pilate will also stand forever as a prime example of someone who knew what was right—but failed to do it. Repeatedly he told the mob clamoring for Jesus' death that he found no basis for condemning Him—but in the end, he caved in to the pressures of the crowd and ordered His death. Publicly he washed his hands and told the crowd that they alone were responsible for Jesus' death (Matthew 27:24), but in reality Pilate's cowardice sent Jesus to the cross.

How often do you cave in to the pressures of the crowd, seeking the approval of others instead of the approval of God? We all like to be liked—but that can be a very dangerous thing. Make it your goal to live for Christ and be faithful to Him, regardless of what the crowd demands.

WISDOM FOR TODAY

You've warned us, Father, of the dangers of living our lives in order to please man. Give us the boldness to stand against the crowd when necessary and to choose obedience to You over popularity with the world.

THE POISON OF PRIDE

The LORD detests all the proud of heart.
Be sure of this: They will not go unpunished.
PROVERBS 16:5

The pride that God loathes is not a healthy self-respect or a legitimate sense of personal dignity. It is the haughty, undue self-esteem out of all proportion to our actual worth. It is the repugnant egotism that is repulsive to both man and God. It is that revolting conceit that swaggers before men and struts in the presence of the Almighty. And God hates it.

Pride may take various forms. Spiritual pride trusts in one's own virtue rather than in the grace of God. Intellectual pride gives its possessor self-confidence rather than God-confidence. Pride in material things enthrones self and displaces God; secondary things are exalted to the place of first importance. Social pride manifests itself in arrogance and status. All forms of pride emanate from the haughty human heart, and pride is the sin that God hates most.

What can you do about it? Confess your pride. Humble yourself in the sight of God. Look then at Christ, who "humbled himself and became obedient to death—even death on a cross!" (Philippians 2:8).

WISDOM FOR TODAY
We live in a world, Father, that encourages pride in a person and misunderstands and mocks humility. We know that every good and perfect gift comes from You, and we will choose the way of humility over pride.

THE POISON OF ANGER

A fool gives full vent to his anger.

PROVERBS 29:11

Anger is one sin that everyone is capable of committing. The tiny baby has a tantrum and spits up her dinner. The little boy has a tantrum and ruins the family gathering. The wife loses her temper and wounds her child's heart. The husband gets angry and terrifies his family. Homes can be destroyed by the swirling tornadoes of anger. Business relations can be shattered by fits of violent temper. Friendships can be broken by anger.

Anger causes murders, assaults, and conflicts. Anger brings out the animal nature of human beings. It hinders our Christian testimony and causes people to lose the joy of living. Too many of us excuse our anger by blaming our natural disposition, but anger is sin.

The first step in finding victory over anger is to want to get rid of it. Next comes confession. Then comes a yielding to God. His Spirit can tame your tongue and your passions when you surrender your heart to Jesus. He who calmed the turbulent Sea of Galilee can calm the tempestuous sea of your anger with His love.

WISDOM FOR TODAY

Help us to recognize our anger for the sin that it is, Father. Create in us, in its place, gentle and quiet spirits that are far more pleasing in Your sight (Philippians 4:5).

THE POISON OF ENVY

A heart at peace gives life to the body,
but envy rots the bones.
PROVERBS 14:30

In ancient Greece, the citizens of a certain city erected a statue of a celebrated champion in the public games. But his rival was so envious that he vowed to destroy that statue. Every night he went after dark and chiseled away at its base in an effort to undermine its foundation and make it fall. At last he succeeded. It did fall—but it fell on him. The jealous athlete died, a victim of his own envy.

Envy destroys our spiritual health, and it takes the joy, happiness, and contentment out of living. Envy becomes a spiritual leprosy, isolating us from both God and other human beings. No wonder God ranks envy on the same level as sexual immorality, idolatry, witchcraft, and drunkenness (see Galatians 5:19–21).

To get rid of this devastating poison, first recognize that you have it. Then confess your sin to God and renounce it. Finally, since envy cannot be overcome in your own strength, open your heart to the transforming power of Christ.

WISDOM FOR TODAY
Envy destroys a person from the inside out. Guard our hearts, Lord, from this evil that can slip in so easily. May we be quick to recognize a jealous spirit and choose, instead, to count the many blessings You've given us.

THE POISON OF IMPURITY

*Among you there must not be even a hint of sexual immorality, or of any
kind of impurity . . . because these are improper for God's holy people.*

EPHESIANS 5:3

In God's eyes, impurity is one of the most revolting sins, because it twists and
distorts one of God's most precious gifts: human love. Impurity drags this gift
down to the level of the beast.

Yet impurity—surrounding us as it does in the form of filthy stories, sugges-
tive remarks, open vulgarity; in magazines, on television, in the movies, through
the Internet—has a better press agent than purity. Purity is considered smug,
but impurity is considered smart—and the consequences of this vicious sin are
played down. Satan fails to speak of the remorse, the futility, the loneliness, and
the spiritual devastation that go hand in hand with immorality.

Christ can do only one thing with the sin of impurity—and every other sin.
Jesus does not condone sin; He forgives it. He will also cleanse you and give you
victory over your sin. Jesus said to the immoral woman, "Go now and leave your
life of sin" (John 8:11). He says that to you as well—and He never told anyone to
do something without offering them the power to do it.

WISDOM FOR TODAY

Give us the strength, Father, to flee sexual immorality. Help us to use wisdom
and discernment in our interactions with other people and in our choice of
activities so we do not needlessly tempt ourselves.

THE POISON OF GLUTTONY

So whether you eat or drink or whatever you do, do it all for the glory of God.
1 CORINTHIANS 10:31

Before the fall of Rome, the Romans were given to gluttony, immorality, and drunkenness. They dug their grave with their teeth, killed themselves by illicit indulgence, and embalmed themselves with alcohol. It is said that, at their sumptuous banquets, men would rush to the windows, eject the contents of their stomachs, and then return to the table for further indulgence. No individual or nation given to drunkenness and gluttony can expect the blessing of God. Rome fell because she overstuffed her body and starved her soul.

Such gluttony is a perversion of a natural, God-given appetite. The gratification of our fleshly appetites is not to receive first importance in our lives. When we cater to the appetites of the flesh—when a normal hunger is extended into abnormality so that it harms the body, dulls the mind, and causes us to neglect the soul—we become guilty of the sin of gluttony.

When we acknowledge that sin and confess it, Jesus will forgive the past and provide the powers of self-discipline, temperance, and restraint for the days ahead.

WISDOM FOR TODAY

We are so grateful, Lord, that You highlight sinful behaviors that are harmful to our spirits and bodies. Help us to learn from those who've gone before us so that we do not suffer the same fate, and may our strongest desire always be for You.

THE POISON OF SLOTH

The sluggard's craving will be the death of him,
because his hands refuse to work.
PROVERBS 21:25

Webster's defines *sloth* as "a disinclination to action or labor; sluggishness, laziness, idleness." In theological contexts, *sloth* carries with it not only the idea of laziness in spiritual things, but also apathy and inactivity in the practice of our everyday lives.

The slothful person is like a piece of driftwood floating effortlessly and heedlessly downstream with the current. It takes no effort, no strength to be lost. A drifting boat always goes downstream, never up. Likewise, a drifting, slothful soul is inevitably moving toward an eternity of destruction.

The sin of doing nothing—the sin of omission—is just as dangerous as any sin of action—of commission. You don't have to do anything to be lost: just do nothing. Just be slothful about your soul. Tragically, thousands of us Christians are slothful also—when it comes to prayer, worship, reading the Bible, witnessing for Christ, helping neighbors in need, giving to charity, or giving to God's work.

A stubborn, slothful spirit is a great hindrance to receiving Jesus' forgiveness and transforming power. Don't let this happen to you.

WISDOM FOR TODAY

Father, we do not want to simply drift through life. We don't want to look back and see missed opportunities for growth and service. Help us to be obedient in our efforts to become more like You.

THE POISON OF GREED

From the least to the greatest,
all are greedy for gain.
JEREMIAH 6:13

A close relative of covetousness, greed is quite possibly the parent of more evil than any other sin. Greed cheats, robs, murders, and slanders in order to achieve its desires—and each of us is born with greed in our nature.

The Bible teaches that greed is idolatry, because it places things at the center of our lives instead of God. We in America, for instance, are so bent on making money that we do not have time for God and the spiritual disciplines. It is not a sin to be rich, but if our riches have choked out our spiritual life, then being rich has become sin—and we are poverty-stricken in God's sight. Furthermore, the love of money corrodes the human heart, spoiling our happiness and setting us in conflict with one another. The Bible says that "the love of money is a root of all kinds of evil" (1 Timothy 6:10).

As long as the prodigal son sang the song of "Give me," his lot was misery, want, loneliness, and famine. But when he changed his song to "Forgive me," he found himself in a state of fellowship, comfort, and plenty. What song are you singing?

WISDOM FOR TODAY
When all we want is You, Lord, we have all that we desire and more. Teach us not to set our hearts on the things of this world, for it promises what it can't provide and leaves us empty inside.

APRIL

LOVE AND JUSTICE MEET

Then Jesus went with his disciples to a place called Gethsemane . . .
and he began to be sorrowful and troubled.
MATTHEW 26:36–37

The word *Gethsemane* means "an oil press." When olives are harvested, they are squeezed under an enormous revolving stone that mashes the fruit to pulp and recovers the valuable oil.

In the garden of Gethsemane, the wheel of humiliation and death would squeeze Jesus to the point of His greatest agony, so He pleaded with His Father for release—but only if it were the Almighty's will.

God did not grant release, for there was no other way for our just and loving God to deal with our sins. Sin must be punished. If God were simply to forgive our sins without judging them, then there would be no justice, no accountability for wrongdoing. God would not be truly holy and just.

But if God were simply to judge us for our sins as we deserve, there would be no hope of salvation for any of us. His love would have failed to provide what we need.

The cross was the only way to resolve the problem of sin. At the cross God's love and justice came together. Jesus took the punishment we deserved, and now we are clothed in His perfect righteousness.

WISDOM FOR TODAY

We never have to question Your love for us, Lord; You proved it once and for all on the cross. Thank You for the life You lived, the death You died, and the way You overcame the grip of the grave.

THE CHOICE

Being in anguish, [Jesus] prayed more earnestly, and his sweat was like drops of blood falling to the ground.

LUKE 22:44

The garden of Gethsemane is the place where Jesus was revealed to be truly human. There He faced the choice between obedience and disobedience. He was not a robot programmed to obey God automatically. He knows what it's like to be tempted. And after three years of selfless giving and the stress of that final week, Jesus was never more vulnerable to temptation than at this moment in Gethsemane.

Some skeptics have said that Jesus' agony in Gethsemane was a sign of weakness. They point out that many martyrs, for instance, died without the intense emotional wrestling of Jesus. But it is one thing to die for a cause or for a country. It is quite another to die for an entire world—for all the accumulated sins of generations past and generations to come.

No one ever experienced greater spiritual suffering than Jesus. His death was a spiritual battle against the powers of darkness, and His resurrection meant the triumph of God over Satan. No mere man could defeat Satan. Only Jesus.

All praise to the Man who was also God—Jesus Christ!

WISDOM FOR TODAY

Thank You, Jesus, for choosing the cross and suffering for sinners like us. There is no other who would be willing to die for the undeserving and able to redeem the wretched. Only You, Jesus.

THE KEY MOMENT IN HISTORY

"I am the resurrection and the life. He who believes in me will live, even though he dies; and whoever lives and believes in me will never die."
JOHN 11:25–26

On that first Easter morning, something happened that had never happened before in the history of the human race—and would never happen again: someone came back from the dead, never to die again.

What difference does that event make? It makes all the difference in the world to us! For one thing, the resurrection proved beyond all doubt that Jesus was who He claimed to be: the Son of God sent from heaven to save us from our sins. Because He rose from the dead, our salvation is secure.

But Jesus' resurrection also tells us that there is life beyond the grave. This world is not all there is; when we die, we continue to live—either in the place of utter darkness the Bible calls hell or in the place of endless joy the Bible calls heaven. And now Jesus has opened the way to heaven for us, by His death and resurrection. Because Jesus rose from the dead, death has been defeated and heaven awaits us. Hallelujah!

WISDOM FOR TODAY

Praise You, Lord, that those who trust in You are no longer slaves to the fear of death. The grave has no hold on us, and death has now become gain, resulting in eternal life in heaven.

JESUS IS ALIVE!

[May you know] his incomparably great power for us who believe.
That power is like the working of his mighty strength, which
he exerted in Christ when he raised him from the dead.

EPHESIANS 1:19–20

Did you know that the same power that raised Christ from the dead is available to you and me today? The moment we receive Jesus as Savior, the Holy Spirit comes into our hearts. He gives us supernatural power to overcome temptations, to smile through tears, to experience joy despite life's burdens and trials. The Holy Spirit will raise you from the mundane, the monotonous, the hopeless; He will raise you out of your spiritual lifelessness and transform you.

In fact, imagine what a difference it would make if people understood that Christ is risen and the Holy Spirit has been given! What a transformation would take place in our families! What a reversal there would be in our culture's deteriorating morals! What a lessening of tensions we would see between individuals, groups, and even nations! And what a new purpose and power we would experience if we caught the wonder of the biblical truth that Jesus is alive!

Believe and share the truth that can fuel this transformation: Jesus is alive!

WISDOM FOR TODAY
What would it look like, Lord, for us to live in the power of Your resurrection? What would we attempt for Your glory? What would we dare to do in Your name? Help us to experience it today.

ALL FOR LOVE

He was pierced for our transgressions,
he was crushed for our iniquities;
the punishment that brought us peace was upon him,
and by his wounds we are healed.
ISAIAH 53:5

Flogged . . . Bits of glass and rocks shredded the flesh of His back . . . Crucified . . . Nailed to the rough wood of the cross and left hanging there to experience the excruciating pain of death by suffocation . . .

Why did Jesus willingly die such a violent death? The Bible says He went to the cross for one reason: to become the final and complete sacrifice for our sins. Each of us has sinned; each of us is guilty before God; each of us deserves to die. God is holy and just, and sin must be punished.

But Christ became our substitute; He died in our place. He was without sin, but all our sins were placed on Him, and He willingly took the punishment and death we deserve. The Bible says, "Christ died for sins once for all, the righteous for the unrighteous, to bring you to God" (1 Peter 3:18). Christ died for you!

Why did He do this? He did it because He loves you, and He wants you to spend eternity with Him in heaven. Have you responded to His love?

WISDOM FOR TODAY
It's difficult to fathom such devotion, Father, that Jesus chose the cross out of love for us. When the world attempts to make us question that love, we will, like Paul, choose to know nothing except Christ and Him crucified.

CAN WE KNOW?

For what I received I passed on to you as of first importance: that
Christ died for our sins according to the Scriptures, that he was buried,
that he was raised on the third day according to the Scriptures.

1 CORINTHIANS 15:3–4

I suppose I'd believe in life after death if I ever met someone who had gone there and then came back to tell about it," a man wrote me once. But that is exactly what Jesus did when He died and then came back to life by the power of God.

When Jesus was put to death, He truly died. The Roman soldiers who nailed Him to the cross attested to that fact when they took His body down and placed it in a tomb. Its entrance was sealed with a huge stone and placed under guard. But that was not the end of the story . . .

Two days later the tomb was empty, and shortly afterward Jesus appeared numerous times to His followers—as many as five hundred on one occasion. His resurrection proved that Jesus was who He claimed to be, the Son of God, sent from heaven to save us from our sins. But it also proved for all time that there is life after death, and that we will go to be with Him in heaven forever if we know Him.

Is your hope in Christ—both for this life and the life to come?

WISDOM FOR TODAY

Help us, Father, to approach each day with a Gospel mind-set. Let every decision we make and every personal interaction we experience reflect the hope we have because of the death and resurrection of Jesus.

"WHERE, O DEATH, IS YOUR VICTORY?"

Our Savior, Christ Jesus . . . has destroyed death and has
brought life and immortality to light through the gospel.
2 TIMOTHY 1:10

Think about the holes children make when they dig in the sand on the seashore. When the waves come in, the holes are swallowed up by the ocean. Similarly, when we know Christ, our physical death is overwhelmed by the love and grace of God. Death is swallowed up in the victory of Christ.

Death is an incident, not an end. It is a transition for a Christian, not a terminus. In death we are freed from all that burdens us here. We lay aside the outward "tent" of our body, and we inherit "a building from God, a house not made with hands, eternal in the heavens" (2 Corinthians 5:1 NASB).

Here our lives are filled with suffering and confusion. We experience pain and problems, and sometimes life seems to have no meaning or purpose. But the resurrection of Jesus Christ changed all that. It gives purpose and meaning to life, and life's greatest joy comes from discovering His will and fulfilling it. His resurrection also gives us hope—hope right now, and hope beyond the grave. May these truths encourage you this day!

WISDOM FOR TODAY
Only You, Lord, could conquer death and make it a source of freedom where it once brought only fear. Because of You, we can approach life and death with hope, knowing that greater things still await us.

GOD'S ONLY SON, OUR SAVIOR

Praise be to God and Father of our Lord Jesus Christ, who has blessed us in the heavenly realms with every spiritual blessing in Christ.

EPHESIANS 1:3

It has often been pointed out that Jesus lived in a small country and never went beyond its borders. He was so poor that He said He had nowhere to lay His head. His only pocketbook was the mouth of a fish. He rode on another man's beast. He cruised the lake in another man's boat. He was buried in another man's grave. And He had laid aside a royal robe for all this.

He never wrote a book. His recorded words would hardly make a pocket edition. Yet if all the words that have been written about Him were brought together, they would fill a thousand libraries.

He never founded a college to perpetuate His doctrines. Yet His teachings have endured for more than two thousand years.

He never carried a sword, He never organized an army, He never built a navy, and He never had an air force. Yet He founded an empire in which there are millions today who would die for Him.

And His name is "Wonderful Counselor, Mighty God, Everlasting Father, Prince of Peace" (Isaiah 9:6). Praise His name!

WISDOM FOR TODAY

You have taught us, Lord, what truly matters in this life. On earth You never sought power, prestige, or popularity. You loved well, served humbly, and sacrificed greatly for us. Help us to follow Your example in our daily lives.

THE CROSS OF CHRIST

For the message of the cross is foolishness to those who are perishing,
but to us who are being saved it is the power of God.
1 CORINTHIANS 1:18

Why is the cross an offense?
First, the cross of Christ is an offense because it condemns the world. It says, "You are sinners"—and we don't like someone pointing out our faults, failures, mistakes, and especially our sins.

The cross also offends and confuses an unbelieving world because blood was shed, and blood is repulsive. But Christ's blood is the blood of redemption, forgiveness, peace, and reconciliation. By His blood—by His death on the cross—we are released from the guilt of sin and accepted as righteous in God's sight (Colossians 1:20).

The cross is an offense as well because it demands a disciplined life: following Jesus will mean denying self and bearing one's own cross.

In addition, the Cross offends because it points to the end of the world as we know it, and that end will be marked by the return of Jesus Christ as Prince of Peace and Lord of lords.

Finally, the cross of Christ is an offense because it claims to be the only way of salvation, the only way to God. Have you chosen to follow the way of the cross?

WISDOM FOR TODAY

Help us, Father, to fully embrace and live out the message of the cross. May it convict us of our sins and challenge us to live more passionately for You.

GLORY IN THE CROSS

God forbid that I should glory, save in the cross of our Lord Jesus Christ.

GALATIANS 6:14 KJV

Why did the apostle Paul say that he gloried in the cross of Christ above everything else?

Paul could have gloried in many things about himself. He could have gloried in his education: he was one of the most brilliant men of his day. A Jew and a Pharisee, Paul could have gloried in his religion. And he could have gloried in his Roman citizenship.

Or Paul could have gloried in other aspects of Jesus' life. He could have gloried in His birth: Jesus was virgin born. Or in the teachings of Jesus: no one had ever taught like Jesus. Paul could have gloried in the resurrection of Jesus or in His future glory when He will return as the victorious and conquering King.

But Paul gloried in the cross. Why? The cross shows the seriousness of our sin—but it also shows us the immeasurable love of God. Furthermore, the cross is the only way of salvation. And the cross gives a new purpose to life. Once you have been to the cross, you will never be the same.

No wonder Paul—and you and I—can glory in the cross.

WISDOM FOR TODAY

For Christ followers, the cross is the center of our lives; it is the essence of our existence. Help us to always and only boast in Your work on the cross and to point others to the salvation found in it.

THE SPIRIT WITHIN YOU

Do you not know that your body is a temple of the Holy Spirit,
who is in you, whom you have received from God?
1 CORINTHIANS 6:19

If you have truly asked Christ to come into your life, you can be confident that the Holy Spirit resides in you—whether or not you feel His presence. The Bible says, "For you . . . received the Spirit of sonship" (Romans 8:15).

Even though the Spirit lives within us, however, we must yield our lives to Him every day because our old nature is still present. Furthermore, Satan will try to tempt us and convince us we must fight our spiritual battles alone. That's why every day we should pray something like this: "Lord, I know that on my own I can't live the way You want me to live—but with Your help I can. Please help me today to step aside and allow Your Holy Spirit to work in me and through me."

Yielding to God's Spirit doesn't mean all your problems will vanish; you and I are engaged in a spiritual battle that will last as long as we live. But we are not alone in that battle. God has provided His armor—including His Spirit—to help us (Ephesians 6:10–18).

Thank God that He lives within you by His Holy Spirit!

WISDOM FOR TODAY
Just as Jesus entered His period of temptation in the wilderness full of the Holy Spirit, we can enter each day filled with the same Holy Spirit. Give us the discipline to seek and to obey His will.

THE GIFT OF GENEROSITY

"Give, and it will be given to you. A good measure, pressed down,
shaken together and running over, will be poured into your lap.
For with the measure you use, it will be measured to you."

LUKE 6:38

Generosity doesn't come naturally to most of us—not the kind of generosity the Bible urges us to have. Most of us will gladly give if we think the cause is worthy and we feel we can afford it. But the Bible urges us to go beyond that: to give sacrificially to God's work.

God's work demands prayer, and dedication, and vision, and reliance on the Holy Spirit. But it also requires our financial resources. Even Jesus' little band of disciples relied on the generosity of others to carry on their work; we read of a group of godly women who "were helping to support them out of their own means" (Luke 8:3).

Never forget: everything you have has been given to you by God. Yes, you may have worked hard and become successful—but who gave you your abilities, and who put you in a society where it was possible to become prosperous? Put Christ first in everything—including your finances. Christ gave His all for you; dare you do anything less for Him?

WISDOM FOR TODAY

When we are tempted to be stingy, Father, we will choose instead to be generous. When we fear not having enough, we will give even more. When we begin to feel pride over any area of our lives, we will remember that it all belongs to You.

THE M WORD

Now about the collection for God's people. . . . On the first day of every week, each one of you should set aside a sum of money in keeping with his income.
1 CORINTHIANS 16:1–2

Sadly, many people who visit churches are put off by what may seem like constant requests for money. And, tragically, some churches and other ministries have given people cause to wonder—or even turn away. But when someone complains to you about the Church always asking for money, gently remind them of two things.

First, invite them to consider what most churches actually do with the money they collect. Almost without exception they use it to reach out to others, seeking—with God's help—to make this world a better place. Who can object to that?

Second, encourage them to look beyond their ideas about Jesus, and discover what He is really like by turning to the New Testament Gospels and letting Jesus speak for Himself. (I often recommend the Gospel of John as a starting point, because it was written to help people know Jesus.)

This is basically an invitation to be honest. After all, how can someone who doesn't know very much about Jesus reject Him? Once you examine who Jesus was and what He did for you, you cannot remain neutral.

WISDOM FOR TODAY
It is a privilege, Lord, to be a part of the work You are doing both locally and around the globe. Help us to be reminded of that fact and to be cheerful givers.

KEEPING MONEY OUR SERVANT

"Do not worry about your life, what you will eat or drink. . . .
Your heavenly father knows that you need them."

MATTHEW 6:25, 32

We aren't supposed to let money become the most important thing in life, but when bills mount, it's hard not to become preoccupied.

The problem is that money can all too easily become our master instead of our servant. That's why the Bible so often talks about money, warning of its dangers and urging us to put it in its rightful place. The writer of Ecclesiastes wisely observed, "Whoever loves money never has money enough; whoever loves wealth is never satisfied" (5:10).

Once we put Christ first in our life, however, we can ask Him to help us trust Him for our needs. Our heavenly Father knows we need clothes, food, and a place to live, so we don't need to worry. That may seem impossible, but God will give us His peace as we learn to trust Him.

We also need to deal with our finances responsibly—following a realistic budget, developing a plan to pay off debt, even cutting up our credit cards if necessary.

Don't become a slave to money, but learn to trust God in everything.

WISDOM FOR TODAY

Help us, Lord, to be very mindful of the importance we place on money in our lives. May we use any financial blessings for Your glory, knowing that every good and perfect gift comes from Your hand.

SIMPLE, BUT NOT ALWAYS EASY

Give everyone what you owe him: If you owe taxes,
pay taxes; if revenue, then revenue.

ROMANS 13:7

Jesus stated it clearly: "You cannot serve both God and Money" (Luke 16:13). Yet too many people try.

Someone wrote to me about money he had made selling some items for cash. He didn't see any reason "to tell the government about it"—but his wife disagreed, and so did I.

First, cheating of any kind will always keep you wondering if you'll be discovered. Second, you won't like the feeling that comes with knowing you lack integrity and are dishonest.

But there is a deeper reason: as the verse above indicates, if we cheat, we are disobeying God. In His eyes, failing to pay the taxes we owe is little different from stealing from an individual. Furthermore, if we fail to pay the taxes we owe, honest citizens will have to make up the shortfall.

If cheating of any kind enters our mind, we need to ask ourselves why we would even consider it. Is money too important to us? Is greed ruling us? Whatever it is, confess it and put Christ first in your life.

WISDOM FOR TODAY

Cheating is often the result of not trusting You to provide what we need, Lord. Help us to handle our financial dealings with honesty and humility, knowing that honoring You should be our highest priority.

ROBBING GOD

A poor widow came and put in two very small copper coins. . . . Jesus said, "I tell you the truth, this poor widow has put more into the treasury than all the others. . . . She, out of her poverty, put in everything—all she had to live on."

MARK 12:42–44

A young man came to me one night and said, "Billy, I pray, read the Bible, and go to church, but I have no victory in my life. What can I do?"

I thought for a moment and asked, "Do you tithe? Do you give to God's work?"

He replied, "No, I don't, but I don't make very much money."

I said, "That's not the point. No one can rob God and expect to experience victory in life."

We can pray all day long. We can go to church every week. We can read our Bible through a thousand times—but if we are robbing God, we will be miserable and spiritually dry.

Do you think you can rob God but have victory in your life? It cannot be done. There is no victory if we aren't giving a portion of our income to the Lord.

The basis of our giving is that the tithe—one-tenth of your income—is God's (Malachi 3:10). It's God's rule, and I believe it is still valid today.

WISDOM FOR TODAY

We will not withhold anything from You, Father. We will freely give of our time, our energy, and our money. Give us the discipline and devotion necessary to honor You with the firstfruits of our labor.

CHRIST IN YOU

For to me, to live is Christ.

PHILIPPIANS 1:21

Christ once lived in history—and today He lives on in people's lives. Jesus not only lived on this earth, but He still lives—and He will live forever.

Year after year we have seen thousands of men, women, and young people receive Christ as Savior throughout the world. People with problems, burdens, and sins have committed their lives to Jesus and seen a light in their eyes and a glow on their faces as they are transformed by the Spirit of God. When Christ takes up residence in their hearts, they become new creations in Him.

Today, as always, many people think they can manage without God. They may manage economically, intellectually, and even socially. But down inside they have a spiritual void that can be filled only by Jesus Christ.

Jesus not only lived in the flesh in history, but He can live right now in you: "Christ in you, the hope of glory" (Colossians 1:27). Has Christ come to live in your life? He can—and He will, as you commit your life to Him.

WISDOM FOR TODAY

Lord, I don't want to merely make it through life as unscathed as possible. I want to live the kind of passionate and purposeful life that is possible only when You, the risen Christ, take up residence in me. Only then will I truly live.

FACING YOUR GIANTS

David said to the Philistine, "You come against me with sword and spear and javelin, but I come against you in the name of the LORD."

1 SAMUEL 17:45

What giants are you facing? The giant of peer pressure? Of different ideologies and philosophies fighting for control of your life? What about giants like social injustice, moral deterioration, or crime? Or maybe the giant of fear, joblessness, broken relationships, or family conflict?

Young David faced a giant named Goliath, a member of the Philistine nation—a bitter enemy of God's people. Goliath was more than nine feet tall and clothed with heavy armor. His spear was about the size of a tree trunk. Goliath was one of the largest men in recorded history. He defied the army of Israel, challenging them to send a man against him. David volunteered.

Goliath had David out-armed and out-experienced. Goliath was a great warrior; David was not. David's only weapon was a slingshot—and a deep dependence on God. And God gave him victory.

Everyone has problems, and Christ wants to help you face yours—if you will let Him. No matter what giants you are facing today, put on the full armor of God (Ephesians 6:10–18) and trust Him to give you victory.

WISDOM FOR TODAY

There is no giant, God, that will not fall at the sound of Your name. Teach us to prepare for battle by being in prayer and in Your Word, to face our giants unafraid, and to trust You for the victory.

A SOLID FOUNDATION

"Whoever comes to Me, and hears My sayings and does them . . . is like a man building a house, who dug deep and laid the foundation on the rock."
LUKE 6:47–48 NKJV

Jesus talked about two men who were building houses. One built his house on a solid rock foundation—and when the storms came, his house stood. The other man built his house on sand—and when the storms came, his house crumbled and fell.

Many people today live in homes built on sand. Lacking the right foundation, their family is in trouble. What about you? When the floods of sorrow, the waves of temptation, and the gales of adversity come, will your home stand?

Make Jesus Christ the foundation of your home—and your life. I believe that no home can stand unless the family in that home has a strong faith in Jesus. There needs to be family prayer, Bible reading, and active involvement in a church where Christ is taught and followed. God's pattern for a strong, Christ-centered home is best fulfilled by a godly father and mother—but even when this isn't possible because of death or divorce, Christ can still help you build your home on His will. On what are you building the foundation of your home? The rock of Christ's teaching or the sand of self-will?

WISDOM FOR TODAY

There are so many storms in this world, Lord, and countless homes have proven unable to withstand them. Help us to have homes and families built on the firm foundation of Your Word.

GOD'S SEVEN WONDERS, PART I

Because your love is better than life, my lips will glorify
you. I will praise you as long as I live.

PSALM 63:3–4

There were seven wonders of the ancient world, and from time to time we read about the seven wonders of the modern world. But God has His seven wonders too.

The first is the wonder of God's love. The Almighty God, the Creator of the whole universe, loves you and is interested in you as if you were the only person who ever lived. Even when we sin against Him, He still wants to put His arms around us and say, "I love you."

The second is the wonder of God coming to live among us. God became a man—and that man was Jesus. He took on flesh so that He might know our trials and heartaches and be tempted as we are. He understands us.

The third is the wonder of the cross. Jesus died for you and for me. Far more than His excruciatingly painful physical death, He suffered spiritually when God laid on Him your sins and mine. He who had never known sin took the penalty for all our sin.

What wondrous love is this!

WISDOM FOR TODAY

Your love for us, Father, truly is a wonder—the way You pursue, protect, and provide. You love us as no other could, and You sacrificed the way no other would. May we never question Your feelings for us.

GOD'S SEVEN WONDERS, PART II

Here I am! I stand at the door and knock. If anyone hears my voice and
opens the door, I will come in and eat with him, and he with me.
REVELATION 3:20

The fourth of God's seven wonders is the wonder of conversion. The word *conversion* means "to change, to turn." You cannot convert yourself: you have to have God help you repent. The Holy Spirit helps us say no to sin and yes to Christ—and He gives us new life.

The fifth wonder is the gift of peace and joy that Christ gives. God's wondrous love and the gracious forgiveness He offers through Jesus Christ bring peace and joy.

The sixth wonder is God's plan for the future. I look forward to that day when He will return. What a glorious day that will be when we see Him face-to-face!

The seventh wonder of God is your own commitment to Jesus Christ. He has come to save you, but He won't force you to make that commitment. Have you committed your life to Him—totally and without reserve?

Love, the Incarnation, the cross, conversion, peace and joy, God's plan, your commitment to Jesus—God definitely is the God of wonders!

WISDOM FOR TODAY

Let us not take for granted the wonder of our conversion, Lord, and the fact that You enable us to turn from the darkness to walk in the light with You. Thank You for the wonder of a brand-new life.

CHOICE, CHANGE, CHALLENGE

*"If anyone would come after me, he must deny himself
and take up his cross and follow me."*

MATTHEW 16:24

What is a true Christian?

First, a Christian is a person who has made a choice. We have to choose—just as Adam and Eve did in the garden of Eden—to obey God or rebel against Him. We make that choice initially when we commit our lives to Christ, but we also make that choice day by day, moment by moment. What kind of choices are you making?

Second, a Christian is a person whose life has been changed, or transformed, by the work of the Holy Spirit. The moment you receive Christ—the moment you choose Him—the Spirit of God comes to live in your heart. What changes have taken place in your life—in your thoughts, feelings, behavior, goals, relationships—since you chose to follow Jesus?

Third, a Christian is a person who has accepted a challenge. The challenge is Jesus' call to deny self—our own selfish ambitions, our own sinful pleasures—and take up our cross. In what ways are you denying yourself in order to follow Jesus?

Choice, change, and challenge—these should characterize every Christian. Are they true of you?

WISDOM FOR TODAY

It is our prayer, Father, that our choice to follow You is evident by a change in our attitudes and actions.

THE WORK OF EVERY BELIEVER

When I preach the gospel, I cannot boast, for I am compelled to preach. Woe to me if I do not preach the gospel!

1 CORINTHIANS 9:16

What is an evangelist? An evangelist is a person with a special gift and a special calling from the Holy Spirit to announce the Good News of the Gospel. It is also a calling from God. Understanding this will help protect us from two dangerous temptations.

First, this understanding will protect us from pride because we know that whatever gift we have and whatever opportunities may open up to us are from God. We cannot take any credit or glory for ourselves. And second, this understanding will save us from discouragement and the temptation to give up, because we know our calling is not from man but from God.

Some are called to be evangelists—but every Christian is called to the work of evangelism, for every Christian is called to tell others about Christ and what He has done for them.

With whom will you share the Good News of Christ today?

WISDOM FOR TODAY

Give us such a passion for the Gospel and such a love for others, Lord, that we can't help but share the Good News. May we never take for granted the part we may play in someone coming to know You.

Your Sin Will Find You Out

Each of you should look not only to your own interests,
but also to the interests of others.

PHILIPPIANS 2:4

When Israel was entering the Promised Land, the two tribes of Reuben and Gad saw that the already conquered territory on the east side of the Jordan was good for their herds and flocks. Thinking only of themselves—of their own needs and the convenience of settling the land they already stood on—rather than being concerned about Israel's inheritance as a whole, they approached Moses with a request: "Let this land be given to your servants as our possession. Do not make us cross the Jordan" (Numbers 32:5).

Moses was an old man, but his eyes blazed, his jaw set, and anger came to his face. Moses said, "Shall your countrymen go to war while you sit here? . . . [If so,] you may be sure your sin will find you out" (Numbers 32:6, 23). Over the years his words proved to be true.

That verse is God's message to any of His people who sit down in apathy and lethargy while their brothers and sisters are in need, or when others are dying and spiritually lost. We can be sure that our sin will find us out.

WISDOM FOR TODAY

Help us not to choose our own comfort over the needs of others, Lord. Let us not rest while those around us struggle in darkness. We will be about our Father's business until He calls us home.

KEEP LOOKING UP!

"Keep watch, because you do not know on what day your Lord will come."
MATTHEW 24:42

Looking across the centuries, the prophets declared that there would be a day when history as we know it would come to an end, with the judgment of God and the return of the Messiah.

What we are seeing today is a shuffling on the stage behind the curtain—a preparation for the day when "the kingdoms of this world [will] become the kingdoms of our Lord and of His Christ; and He shall reign forever and ever" (Revelation 11:15 NKJV).

The Bible is filled with promises of that coming day of glory. Its pages indicate that when Christ returns, the world will not be expecting Him. Just as the people in Noah's day did not believe that a flood was coming, multitudes today do not believe that God's judgment is coming. The flood did come, though, and so will His judgment.

Jesus calls us who know Him to wait in expectation. Our hands should be busy with His work—but our eyes should be looking up. May your watching for Jesus make you even more active in His service!

WISDOM FOR TODAY

Help us, Lord, to live daily with an urgency to share the Gospel with those around us, knowing that Your return is imminent. While we cannot know the exact day, we will live in expectation of seeing You again.

God's Unchanging Standards

And God spoke all these words: "I am the Lord your God, who brought you out of Egypt, out of the land of slavery."

EXODUS 20:1–2

The Ten Commandments serve as the constitution of God's moral universe. The first four commandments show that our main priority is to love God; the other six guide our love of other people.

First, we are to serve God alone. Whatever our heart clings to is our "god," and when we cling to anything or anyone other than God we are guilty of idolatry. God alone must be first in our heart and our life. Next, we are to avoid anything that excludes or obscures the divine nature of God. We are also to honor His name and enter His presence with reverence and respect. In addition, we are to set aside one day in seven for rest and the worship of God.

In the last six commandments, God tells us to honor and obey our parents, not to murder (literally or with our words), to be true to our marriage vows, not to steal from people or from God, not to lie or misrepresent anything, and not to covet what belongs to someone else.

What do these commandments reveal about your love for God and your love for others?

WISDOM FOR TODAY

Thank You, Lord, for the Ten Commandments and the way they remind us how we are to act in relation to You and to the people around us. Only through honoring the first commandment can we attempt to live out the rest.

SIGNS OF THE TIME

"This gospel of the kingdom will be preached in the whole world
as a testimony to all nations, and then the end will come."
MATTHEW 24:14

Parousia, "the coming." *Epiphaneia*, "the appearing." *Apokalupsis*, "the unveiling." As their meanings suggest, these three Greek words in the New Testament all refer to the return of Christ.

And He will come back. Jesus said that only the Father in heaven knows exactly when—and this should keep us from wild speculations. But Jesus did say that we should watch for certain signs.

We should be on guard against false Christs and false prophets. Scripture also teaches that there will be "wars and rumors of wars" (Matthew 24:6) as well as unprecedented natural disasters. Christians will be persecuted for their faith. Hearts once passionate for Jesus will become cold toward Him. This loss of love will create a breakdown of morals—another sign the end is near.

Finally, the worldwide proclamation of the Gospel will point to Christ's return. Only when the whole human race has had an opportunity to respond to the Gospel will the way be clear for His coming.

Are you certain that if He came today, you would be ready?

WISDOM FOR TODAY

You've made it clear, Father, that only You know the time of Christ's return. Give us the wisdom to recognize the signs and to respond appropriately while still being faithfully engaged in the work You've given us to do.

EARNEST, FOCUSED PRAYER

"When you pray, do not keep on babbling like pagans."
MATTHEW 6:7

O bserve carefully the prayer life of Jesus, and notice the earnestness with which He prayed. In Gethsemane He cried out with a loud voice, and in the intensity of His supplication He fell headlong on the damp ground and pleaded before His Father until "his sweat was like drops of blood falling to the ground" (Luke 22:44). Too often—and in very sharp contrast—you and I use petty petitions, oratorical exercises, and the same words we have used for years rather than the cries of our inmost being.

Also, too often when we pray, our thoughts roam. We insult God by speaking to Him with our lips while our minds and hearts are far from Him. Suppose you were talking to a famous person. Would you let your thoughts wander for one moment? No, you would be intensely interested in everything that was said—and very careful about what you were saying. How dare we treat the King of kings with less respect!

May our prayers today—and every day—be from our hearts, and with the focus of our whole being!

WISDOM FOR TODAY

Instill in us, Father, a fresh passion for prayer. May our prayer lives model Christ's in intensity, humility, devotion, and reverence. Let us not take lightly the promise given in Your Word that the prayer of a righteous person has great power.

LESSONS ON PRAYER

"If you remain in me and my words remain in you, ask
whatever you wish, and it will be given you."
JOHN 15:7

Consider what Jesus teaches about prayer.
Jesus tells us to "pray for those who persecute you" (Matthew 5:44). We are to plead for our enemies—just as Jesus prayed for His crucifiers—asking God to lead them to Christ and, for His sake, to forgive them. Jesus also tells us to pray for the conversion of sinners. Prayer is key to our effort to communicate the Gospel and win men and women to Christ.

Another lesson Jesus teaches is the victorious assurance that God answers every true petition (although not always the way we wish He would). We need to trust in the promise of John 15:7 and in the complementary intercession of the Holy Spirit (Romans 8:27).

We also need to remember that with God nothing is impossible. No task is too arduous, no problem too difficult, no burden too heavy for Him. Do not, however, put your will above His. Do not insist on your way. And don't expect an immediate answer to come in exactly the way, the place, and the manner that you are seeking. Rather, learn to pray as Jesus Himself prayed: "Not my will, but yours be done" (Luke 22:42).

WISDOM FOR TODAY

Father, prayer is an opportunity for us to pause and align our wills with Your will. Help us to pray more fervently for the lost, more humbly for our enemies, and more submissively for Your will in our lives.

KNEEL AND SEE

Far be it from me that I should sin against the LORD by failing to pray for you.

1 SAMUEL 12:23

In this world all of us have trials and tribulations, and each one is an opportunity to pray. But far too often we Christians close our conversation with someone who is struggling with "I'll pray for you"—and sadly, that's the last of it. We need to be true to our word; we need to live according to the Golden Rule and actually pray for our brothers and sisters the way we would want them to pray for us. But the blessing of such prayer isn't just for the other person. Consider this story.

In a city in Scandinavia is a famous statue of our Lord. One day a visitor standing before it was very disappointed, and he didn't hesitate to share his feelings with an attendant. "I can't see the face of the Christ," he complained.

The attendant replied, "Sir, if you want to see His face, you must kneel at His feet." The visitor knelt and he saw!

Do you want to see Jesus' face? Kneel in prayer—for others, for yourself, for the world, for His kingdom—and be blessed.

WISDOM FOR TODAY

Father, when we are tempted to panic, let us choose to pray. When we're overwhelmed by the needs of others, let us intercede on their behalf. May we be known as people of prayer.

MAY

LIGHT IN THE DARKNESS

I urge, then, first of all, that requests, prayers, intercession and thanksgiving
be made for everyone—for kings and all those in authority, that we
may live peaceful and quiet lives in all godliness and holiness.
1 TIMOTHY 2:1–2

Looking around at all the evil that happens today, we may find ourselves wondering if some people must have been born without a conscience! But the Bible teaches that God has placed within every human being some sense of right and wrong.

We can, however, ignore the voice of our conscience, and over time we can become so hardened by sin that we almost can't hear its voice. In fact, some people lose almost all sense of right and wrong—and when that happens the results are always tragic. This is one reason why Christians need to take a stand for what is right and not let evil go unchallenged.

But most of all we need to pray. During this first week in May, many people will celebrate an annual Day of Prayer, praying especially for our world and its leaders—its politicians, trendsetters, media powers, athletes, and others in a position of influence. Pray that they may use their influence for good and not for evil. Remember: God is sovereign and is still at work, and He alone is our hope for a better world.

WISDOM FOR TODAY

Things happen in unseen places when we pray. Remind us, Father, that prayer isn't our last resort; it's our first line of defense. God's people are never powerless when we choose to be people of prayer.

WHY PRAY?

Your Father knows what you need before you ask him.
MATTHEW 6:8

If God already knows our needs, why pray? Perhaps this question has even kept you from praying—but in reality it should make us pray more.

If you are a parent, do you discourage your children from coming to you with their requests—even if you already know what they want? No, of course not. You love them, and you take delight in listening to them. Even if you say no to their requests, it's because you know better than they do what is best for them.

God, our heavenly Father, loves us, His children—and one of our greatest privileges is coming to Him in prayer. And because He already knows our needs, we can be confident His answer will be best. If He didn't know our needs, why bother to pray? But He does, and this should give us confidence in prayer.

Thank God that He knows your needs and wants you to come to Him in prayer. Remember: His Son gave His life "so that we may receive mercy and find grace to help us in our time of need" (Hebrews 4:16).

WISDOM FOR TODAY

We're so grateful, Lord, that You know exactly what we need and that Your plans are always to prosper us and not to harm us. Help us to trust in Your faithful love and to know that Your ways are always good.

JESUS' PRAYER PROGRAM

He went up on a mountainside by himself to pray.
MATTHEW 14:23

It may surprise you to read this, but we were created to live a life of prayer. The problem is that sin has erected a barrier between God and us. To recover the role God intended prayer to have in our life, we would do well to follow Jesus' example: in spite of His hectic public ministry, He was never too hurried to spend hours in prayer.

By contrast, how quickly and carelessly we pray (if we pray at all). In the morning we hastily ask for His blessing on our day, then say good-bye to God for the rest of the day until we rush through a few closing thoughts at night. This is not what Jesus modeled. Jesus prayed deeply and repeatedly. He spent entire nights in fervent appeal to God. How different is our pattern of prayer!

One more note. Our Lord frequently prayed alone, separating Himself from every earthly distraction. I urge you to select a room or corner in your home where you can regularly meet alone with God. That quiet, secluded, one-to-one praying can be your day's greatest blessing.

WISDOM FOR TODAY

Help us, Father, to make prayer a priority in our lives. May we take seriously the privilege of speaking intimately with You and may our prayers be deliberate, focused, and frequent.

REASONS TO PRAY

Let us then approach the throne of grace with confidence.

HEBREWS 4:16

Can you relate to this? "I have many people I should pray for, but I wonder if it will do any good. How can we expect God to keep track of every person on the planet?"

The real question here is "How big is God?" If God is limited—if He isn't all-powerful and all-knowing—then we would be right to think He might not answer our prayers.

But God isn't limited! He isn't like a computer without enough memory. God is infinite in His knowledge and wisdom. Since He created this universe—right down to the smallest subatomic particle—isn't He able to know every detail of what goes on in the world? Of course!

Another reason to pray is because God loves us. He is more concerned about you and about those you love than you are. As Jesus said, "Are not two sparrows sold for a penny? Yet not one of them will fall to the ground apart from the will of your Father. . . . So don't be afraid; you are worth more than many sparrows" (Matthew 10:29, 31).

So pray with confidence to your great God!

WISDOM FOR TODAY

There is nothing too small or too big to bring before You, God. You are never overwhelmed, preoccupied, or caught off guard. We can come to You with confidence, knowing that You are still in control of the world You created.

IN JESUS' NAME

We have peace with God through our Lord Jesus Christ, through whom we have gained access by faith into this grace.
ROMANS 5:1–2

Do you know why we often close our prayers with the phrase "in Jesus' name"? Those words remind us that Jesus has opened the door to heaven for us, and we can approach God only because of what He has done for us. But this phrase isn't a magic formula we add in order to make God answer our prayers. God answers our prayers solely because of Christ.

Does this mean God always answers our prayers the way we wish He would? No, not necessarily—and the reason is because He loves us and knows what is best for us. What if parents gave their young children everything they asked for? You know what would happen: the children would not only be spoiled, but they might end up in great danger. Wise parents know when to say no.

In a far greater way, God knows what is best for us. When you pray, therefore, seek God's will. Thank God for the privilege of prayer, and make it part of your life every day.

WISDOM FOR TODAY
We are so thankful, Father, for the sacrifice Jesus made on the cross that tore the veil of separation between God and man and gave us access to You. Give us the boldness to approach the throne with our needs and requests, knowing You will hear us.

REVIVE YOUR PEOPLE, LORD

Will you not revive us again,
that your people may rejoice in you?
PSALM 85:6

Jesus said, "Blessed are the peacemakers, for they will be called sons of God" (Matthew 5:9), and the desire for peace is universal. But simply telling people to stop fighting and love each other isn't the solution for the tension, discord, and violence that exist around the globe. Diplomats and leaders have tried to do this for centuries, yet world history is filled with wars and conflicts.

The problem lies within the human heart; by nature we are selfish and greedy. Even leaders aren't exempt from these sins. As the Bible says, "What causes fights and quarrels among you? Don't they come from your desires that battle within you?" (James 4:1). Even when we want peace, it often eludes us because of our greed or anger or jealousy.

Only God can change the human heart, and that is why our greatest need is spiritual renewal. Pray today for our world and its leaders—and pray as well for spiritual renewal in our time.

WISDOM FOR TODAY

Father, teach us to pray in accordance with Your will and not our fleshly desires. Please give us insight as to how to pray for our country's leaders so that they can lead with humble hearts, godly wisdom, and the boldness to stand for what You say is right and true.

PRAY FOR PEACE

War will continue until the end.

DANIEL 9:26

In the Bible, God calls us to work for peace and pray for peace. But He also warns us that conflicts and wars will always be part of human society until Jesus comes at the end of history to set up His kingdom of peace and justice. In that day all evil will be eliminated, and perfect peace will reign upon the earth. Until that day, however, the world will always be subject to "wars and rumors of wars" (Matthew 24:6).

Why is this? Why can't we live together in peace? The reason is that our hearts are selfish and filled with anger and greed and a lust for power. Until our hearts are changed, we will never know lasting peace.

Tragically, we are a planet in rebellion against God. That is why the world's greatest need is to turn to Christ. Only He can change us from within by His Holy Spirit.

But even when wars rage, we can have peace in our heart as we open our life to Christ. Ask God to give you that peace—and pray that others will know it too.

WISDOM FOR TODAY

There is peace available to us, Lord, even in the midst of earthly conflict and chaos. Help us to seek and pursue it as Your Word commands, both for ourselves and for those around us.

PRAYERS AND TEARS OF LOVE

Dear friends, let us love one another, for love comes from God.

1 JOHN 4:7

I've learned that serving the Lord requires prayer, and often means tears. Any day that I leave my room without a quiet time with God, I look for the devil to hit me from every angle. Power for life, for ministry, doesn't come from our own ability; it comes from God. We need a fresh, daily anointing from the Holy Spirit, and that comes from the time we spend with God in His Word and in prayer. Are you a person of prayer?

In Boston, Massachusetts, the great soul winner John Vassar knocked on the door of a person's home and asked the woman if she knew Christ as her Savior. She replied, "It's none of your business" and slammed the door in his face. He stood on the doorstep and wept and wept, and she looked out her window and saw him weeping. The next Sunday she was in church. She said it was because of those tears. Where are your tears?

A life fueled by prayer and characterized by His love is a life God will use.

WISDOM FOR TODAY

Give us such a love for others, Father, that we mourn with the mourning, as if their pain was our own, and genuinely rejoice with those who rejoice. This is possible only through spending time daily in Your presence.

AN ALL-IMPORTANT APPOINTMENT

If any of you lacks wisdom, he should ask God, who gives generously
to all without finding fault, and it will be given to him.
JAMES 1:5

Every day the young president of an East Coast company instructed his secretary not to disturb him because he had an important appointment.

One morning the chairman of the board arrived unannounced and said, "I want to see Mr. Jones."

The secretary answered, "I'm sorry. He cannot be disturbed. He has an important appointment."

The chairman became angry and banged open the door. Upon seeing the president of the corporation on his knees in prayer, the chairman quietly backed out of the office and softly closed the door. He asked the secretary, "Is that usual?"

When she answered, "Yes, sir. Every morning," the chairman replied, "No wonder we come to him for advice."

This company president offers each of us a good example. Do you make a regular appointment with God each day—and do you keep it? And when you meet with your Father, is a request for wisdom for your day part of the conversation?

WISDOM FOR TODAY

Help us to have the discipline, Lord, to begin each day with You, seeking wisdom for all that the day will hold. Thank You for the way You generously give grace to all who seek it.

HISTORY-CHANGING PRAYER

[Hezekiah prayed,] "O LORD our God, deliver us from [the enemy's] hand, so that all kingdoms on earth may know that you alone, O LORD, are God." . . .

That night the angel of the LORD went out and put to death a hundred and eighty-five thousand men in the Assyrian camp.

2 KINGS 19:19, 35

As someone has said, "Prayer is the highest use to which speech can be put." But today we often regard prayer as merely an honored tradition or a polite formality. But prayer—sincere, believing prayer—is so much more.

Cover to cover, the Bible tells of people whose prayers were answered and who turned the tide of history as a result. Hezekiah prayed, and God spared his nation when the Assyrians attacked. Elijah prayed, and God sent fire to confound the false prophets and consume the offering on the waterlogged altar. Elisha prayed, and the son of the Shunammite woman was raised from the dead. Jesus prayed, and Lazarus came forth from the tomb. Paul prayed, and new churches were born. The early church prayed, and Peter was delivered from prison.

We can change the course of events if we go to our knees in believing prayer. What will you pray about today?

WISDOM FOR TODAY

How much more would we pray, Father, if we truly believed that our prayers were effective? Let us not take lightly the command to "pray without ceasing," for it is powerful and important.

KEEP AT IT!

Will not God bring about justice for his chosen ones,
who cry out to him day and night?
LUKE 18:7

Almost every week I get at least one letter from someone who has been praying for years for a family member, friend, neighbor, or coworker who doesn't know Christ. In many cases that person has eventually turned to Christ, and his or her life has been changed. But what if the person writing to me had stopped praying?

Whenever we pray, we need to remember that God's ways and God's timing aren't always the same as ours. In fact, His time frame rarely matches ours.

We also need to remember that God is able to do what we can't do. Only He can convict nonbelievers of their sins; only He can convince them of the truth of the Gospel. That is why no one is hopeless, for God can break through even the hardest heart. "Is not my word . . . like a hammer that breaks a rock in pieces?" (Jeremiah 23:29).

For whom are you praying? Keep at it!

WISDOM FOR TODAY

May we not grow weary, Lord, as we pray for our loved ones who don't know You. Today may just be the day that You choose to soften their hearts and open their eyes to the truth of the Gospel.

ONE MORE TIME!

"[My word] will not return to me empty,
but will accomplish what I desire
and achieve the purpose for which I sent it."
ISAIAH 55:11

I remember hearing a professor say that during His earthly ministry Jesus probably repeated Himself more than five hundred times.

In college I had a professor who deliberately repeated himself three times. He said that the people in the first two or three rows will get the message the first time. The second time the people in the middle of the lecture hall will get it. The third time the people in the back will get it. And the ones in the front row will never forget it.

We need to keep that fact of human nature in mind as we share God's love with the people He puts in our path. We need to repeat ourselves—to repeat our acts of service, our deeds of love, and, yes, our words of truth. The Bible says, "Let us not become weary in doing good, for at the proper time we will reap a harvest if we do not give up" (Galatians 6:9).

Let us saturate ourselves in the Word of God and in prayer. Then we will be equipped to share His truth—and to repeat it again and again!

WISDOM FOR TODAY

Give us the discipline, Father, to be consistent in our conduct around others as we share the Gospel with them in word and deed. Let us love and serve them tirelessly, knowing that their eternity is at stake.

FLEE!

Flee from all this, and pursue righteousness, godliness,
faith, love, endurance and gentleness.
1 TIMOTHY 6:11

God intends for us to have victory over sin, and when we don't, it's not because God's power has failed. By His Holy Spirit, He is able to give us the power to live just as good a life as Paul or Timothy lived. However, we need to do our part and, by prayer, appropriate the Holy Spirit's power.

We also need to flee these things that God has labeled wrong. We need to flee pride—that tendency to think of ourselves more highly than we ought—and instead live with humility. We need to flee envy and jealousy. We need to avoid causing strife, and the anger, bad temper, irritability, and self-centeredness that prompt it. We need to avoid abusive language and instead develop a Spirit-controlled tongue. We are also to flee lust, the love of money, and evil thoughts about other people.

And you and I can do all this by the power of God's Spirit. Don't depend on yourself and your ability to fight sin, but ask God to fill you with His Spirit—and He will.

WISDOM FOR TODAY

Without You, Lord, we could not pursue the things of the Spirit as we ought. Give us a healthy fear of the desires of the flesh and a passion for the disciplines that lead to godliness.

GOD'S UNCHANGING WORD

All Scripture is God-breathed and is useful for teaching,
rebuking, correcting and training in righteousness.

2 TIMOTHY 3:16

Early in my life I had some doubts about whether or not the Bible was really God's Word. But one night in 1949 I knelt before a stump in the woods of Forest Home, California, opened my Bible, and said, "O God, there are many things in this Book I do not understand. But by faith I accept it—from Genesis to Revelation—as Your Word."

By God's grace that settled the issue for me once and for all. From that moment on I have never had a single doubt that the Bible is God's Word. When I quote Scripture, I know I am quoting the very Word of God.

This confidence in God's Word not only gives authority to one's ministry; it provides a solid foundation for one's life. We who trust in God's Word aren't living according to what someone says about the Bible or on some human philosophy. We are basing our faith, our ministry, even our life itself on God's unchanging truth as it is presented in His unchanging Word. Is God's Word the foundation of your life?

WISDOM FOR TODAY

We believe all of Scripture to be truth, God. Help us base our lives on Your Word and use its truths as the foundation for every decision, relationship, and trial we encounter.

HEART MEDICINE

"For God so loved the world that he gave his one and only Son, that whoever believes in him shall not perish but have eternal life."
JOHN 3:16

One time I was preaching in Africa to a small group of tribal people. I had been told that they had heard very little about the Gospel, and I wanted to bring a basic, straightforward Gospel message they could understand. So I preached on John 3:16 as simply as I knew how. Trying to explain John 3:16, I used every illustration I could think of that would help make the message clear. Afterward—by the work of the Spirit—several people indicated that they wanted to receive Christ.

The next Sunday I was to preach at the parish church of Great St. Mary's at Cambridge University in England, and I thought, "I'm going to try something. I am going to preach the same simple sermon at Cambridge that I preached to the people in Africa." And I did. That Sunday many students in the congregation came to know Christ as Lord and Savior.

Human hearts are the same the world over—in rebellion against God, suffering from the disease of sin, and dying . . . until they discover the simple (and yet profound) truth of God's love for us in Jesus Christ.

WISDOM FOR TODAY

There are many truths in Scripture that are profound and difficult to comprehend. But the essence of the Gospel message, Lord, is beautifully simple. Your love for us compelled You to give Your only Son so that we could spend eternity with You.

SALT AND LIGHT

"You are the salt of the earth. . . . You are the light of the world."
MATTHEW 5:13–14

Many people doubt if there are any answers to life's basic questions. What is the purpose of life? What happens after I die? Is there any hope for the world today?

However, the human mind—like nature itself—abhors a vacuum. If our minds and hearts are not filled with God's truth, something else will take His place: cynicism, occultism, false religions and philosophies, drugs—the list is endless.

Already a terrifying spiritual and moral tide of evil has loosed our society from its spiritual moorings. Ideas that could easily destroy our freedoms are rushing into the vacuum that results when societies turn from the moral truths found in Scripture. Moral and spiritual chaos is the inevitable result.

May we who know God's truth stay committed to the principles outlined in His Word. Above all, may we be salt and light in this world, proclaiming God's righteousness and love to a confused and dying world.

WISDOM FOR TODAY

Fill us with Your truth, God, until we're overflowing with the things of the Spirit and no room remains for the lies of the world. May all we do be done with the love that comes from being saturated with Scripture.

143

CRYING OUT

When [blind Bartimaeus] heard that it was Jesus of Nazareth, he
began to shout, "Jesus, Son of David, have mercy on me!"
MARK 10:47

B lind Bartimaeus probably never expected to be able to see—and then Jesus Christ came to town.

When He did, Bartimaeus cried out, and he cried out for the right thing: he cried for mercy. He needed other things, but what he—like you and I—needed most of all was God's mercy.

Bartimaeus also cried out to the right Person. He cried to the Lord Jesus Christ, the only One in all the world who could help him. And He is there for us, because "salvation is found in no one else, for there is no other name under heaven given to men by which we must be saved" (Acts 4:12).

Third, Bartimaeus cried out at the right time. Suppose Bartimaeus had said, "I'm going to find out what other people think about Him, or perhaps I'll wait until He comes to Jericho again." But Jesus never returned to Jericho.

The Bible says, "Now is the time of God's favor, now is the day of salvation" (2 Corinthians 6:2). What do you need to cry out to Jesus about today?

WISDOM FOR TODAY
The world can never satisfy the desires of the human heart, Father. Only You, the One who created us, can do that. May we always cry out to You in our moment of need.

HOLY SPIRIT WITHIN US

When [the Holy Spirit] has come, He will convict the world
of sin, and of righteousness, and of judgment.

JOHN 16:8 NKJV

The Holy Spirit is God Himself, as He comes to live within us. But why has He come?

First, the Holy Spirit comes to convict us of our sin. He reveals to us that we are sinners. We cannot come to Christ unless the Holy Spirit convicts us of our sin. He also convinces us of the truth about Christ as the Savior.

In addition, the Holy Spirit gives us new life. When we give our lives to Jesus and trust Him as our Savior and Lord, the Spirit renews our souls and brings the life of God into us. We have joy and peace, and we have a new direction to our lives because the Spirit of God has imparted to us the very life of God.

The Bible also teaches that the Holy Spirit produces fruit in our lives. Our thoughts, words, actions, motives—all that we are and all that we do—begin to reflect the Spirit's fruit of love, joy, peace, patience, kindness, goodness, faithfulness, gentleness, and self-control (Galatians 5:22–23). This fruit comes as we yield ourselves to the Spirit.

How yielded is your life today?

WISDOM FOR TODAY

Lord, we give You complete control over every aspect of our lives. Reveal to us any areas of sin so we may repent, and give us hearts for the things of the Spirit.

THE FACT OF CHRIST'S RETURN

"I will come back and take you to be with me."
JOHN 14:3

C. S. Lewis, one of the greatest Christian writers of the twentieth century, said that there are three reasons people don't want to believe in the return of Christ.

First, they claim that Jesus' return did not take place as the early church hoped—so it must be a myth. This argument is not new; in his second letter the apostle Peter put it this way: "First of all, you must understand that in the last days scoffers will come, scoffing and following their own evil desires. They will say, 'Where is this "coming" he promised? Ever since our fathers died, everything goes on as it has since the beginning of creation'" (2 Peter 3:3–4).

Second, the theory of inevitable progress keeps some people from believing that Jesus is coming back. If we believe that humanity is constantly progressing, we will never see the need for the return of Christ. Why do we need Christ to come back if we can reach perfection on our own?

Third, the teaching of Christ's return cuts across the plans and dreams of millions of people. They want to eat, drink, and be merry. Christ's return would interrupt what they are doing—and they don't want that.

But Jesus will return despite these denials. Are you ready?

WISDOM FOR TODAY

Lord, we eagerly anticipate Your return, knowing that it will indeed occur. Your Word tells us as much, and we believe it to be true. Help us live faithfully for You until that day.

WHEN CHRIST RETURNS

They will beat their swords into plowshares
and their spears into pruning hooks.
Nation will not take up sword against nation,
nor will they train for war anymore.

MICAH 4:3

First, the sobering news.

When Jesus returns, there will be an accounting given, a judgment held. Every person outside of Christ will give an account not only of the things done and the things said, but also an account of all their thoughts and motives.

Now for the glorious news: when Jesus returns, all evil will be destroyed. There will be worldwide justice and complete safety and security. There will be no more war, no more fighting—for Jesus Christ will rule as King of kings and Lord of lords, and "his kingdom will never end" (Luke 1:33).

And under His rule there will be universal joy: "Everlasting joy will crown their heads. Gladness and joy will overtake them, and sorrow and sighing will flee away" (Isaiah 51:11). Everlasting joy—think of it—forever! So, with joyful anticipation, "we wait for the blessed hope—the glorious appearing of our great God and Savior, Jesus Christ!" (Titus 2:13). Is your hope in Him?

WISDOM FOR TODAY

The Gospel is truly Good News for those who have placed their faith in You, Lord. We eagerly await Your return and the peace and joy that will be ours to enjoy. Help us remain steadfast as we wait.

GOD'S FORMULA OF GRACE

It is by grace you have been saved, through faith—and this not from yourselves, it is the gift of God.

EPHESIANS 2:8

Astronomers tell us that every star moves with precision along its celestial path. To ignore the detailed rules of the universe would spell ruin to a star. The laws of nature are fixed, and for a star to ignore those laws would be folly—if it were even possible.

If the laws in His material realm are so fixed and exact, would God be haphazard in the spiritual realm, where the eternal destinies of billions of people are at stake? No! Just as God has equations and rules in the material realm, He also has equations and rules in the spiritual realm. For instance, the Bible says, "The wages of sin is death" (Romans 6:23). This is God's formula: when a person sins, he or she will pay for it—in this life and in the life to come.

The formula continues, though, and it is the way of God's grace—Jesus' death on the cross for our sins. We cannot be saved by our own good works, but only through faith in the One who took our sins upon Himself and died in our place. That is grace!

WISDOM FOR TODAY

Thank You, God, for Your grace that made a way for sinners to be made right before You. There is nothing in us that would have made that possible. It is only through Jesus' work on the cross.

TWO SETS OF BOOKS

If anyone's name was not found written in the book
of life, he was thrown into the lake of fire.

These are sobering words—the most sobering words imaginable.

The Bible says that in heaven there are two sets of books. One set records every detail of our lives: everything we have done since the day we were born. All of that will be held against us at judgment.

But Scripture tells us there is another book in heaven: the Book of Life. When we come to Christ—when we receive Him, when we come to the cross where He died for us, when we believe that He is risen and we receive Him into our lives—our names are blotted out of the first set of books. God no longer even remembers our sins because they have been blotted out by the blood of Christ, shed on the cross for us.

The moment our names are blotted out of the first set of books, God writes them in the other book called the Book of Life. Only those whose names are recorded there will enter the kingdom of heaven.

Is your name written in the Book of Life? Make sure by opening your heart to Christ and committing your life without reserve to Him today.

WISDOM FOR TODAY

Father, we believe that Jesus died for our sins, rose from the grave, and lives again. We know that because of His work on the cross, our names are written in the Book of Life, and You remember our sins no more!

FEAR NOT!

There is no fear in love. But perfect love drives out fear.
1 JOHN 4:18

The world of Jesus' day was filled with fear. The Romans feared rebellion, and their subjects feared Rome's power. The Sadducees feared the Pharisees, and both were suspicious of the publicans. The hearts of people everywhere were filled with fear and distrust. Life was precarious, and above all, people feared death.

The world lives with fear even today. What is your fear? Do you fear the future? Do you fear life's burdens that sometimes seem almost overwhelming? Do you fear death? Most of us fear everything except God—yet it is God whom we should fear most of all!

Jesus can put an end to fear for all who trust in Him. "Do not be afraid, little flock" is a phrase typical of His teaching and preaching (Luke 12:32). He is the answer to any fear you have. After all, God's power is greater than the powers of evil, and "neither death nor life, neither angels nor demons, neither the present nor the future . . . nor anything else in all creation, will be able to separate us from the love of God that is in Christ Jesus our Lord" (Romans 8:38–39).

WISDOM FOR TODAY

Your love is perfect, Lord, and it leaves no room for fear. Help us to draw near to You so we can focus on the wonder of that love and not the worries of the world.

OUR HOPE OF HEAVEN

God made him who had no sin to be sin for us, so that in
him we might become the righteousness of God.

2 CORINTHIANS 5:21

You'll never be good enough to go to heaven.

That statement may shock you, but I hope you keep reading, because it is true. The reason is because God is absolutely holy and pure—and because of that, He cannot tolerate sin. To put it another way, even one sin would be enough to keep you out of heaven. The Bible is clear: "Nothing impure will ever enter [heaven], nor will anyone who does what is shameful or deceitful" (Revelation 21:27).

Does that mean there is no hope? No! Because of Jesus, you and I have hope. God loves us and wants us to be with Him in heaven forever. To make that possible, He sent Christ into the world. Jesus, who was God in human flesh, was without sin—but on the cross all our sins were transferred to Him and He died in our place. We deserve to die for our sins, but Christ took our death and our hell. Now we can be forgiven! Now we can enter heaven! Is your trust and hope in Him?

WISDOM FOR TODAY

Thank You, Lord, for making it possible for us to have the hope of heaven when we die. We know that, on our own, it would not be possible, and we would spend eternity apart from God.

GOD WINS!

Blessed is the one who reads the words of this prophecy, and blessed are those who hear it and take to heart what is written in it, because the time is near.
REVELATION 1:3

God gave us the book of Revelation to encourage us and show us there is hope for the future—and the reason is because the future is in His hands.

Look at it this way: How would you feel if you read only the daily headlines? You'd probably conclude that the world is caught in a never-ending cycle of war, crime, and violence; it would be easy to become cynical and discouraged. Like the writer of Ecclesiastes, you would be tempted to ask in despair, "What does man gain from all his labor at which he toils under the sun?" (Ecclesiastes 1:3).

But Revelation gives us a different picture. Someday, it says, Jesus will triumph over all the forces of death and hell and Satan. Someday the heavenly hosts will sing, "The kingdom of the world has become the kingdom of our Lord and of his Christ, and he will reign for ever and ever" (Revelation 11:15). All evil and death will be destroyed, and His victory over sin and Satan will be complete.

No matter what you are facing today, you can have hope—because of Christ.

WISDOM FOR TODAY

Remind us, Father, that there is life beyond what we see here on earth. Because of our faith in Jesus, we have joy, peace, and hope available to us, no matter what earthly trials we encounter.

A Reason to Do Right

Nothing in all creation is hidden from God's sight.

HEBREWS 4:13

Do people who have died and gone to heaven know what happens on earth? The Bible doesn't give us an absolutely clear answer about this, but it does hint that they may be aware of what takes place here on earth.

The writer of Hebrews reminds us of some great Old Testament heroes who lived for God, often despite great opposition (Hebrews 11). Then he concludes, "Since we are surrounded by such a great cloud of witnesses, let us throw off everything that hinders and the sin that so easily entangles, and let us run with perseverance the race marked out for us" (12:1).

Here the writer paints a picture for us—a picture of a stadium filled with spectators, perhaps watching us as we live out our lives and cheering us on as we stretch toward the finish line. So perhaps those who have entered heaven are watching us, even now.

What we do know for sure is that God sees us—and that should be enough to encourage us to live for Christ and do what is right.

Wisdom for Today

What a comfort to know, Father, that You see us in both our trials and our triumphs. May all we say and do be pleasing in Your sight and bring glory to Your name.

MYSTERIOUS EVIL

In this world you will have trouble. But take heart! I have overcome the world.
JOHN 16:33

I have to admit that I do not know why some people suffer more than others do. There is a mystery to evil that we will never fully understand this side of eternity; the Bible speaks of "the mystery of iniquity" (2 Thessalonians 2:7 KJV).

But I do know this: we live in a world that is in the grip of evil, and in this present age God's plans are often blocked by Satan's supernatural force. This world is not the way God meant it to be; it is in the grip of "spiritual forces of evil in the heavenly realms" (Ephesians 6:12).

In light of that truth, we must not blame God for everything that happens in our lives, especially the bad things. Instead, we need to remember that God has already entered the battle against evil—and someday His victory will be complete. In His death and resurrection, Jesus Christ confronted Satan—and won! That is our hope—and that is our comfort.

WISDOM FOR TODAY

Help us, Lord, to trust You when we don't understand why certain things happen. Teach us to focus on and have faith in You, the One who is ultimately in control and will reign victorious in the end.

NOT THE RIGHT TICKET

"There is no one righteous, not even one."

ROMANS 3:10

Do you know people who are trusting in their good deeds to get into heaven? If so, you might want to ask them this important question: "By what standard do you think God will judge you?"

Their reply might run something like this: "I'm a good person. I may not be perfect, but I've always tried to do what's right. Isn't that what God expects?"

But God's standard is higher than that; His standard is nothing less than perfection. That means we can't make it into heaven on our own, for no matter how good we are, we still aren't perfect. Even the best person sins in words and actions as well as in thoughts and motives. God's standard is perfection, and even one sin will keep us out of heaven.

So if you know someone who thinks good deeds are their ticket to heaven, urge them not to gamble with their soul. Instead, urge them to repent of their pride and trust Jesus alone for their salvation.

WISDOM FOR TODAY

Father, we could never be good enough to deserve heaven, and that knowledge is freeing to those of us who accept and believe it, because we don't have to try to earn Your favor. We can stand before You only because of Christ.

LEARNING FROM BAD EXAMPLES

These things happened to them as examples and
were written down as warnings for us.

1 CORINTHIANS 10:11

I find it very encouraging that God included real-life, flesh-and-blood sinful people in His Word. David committed adultery, Abraham lied about his wife—the list goes on and on. Why are they in the Bible? So we will learn from their wrongdoings.

One lesson is that sin always has consequences. Take David. He was a great leader and a good man in many ways. But over the years he became complacent, and instead of carrying out his responsibilities, he fell into immorality (2 Samuel 11–12).

And consider the tragic consequences of his sin. Not only did the child born of that illicit union die, but David committed other sins—lying, murder—in a vain attempt to cover it up. Furthermore, his influence for good was lost, and his latter years as king were marked by rebellion and tragedy.

God has much to teach us from the examples of His people who failed. But most of all His Word points us to Christ, who alone can forgive us and set our feet on the right path.

WISDOM FOR TODAY

Every Word of Scripture is useful for teaching and correcting. Help us, Father, to learn from the mistakes of others who have gone before us and to see Your grace at work in their stories.

LOVING PEOPLE INTO THE KINGDOM

Let your conversation be always full of grace, seasoned with
salt, so that you may know how to answer everyone.

COLOSSIANS 4:6

Have you noticed that you can seldom argue a person into the kingdom of God? That's because the real reason for disbelief in God usually has nothing to do with logic.

Instead, the real reason usually has to do with their emotions and their will. In other words, people don't believe in God because they don't want to believe—and they don't want to believe because they want to run their own lives. If they admitted God exists, they know they'd have to humble themselves before Him and yield control of their lives to Him. They don't want to do that.

We must do our best to answer—with gentleness and respect—any question we're asked, even if we think it isn't sincere or is only meant to put us on the spot. But the most important thing we can do is to show by our life and love that Jesus is real. Our actions often speak far louder than our words. Do others see Christ in you, both by what you say and by what you do?

WISDOM FOR TODAY

Help us approach each conversation, Lord, with a desire to honor You and not simply to make our own opinions or desires known. May our gentleness be evident to all who come in contact with us.

TRANSFORMING POWER

They saw what seemed to be tongues of fire. . . . All
of them were filled with the Holy Spirit.
ACTS 2:3–4

Within fifty days of Jesus' death and the apparent collapse of His cause, the city of Jerusalem rang with the cries of those who boldly declared that God had raised Jesus from the dead and that they were eyewitnesses to that truth. Hundreds had seen the resurrected Jesus!

As the Holy Spirit descended on the day of Pentecost, craven cowards were changed into courageous confessors. Humble fishermen became heralds of the King. All who saw and heard them were compelled to acknowledge that something had utterly transformed their lives. When questioned by their critics, the apostles did not hesitate to reply: they accounted for their boldness by pointing to the risen Christ. On that day of Pentecost, the resurrection was the keynote of Peter's sermon, causing three thousand people to confess Jesus as Lord (Acts 2:14–41). The resurrection was the dominant theme in Paul's preaching. The earthshaking fact that God had raised Jesus from the dead was the axle and wheels of the early Christian church.

What difference will the resurrection and the Holy Spirit's power make in your life today?

WISDOM FOR TODAY

The same power that enabled Jesus to leave the grave behind lives in believers today. Lord, may the knowledge of Your resurrection make us bold in our witnessing and brave in our stance against evil.

JUNE

GIVE YOUR FEARS TO JESUS

*"I know the plans I have for you . . . plans to prosper you and
not to harm you, plans to give you hope and a future."*
JEREMIAH 29:11

What are you afraid of?

A young person I know would like to get married, but she is afraid of getting into a serious relationship because her parents went through a bitter divorce. She is afraid her marriage will also fail.

Intellectually, she knows that just because her parents failed in their marriage doesn't mean she is also destined to fail. In fact, she knows she can learn from their mistakes and be better prepared for marriage than they were.

Emotionally, however, this woman feels trapped by fears and insecurities that are constantly telling her she will always be a failure. But it isn't necessarily true. Our emotions can lie to us, and we need to counter our emotions with truth.

And the greatest truth you can use to counteract your fears is the truth that God loves you and His plans for you are good. So give your fears—and every aspect of your life—to Christ. Then let the truth of His Word, the Bible, take root in your soul every day, and trust your future to Him who knows your needs and loves you deeply.

WISDOM FOR TODAY

If we don't fill ourselves with Your truth, Lord, we could easily succumb to all the fears the world throws at us. When we meditate on Scripture, we are more able to choose faith over fear and worship over worry.

LOTS OF QUESTIONS

"Take my yoke upon you and learn from me."

MATTHEW 11:29

H ave you ever known someone who had lots of questions about God and the Bible? No matter how many you answered, they always had more!

Our faith can stand up to any question, but sometimes people ask questions—and keep asking questions—just to avoid facing their own spiritual needs and acknowledging who Jesus really is. Their questions may only be an excuse to keep from turning their lives over to Christ.

In that situation, consider asking this question: "If I could answer every question you have, would you be willing to repent of your sins and commit your life to Jesus?" If they are honest, their answer may be no, but even if it is, let them know you still care about them and want to be their friend. But don't hesitate to warn them that someday they "will have to give an account to him who is ready to judge the living and the dead" (1 Peter 4:5).

In addition, make sure your friend knows what the Gospel is; many people really don't understand it—although they think they do. Never give up hoping that someday they will give their life to Jesus.

And of course pray for them; only God can change hearts.

WISDOM FOR TODAY

We don't have to be afraid, Lord, of the questions people may ask. Help us share confidently the things we know to be true, admit the things we aren't sure about, and never miss an opportunity to point someone to You.

GOD'S OLD TESTAMENT

Man does not live on bread alone but on every word
that comes from the mouth of the LORD.
DEUTERONOMY 8:3

The Old Testament may not seem relevant to us today—but it is, because it is part of God's holy Word, and He has much to teach us through its pages. After all, the Old Testament was the Bible Jesus knew and often quoted. One reason it is so important, He declared, is because it points to His coming as the promised Messiah. Some parts may seem hard to understand, such as the detailed instructions that governed the Old Testament sacrificial system. These no longer strictly apply to us, however, because they have been fulfilled in Christ's sacrifice of Himself on the cross—and yet they still have much to teach us about the holiness of God and the seriousness of sin.

If the Old Testament is unfamiliar to you, I suggest you begin with the book of Psalms, the Bible's hymnbook. It will show you what it means to walk with God in prayer and praise. Later you can begin reading other parts, such as the prophets and historical sections. There you'll see how God dealt with His people in times past—and how He wants to deal with us today. Remember: "All Scripture is given by inspiration of God, and is profitable for doctrine, for reproof, for correction, for instruction in righteousness" (2 Timothy 3:16 NKJV).

WISDOM FOR TODAY
It is Your desire, Father, that we would know and meditate on every Word of Scripture. May Your Word accomplish its purpose in us.

WHAT TO DO WITH ANGER

The tongue also is a fire, a world of evil among the parts of the body.

JAMES 3:6

Have you ever been falsely accused of something? Even when it was later proven false, did you suspect that some people still wondered if it was true? Did that unfounded accusation damage your reputation?

That kind of experience vividly demonstrates the dangerous power of a lying tongue. And when it happens to us, the temptation is to strike back and hurt the person who hurt us, perhaps by telling lies about them. But in the long run, doing so only damages our own credibility and makes people even more suspicious of us.

Anger and bitterness—whatever the cause—only end up hurting us. So, whenever a situation causes you to be angry, turn that anger over to Christ. Ask Him to forgive your anger, and then ask Him to help you get rid of it and even forgive the person who hurt you.

Remember that Jesus was falsely accused of sin. Rather than strike back at His accusers, He willingly went to the cross so that we could be forgiven for all our sins—including anger.

WISDOM FOR TODAY

To live with anger is to live in bondage, Lord. Set us free by softening our hearts and giving us a humble spirit that chooses to bestow grace on those who have wounded us and prays for those who wish us harm.

THE BASICS

May we know what this new teaching is that you are presenting?
ACTS 17:19

P aul's preaching in Athens's main marketplace attracted great curiosity, and
eventually a well-known group of intellectuals invited him to speak to them.
He accepted, and in his address he covered three important points.

First, Paul talked about the one true God, the Creator who is the holy,
unchangeable God of love. Calling their attention to an altar Paul had seen dedicated "To an Unknown God," he pointed them to the God who made them and
sustained them—a God they could have fellowship with.

Paul also talked about the need to repent and the coming judgment.
Repentance means changing our minds about God and about ourselves. It means
recognizing God's holiness, our sinfulness, and Jesus' sacrificial death for us.

Paul finally talked about the resurrection, which gives us hope for the future.
There will be a glorious tomorrow for those who have trusted Christ—when we
come to Christ, we know we will spend eternity with Him!

Most in Athens rejected Paul's message—but some believed and became followers of Jesus. Have you committed your life to Christ, and are you seeking to
tell others about Him?

WISDOM FOR TODAY

May we never assume, Lord, that others know and understand the message
of the Gospel. What is familiar to us may be a new teaching to someone else,
and we do not know when someone may be hearing it for the first time.

OUR TIMELESS GOD

Before the mountains were born
or you brought forth the earth and the world,
from everlasting to everlasting you are God.
PSALM 90:2

An eight-year-old asked me the other day, "How old is God?" I told him he'd asked a very good question and said I was glad he wanted to know more about God.

Then I told this young child that God is timeless: He has always existed. God has no beginning—and He has no end. He was never young, and He will never grow old.

I know that statement was hard for him to understand, because everything around us grows old or wears out. Perhaps, I told him, you have a grandfather or a grandmother; you probably think of them as old. At one time, however, they were just as young as you are. Now the years have passed, and they have grown old. But God isn't like that. He doesn't change, nor does He grow old and weak.

Why is this important? Because this means you can trust God with your life. He won't die or grow weak or forgetful; He loves you, and He is always there to take care of you. That's an important truth, whatever our age!

WISDOM FOR TODAY
We're so grateful, God, that You exist outside the boundaries of time. You are who You have always been, and there is great comfort in that knowledge.

GOD'S GRACE

Your eyes are too pure to look on evil;
you cannot tolerate wrong.
HABAKKUK 1:13

What do pastors mean when they talk about "the grace of God"? It refers to much more than His kindness and mercy, although those traits are certainly evidence of His grace.

Grace means "undeserved favor or goodness." God doesn't owe us anything—yet in His grace, He still gives us good things. We don't even deserve the next breath we take, but God in His grace grants it. Most of all, we don't deserve to go to heaven, but in His grace God has provided the way: He sent Jesus Christ to die for our sins.

Remember: by nature we have no right to expect anything from God—except His judgment. That's because we are sinners, and sin is rebellion against God. We don't like to admit this. We like to think we aren't so bad after all, and God ought to overlook our sins. But that's just not true.

Thank God for His saving grace to you in Jesus Christ, and then seek—by His power—to glorify Him in your life.

WISDOM FOR TODAY

When we begin to see every good thing as a gift from You, God, we realize just how generous You are with Your grace. Teach us to live lives of gratitude for the grace lavishly bestowed on us, to recognize the gifts, and to glorify the Giver.

CONFIDENCE ABOUT THE FUTURE

"Trust in God; trust also in me. . . . I am going there to prepare a place for you."
JOHN 14:1–2

Almost since the dawn of the human race, people have tried to discern the future. The horoscopes published in many daily newspapers are evidence that it still goes on today.

As a Christian, though, I believe only God knows the future and that we are to look to Him—not to the stars or the tea leaves or the lines on the palm of our hand—for our confidence in the future. Some of these attempts to learn what the future holds are merely foolish or useless, but others involve occult practices that can bring people into contact with spiritual forces that are not from God but from Satan.

This is one reason why the Bible strongly urges us to avoid any practice that may be linked with the occult. Astrology can never give you the answers to life's deepest questions—especially where you will spend eternity. Committing your life to Christ means having the joyous confidence that your future is securely in His hands—tomorrow and forever.

WISDOM FOR TODAY

You are well acquainted, Father, with the weaknesses of our flesh, including our tendency to fear the unknown. Thank You for the assurances You provide regarding the certainty of heaven for those who put their faith in Christ.

FAITH IN THE DARKNESS

I do believe; help me overcome my unbelief!
MARK 9:24

E vil is real, and at one time or another most of us have wondered why God doesn't just reach down and stop it. Sometimes He does—but not always, and the Bible says evil is a mystery that we won't fully understand until we get to heaven. In the meantime, God calls us to trust Him and have confidence in His love, no matter the circumstances.

Maybe someone you love has cancer, or just lost a job, or is dealing with a prodigal child, or . . . the list of the ways that evil intersects our daily life goes on and on. Bitterness and anger can result, but don't let those emotions drive a wedge between you and God. That gains you nothing, and in the long run it will only destroy you.

Instead, let your attitude be that of the Psalmist: "But as for me, it is good to be near God. I have made the Sovereign LORD my refuge" (Psalm 73:28). Ask God to help you trust Him even when the way is dark.

WISDOM FOR TODAY

Lord, there are so many things we just don't understand about the way life turns out sometimes. Protect our hearts from the danger of discouragement that can sometimes turn into doubt. Help us stand firm in our faith and remain certain what You've told us is true.

JESUS' QUESTION FOR YOU

"Who do you say I am?"
MATTHEW 16:15

S ome years ago Christian writer C. S. Lewis pointed out that there are only four possible conclusions you can reach about Jesus. Either He was a liar, or He was self-deceived, or He was insane—or He was in fact who He claimed to be: the Son of God.

Which was He? The only logical conclusion is that Jesus was the Son of God. A liar couldn't have taught the lofty moral principles He did. A self-deceived person couldn't have performed the miracles He did. A lunatic couldn't have held up under pressure the way Jesus did. After closely observing His life every day, His disciples reached their conclusion: "You are the Christ, the Son of the living God" (Matthew 16:16).

But there is an even more compelling reason to believe that Jesus was who He claimed to be: His resurrection from the dead. In all of human history, only one Person came back permanently from the grave; Jesus Christ "was declared with power to be the Son of God by his resurrection from the dead" (Romans 1:4). Who do you say He is?

WISDOM FOR TODAY

Jesus, You are the Messiah the Old Testament saints eagerly anticipated. You are the virgin-born, sinless, and resurrected Savior of the New Testament. You are our Lord, our Redeemer, and our hope of heaven.

WHITEWASHED TOMBS

Rid yourselves of all malice and all deceit, hypocrisy,
envy, and slander of every kind.
1 PETER 2:1

Unfortunately, sometimes those of us who are Christians are the worst advertisements for our faith. We keep sinning even after we name Jesus as our Savior and Lord, and we often appear to others as insincere and hypocritical. And all too often we are.

Some of Jesus' strongest words were reserved for hypocrites—for people who claimed to believe in God yet were insincere and only used their religion to try to impress others. Jesus called those people "whitewashed tombs, which look beautiful on the outside but on the inside are full of dead men's bones" (Matthew 23:27). What an indictment!

Ask God to reveal hypocrisy in your life—an inconsistency between what you profess and what you practice. Then ask God to bring you so close to Christ that you won't have any desire to live an inconsistent, deceitful life. Not only will you be a better person, but God will begin to use you to point others to Christ and His transforming love.

WISDOM FOR TODAY

Let us never be the reason, Father, that someone does not come to saving faith in Christ or doubts the change You make in a person's life. Help us live out a genuine and consistent faith that will cause others to see You in us.

GOD'S TRUTH, YOUR LIFE

You are a chosen people . . . that you may declare the praises of
him who called you out of darkness into his wonderful light.

1 PETER 2:9

I have found that people who say, "You can't trust what the Bible says" often have never actually read it for themselves. Instead, they are only using this as an excuse to avoid God.

The real issue for them isn't the trustworthiness of the Bible but their determination to keep God away. Down inside, they sense that if they took God seriously and gave their lives to Christ, they would have to change their way of living—and they don't want to do that.

So don't be afraid to challenge your nonbelieving friends to read the Gospels and learn about Jesus for themselves. God can use it to break down their barriers and bring them to Himself.

Also pray for them. You can't change their hearts and minds—but God can. Ask Him to awaken your friends to their need for Christ.

Finally, be a good witness by the way you live. Let these friends know you really care; let them see Jesus' love and peace and joy in your life. The way we live is often more convincing than the words we say.

WISDOM FOR TODAY

Father, in an attempt to convince people of the truth, we mistakenly try to explain or defend You to others. Teach us, instead, to live a life consistent with the Gospel, to encourage others to search Scripture for themselves, and to pray that they would have a personal encounter with You.

LEARNING FROM DEATH

There is a time for everything . . .
a time to be born and a time to die.
ECCLESIASTES 3:1–2

Have you ever watched a loved one struggle with pain, growing disability, and even approaching death? Perhaps you asked yourself, "Why doesn't God just let her die?"

I don't have a complete answer for you. We live in a fallen, sin-scarred world, and much of what happens falls far short of God's original plan.

But I do know this. Even when we can't understand why God allows things like this to happen, He still can be trusted to do what is right. God is sovereign, and He knows what is best—for you, for the person who is suffering, and for all those affected by their suffering. In God's time, He will take the suffering saint to be with Him.

When someone is suffering or dying, we should ask God to teach us whatever lessons He has for us in this experience. Sometimes, I believe, God allows a loved one to linger because family members need to come together and be reconciled to one another. God also may use situations like this to teach us how to love others who are in need and to remind us of the brevity of life.

WISDOM FOR TODAY

Because we trust You, Father, we know that our suffering or the suffering of a loved one is never in vain. Help us cling tightly to You in times of sorrow, knowing that You will work all things for our good and Your glory.

BEFORE IT'S TOO LATE

*Instead you ought to forgive and comfort him, so that he
will not be overwhelmed by excessive sorrow.*

2 CORINTHIANS 2:7

The situation was heartbreaking. The father had abused his children and abandoned the family. Years later, when he was sick, he wrote to his children asking to see them, asking for their forgiveness.

Situations like this make Jesus' command to forgive seem impossible to obey. But when the guilty party is near the end of life—and especially if that person has requested reconciliation—we need to prayerfully consider honoring their request. Although we may not realize it at the time, someday we will regret never being reconciled to the family member or friend who hurt us.

Forgiveness isn't easy. In fact, often we can't forgive the person who hurt us deeply without God's help. But is it impossible for God to overcome those hurts and heal the wounds? No, of course not.

Remember what it cost Christ to forgive you—and then ask Him to help you forgive others. What the person did was wrong, and you may still bear the emotional scars. But God doesn't want you to carry those hurts forever.

Whom do you need to forgive before it's too late?

WISDOM FOR TODAY

Forgiveness doesn't come naturally to us, Lord, but it is always an act of obedience. Soften our hearts toward those we need to forgive, and give us the humility necessary to seek forgiveness for times we have wronged other people.

What God Hates

To fear the Lord is to hate evil; I hate pride and
arrogance, evil behavior and perverse speech.
Proverbs 8:13

From our human standpoint some sins are certainly worse than others—sins like murder, assault, or stealing that deeply hurt others. But the Bible doesn't tell us which sin is worst in God's eyes, and the reason is because God hates all sin. God is absolutely pure and holy; even the smallest sin is evil in His sight.

I'm afraid we have largely lost sight of the holiness and purity of God today. This is one reason why we tolerate sin so easily and casually dismiss so many sins as minor or insignificant. It is also the reason why we ignore sin in our lives and neglect to repent of it.

We need a new vision of who God is, and who we are as sinners in His sight. No matter how good we think we are, God's judgment still stands: "There is no one who does good, not even one" (Romans 3:12).

But God loves us despite our sin, and He yearns to forgive us and welcome us into His family forever. Don't excuse your sin or tolerate it any longer, but repent of it, and with God's help begin following Christ every day.

Wisdom for Today

Lord, the enemy attempts to blur the lines between right and wrong until we are able to convince ourselves that our sin isn't that bad or, perhaps, even sin at all! Open our eyes to the seriousness of our sins and the grace available to us through Christ.

THE SPIRIT OF ANTICHRIST

As you have heard that the antichrist is coming,
even now many antichrists have come.

1 JOHN 2:18

One of the characteristics of the antichrist who will come in the last days is that he will be "the deceiver" (2 John 1:7) who turns many away from God by his lies and apparent miracles.

His very name—Antichrist—clearly indicates his character as well as his mission: he will be sent into the world as Satan's representative to oppose God at every turn. The Bible calls him "the man of lawlessness . . . [who] will exalt himself over everything that is called God or is worshiped . . . proclaiming himself to be God" (2 Thessalonians 2:3–4).

Is the antichrist alive today? No one can say for sure.

But the Bible tells us a very important truth: the spirit of antichrist has often been among us. Satan is always at work to oppose God's work, and some people deliberately take their stand with Satan, not God.

What does all this mean? It means we must be sure of our own commitment to Christ. If our lives are not built on Christ's truth, we can easily be led astray. Don't let this happen to you!

WISDOM FOR TODAY

Let us not be led astray by Satan's tricks, Lord. May we be so immersed in the truth found in Your Word that we are able to immediately recognize the enemy's attempts at distraction and deception.

Evil Hearts

The hearts of men, moreover, are full of evil and there
is madness in their hearts while they live.
Ecclesiastes 9:3

As the headlines any day of the week indicate, terrible things happen in our world—wars, conflicts, terrorist attacks, injustice, and so forth. Why? Because the human heart is capable of incredible evil.

We like to pretend this isn't the case; we may even think that the more civilized or educated we are, the less likely we will be to do something evil. But that isn't necessarily so. Even people who are decent and respectable on the surface may be harboring deep hatred and anger in their hearts.

Only Jesus can cleanse us from the moral and spiritual filth we have allowed to accumulate in our hearts. When we go to Him, God not only forgives us of our sins, but He comes to live within us by His Holy Spirit. God's promise is for all who turn in faith to Christ: "I will give you a new heart" (Ezekiel 36:26).

Are you, day by day, seeking Jesus' help to do His will? And are you praying that He will restrain evil and hasten the coming of His kingdom?

Wisdom for Today

Apart from Your Spirit dwelling in us, Lord, there isn't any sin that we are incapable of committing. Once we accept this truth, we will more earnestly seek Your guidance in our lives and desire to live daily in Your presence.

TRUE BEAUTY

Your beauty should not come from outward adornment.

1 PETER 3:3

Our world bombards us with messages about what is beautiful and hand-some. It sets standards for our physical appearance and our material success that penetrate our minds and shape our personalities and our goals—often without us even realizing it. It's difficult to ignore these loud and ever-present voices as they speak to us from magazines, television, movies, the Internet, and advertising. The problem is, these messages will lead us astray.

To cope with all this, first ask God to help you be content with the way you are. God made you, and He didn't make a mistake. Some of the most unhappy people I have ever met possessed great beauty or wealth, yet their lives were empty and without meaning. God loves you just as you are!

Second, focus on what the Bible calls true beauty—the beauty of a godly character, "the unfading beauty of a gentle and quiet spirit, which is of great worth in God's sight" (1 Peter 3:4).

Take care of your body; the Bible calls it "a temple of the Holy Spirit" (1 Corinthians 6:19). But most of all take care of your soul—your inner self—by feeding on the Word of God and letting His Spirit transform you from within.

WISDOM FOR TODAY

It's easy to become obsessed with meeting the world's standards of beauty and success. Help us, Lord, to be more concerned with Your standards and with becoming what is pleasing and beautiful in Your sight.

ATTENTION!

No man knows when his hour will come:
As fish are caught in a cruel net . . .
so men are trapped by evil times
that fall unexpectedly upon them.
ECCLESIASTES 9:12

H as God ever tried to get your attention? Sometimes a narrow escape in a car accident or a false-positive test for cancer or a major surgery can make us realize that we aren't ready to die—and make us wonder if God is trying to get our attention.

Perhaps, for instance, God is trying to tell you that you are on the wrong road. You may have chosen a self-centered, self-indulgent path—but where does it lead? Jesus warned, "Wide is the gate and broad is the road that leads to destruction, and many enter through it" (Matthew 7:13).

Or God may be warning you that life is short; you cannot count on having time to turn to Him later on. If you are going to turn to Christ, the time is now.

Above all, God wants to tell you that He loves you. He loves you so much that He gave His Son to die on the cross for you. When we know Christ we have joy and peace, because we know our future is secure—and someday we will be with Him forever.

WISDOM FOR TODAY
Let us live in such a way, Father, that we will not have regrets on the day You call us home. May we be quick to repent of any sinful practices in our lives.

HEAVEN OR HELL?

In hell, where he was in torment, he looked up and . . . called to him, "Father Abraham, have pity on me . . . because I am in agony in this fire."

LUKE 16:23–24

I t isn't fashionable today to talk about hell—but the Bible is clear: God created us with a soul or a spirit that will live forever—and when we die, we will continue to exist—either in the place the Bible calls heaven or in the place it calls hell.

Hell, the Bible says, is reserved for those who reject God and turn their back on Him. If you want nothing to do with Him in this life, then you will have nothing to do with Him in the next life.

And let me be as clear as possible: you don't want to go to hell. The Bible speaks of hell as a place of "darkness, where there will be weeping and gnashing of teeth" (Matthew 25:30). Hell is a place of absolute loneliness and hopelessness.

But the good news is that God doesn't want you to go there! Jesus paid the price for your sins; He took upon Himself the death and hell we deserve through His death on the cross. Trust Jesus as your Lord and Savior, and then thank Him that you will spend all eternity with Him in heaven.

WISDOM FOR TODAY

Thank You, Lord, for making a way for us to spend eternity in Your presence. Give us a passion and a love for the lost that compel us to share the truth with them so that they, too, may trust in You and go to heaven.

THE ONLY SPIRITUAL REALITY

No one has ever seen God, but God the One and Only, who is at the Father's side, has made him known.

JOHN 1:18

Many today sense there must be something more to life than material things, and they are searching for a deeper spiritual reality. Often, however, their search takes them down paths that will not lead them to the living God.

If you know people like that, urge them to put aside whatever prejudices they may have against Jesus Christ and encourage them to seek God with an open heart and mind. God hasn't left us in the dark: He has revealed Himself to us through His Word and His Son.

Remember: God took upon Himself human flesh and became a man—a fact that should stagger our imagination. If we want to know what God is like, we only need to look at Jesus, for He was God in human flesh.

Pray for people you know who are seeking God, that they won't be deceived or led down a path that will only take them away from God. And ask God to use you to point them to Jesus' love and truth. Only Christ can meet the deepest hunger of our souls.

WISDOM FOR TODAY

You've put eternity in our hearts, Father, and we instinctively know that there is more to this life than what we see. Keep us grounded in Your truth so our longing for something more does not cause us to be deceived by the enemy.

THE CURE FOR SPIRITUAL "CANCER"

Now in Christ Jesus you who once were far away have
been brought near through the blood of Christ.

EPHESIANS 2:13

Suppose you had a deadly form of cancer, and one day you discovered a cure for it. Wouldn't you want other people who had that same disease to know what you had learned? Wouldn't you try to point them to the same discovery you had made? I'm sure you would; it would be monstrous to do otherwise.

The Bible teaches that we all have a spiritual "cancer"—a deadly spiritual disease called sin. Not only does it cripple us right now morally and spiritually, but it will also destroy us in the future and keep us from the blessings God has for us in heaven.

Is there any answer to this spiritual cancer? Yes! The answer is Christ, who came "to reconcile to himself all things . . . by making peace through his blood, shed on the cross" (Colossians 1:20).

Show that you care about your friends by letting them know that you've found the cure for our spiritual cancer. Who in your life needs to know that Good News today?

WISDOM FOR TODAY

God, give us such a passion for the lost that we can't be silent about the Good News of Jesus Christ. May everyone who comes in contact with us hear the message of salvation.

LOVING AND JUST

The LORD our God is righteous in everything he does.
DANIEL 9:14

The Bible tells us that God is loving and merciful—and this is absolutely true. That truth, however, makes some people wonder how He could send anyone to hell.

But do you honestly think God ought to excuse people like Hitler or Stalin, and tell them He doesn't really care that they killed tens of millions of innocent people? Do you really think God should welcome them into heaven, in spite of their relentless evil? I doubt if you do.

Sins like murder and rape and violence are an offense to our holy and pure God—as is every sin. God can't simply ignore evil or pretend it doesn't exist; to do so would be unjust. If someone hates God and chooses to do evil, God should not overlook their lifelong rebellion. The Bible is very clear: "He has set a day when he will judge the world with justice" (Acts 17:31).

Those of us who name Jesus as Savior and Lord, however, have trusted Him for our eternal salvation. And someday we know evil will be destroyed and Christ will reign forever.

WISDOM FOR TODAY

You are perfectly just, Lord, and will rightly judge every person. Thank You, Father, that those who believe are judged based on the righteousness of Christ and not our own worthiness.

BE ALERT!

*"Keep watch because you do not know when the owner of
the house will come back—whether in the evening, or at
midnight, or when the rooster crows, or at dawn."*

MARK 13:35

Are we living in the end times? Will Jesus return soon? The world does seem to be getting worse, and this should remind us that someday Christ will come again to bring an end to this present world.

Jesus taught that certain events or signs would point to His coming, and we certainly see many of these today. Jesus warned, for instance, that before He comes again "you will hear of wars and rumors of wars . . . famines and earthquakes in various places . . . false prophets will appear and deceive many people" (Matthew 24:6–7, 11). Satan will thrash about in one last burst of evil, hoping to capture as many souls as possible before his inevitable end.

So is Christ's coming near? It may well be—although the Bible warns us not to make precise predictions. But we must be alert and ready for His coming by being certain of our commitment to Christ, and approaching every day as if it were our last.

WISDOM FOR TODAY

We look forward to Your return, Lord, with eager anticipation, knowing the day will come when we will see Your face. We will continue faithfully serving here on earth until that day.

BE A BLESSING

Carry each other's burdens, and in this way you will fulfill the law of Christ.
GALATIANS 6:2

Sadly, we often don't realize how heavy another person's burden is until we walk along a similar path. Most of us are insensitive to the sufferings of others until we experience them ourselves. We become wrapped up in our own circumstances, and overlook the needs of those around us—even members of our own family. But this isn't God's plan. We are to show our love by bearing one another's burdens.

We can't change the past; it may be too late to apologize to someone for our thoughtlessness. But we don't need to carry around a burden of guilt over this. When Jesus died on the cross, He died for every sin you ever committed, including this one. If you confess your sin, He will cleanse you (1 John 1:9).

We can't change the past—but we can change our behavior now. Ask God to help you be a burden-bearer to those around you. Ask Him to show you how and to whom you can be a blessing and an encouragement. Whose burden will you help shoulder today?

WISDOM FOR TODAY

Give us eyes that see others in need, Lord, and a heart that is moved with compassion to help bear their burdens. Let us use any strength You've given us to help those in a season of weakness.

LISTENING AND . . .

There is a time for everything . . .
a time to be silent and a time to speak.
ECCLESIASTES 3:1, 7

When we are hurting, we value the presence of a friend who will just listen. But when someone we know is hurting, we often are tempted to do anything but listen—chattering away and giving unwanted advice to them instead of letting them share their burden with us.

But remember: sometimes the best thing we can do is listen quietly when a friend has a problem, letting them share their feelings and assuring them that we care, even if we don't have any answers. In the midst of his suffering, Job cried out to those who were constantly giving him advice, "If only you would be altogether silent!" (Job 13:5).

In addition to listening, pray for your hurting friends—and let them know you are praying. And when you do talk with them, encourage them and urge them to commit their problem—and their entire life—into Jesus' hands. God can work in unexpected ways to bring good out of bad.

When your friends are hurting, ask God to help you be an encourager and a burden-bearer—for Jesus' sake.

WISDOM FOR TODAY
Give us the wisdom, Father, to know when to speak and when to simply sit in silence with the hurting. Let us be sensitive to the Holy Spirit so that we know what is appropriate for each situation.

185

GOD WILL FORGIVE

Cleanse me with hyssop, and I will be clean;
wash me, and I will be whiter than snow.
PSALM 51:7

Do you believe that God can't forgive you for something you've done, even a long time ago? If so, know that those thoughts are actually from your enemy, Satan. He will do almost anything to make us think God hates us and won't forgive us. One of his favorite tricks is to encourage us to keep dredging up the sins of the past, and he uses our memory of them to condemn us and tell us how terrible we are. That is why the Bible calls Satan "the accuser of our brothers" (Revelation 12:10). But his accusations are false!

Here is the truth: if you have honestly turned to Jesus and asked Him to forgive you, then you are forgiven—totally and absolutely. When Jesus died on the cross, every sin you ever committed—every one—was placed on Him. He died to pay the penalty for all your sins.

So don't believe your emotions and don't let the memories of the past defeat you. The Bible says, "The blood of Jesus Christ His Son cleanses us from all sin" (1 John 1:7 NKJV). That is God's promise to you—and God cannot lie.

WISDOM FOR TODAY

Guilt is a tool of the enemy, Lord, but You are a God of grace. When Satan reminds us of our past failings, remind us that there is no condemnation for those in Christ Jesus. Help us to live in the freedom that You provided through the cross.

NEVER TOO LATE

Humble yourselves before the Lord, and he will lift you up.

JAMES 4:10

He and his brother were in prison awaiting trial for selling drugs. In his letter he said, "We both know we've messed up our lives and . . . hurt our parents a lot." It was my privilege to reassure him that it is never too late to get back on God's path, the path his Christian parents had raised him to know. Nor is it ever too late for you to honestly face your sins and turn to Jesus in repentance and faith.

One reason this young man's parents are hurting is because they love him, yet he rejected them by his actions. In a far greater way, God loves each one of us, and yet we hurt Him deeply when we turn our backs on Him. But He loves us despite our sin, and He stands ready to forgive us. Forgiveness is not something we deserve; it comes only as a gift of God's grace.

I told this young man something that you, too, may need to hear: don't let another day go by without Christ. No matter what the future holds, you will never be alone when Jesus lives within.

WISDOM FOR TODAY

It's never too late to repent and seek Your forgiveness, Lord. There isn't a place where our sin could take us that Your grace can't reach and redeem us. Thank You for Your love that lifts us from the pit and makes us brand new.

Hope for the Future

[Jesus] is able to save completely those who come to God through
him, because he always lives to intercede for them.
Hebrews 7:25

Sometimes life brings us to the point where we don't see much hope for the future. If you're there right now—whatever the situation, whatever the reason—let me assure you that God cares, and because of Him your future can be different.

Committing our lives to Christ or renewing our commitment to Him doesn't mean all our problems will suddenly vanish. We can't undo the past, and when we have made unwise decisions, we often have to live with the consequences. But isn't it better to face the future with God than without Him? God loves you, and even when life is dark and uncertain, that truth will bring you encouragement and strength.

Jesus knows what you are going through, and—as the verse above says—He is praying for you. So commit your problems and your future into His hands. Ask Him to help you make wise decisions about your future and to follow Him every day. Then "the God of hope [will] fill you with all joy and peace as you trust in him" (Romans 15:13).

Wisdom for Today

If the prayer of a righteous man availeth much (James 5:16), how much more powerful are the prayers of Jesus interceding on our behalf! Thank You, Lord, that You see us, care about us, and know exactly how to petition the Father on our behalf.

RIGHT AND WRONG

Everyone did what was right in his own eyes.

JUDGES 21:25 NJKV

Is our society today any different from the ancient society reflected in this verse? Sadly, not different enough. Too many people today feel that the old moral standards are useless and out of date, and they ought to be free to make up their own minds about what is right and what is wrong.

I wonder if we have honestly faced the logical result of this belief. What is actually being said is that there is no such thing as right or wrong, and we should be free to decide how we want to behave. But aren't things like racism and injustice and genocide always wrong? Shouldn't we always condemn an immoral tyrant who allows millions of children to die of starvation?

The moral standards God has given us are always best—for society and for us as individuals. The reason is because He created us, He loves us, and He knows what is best for us. Don't be misled by those who deny God's moral standards. His way is always best.

WISDOM FOR TODAY

Lord, we trust that You know what is best for Your people. Give us the wisdom to live according to Your commands, to trust in Your plan for us, and to always do what is clearly laid out in Scripture as good and right in Your eyes.

JULY

THE BUSINESS OF OUR LIVES

The proverbs of Solomon . . . for acquiring a disciplined and prudent life, doing what is right and just and fair.

PROVERBS 1:1, 3

The great eighteenth-century American preacher Jonathan Edwards wrote this about the Puritans who settled in America: "The practice of religion is not only their business at certain seasons, but the business of their lives."

The Puritans were ready to order their personal lives, worship, church, business affairs, political views, even recreation according to the Bible's commandments. What a contrast between the conduct of those earlier Christians and the permissiveness of our day!

Millions today want instant gratification. The whole world seems bent on pleasure, and there is an alarming preoccupation with self. When nations or individuals live only for pleasure, they begin to die morally and spiritually, oblivious to God's will and scornful of His judgment.

The Puritans knew that the life of faith is a struggle. They knew, too, that sin is a stubborn reality and that believers are not immune to affliction, poverty, and suffering. Still they persevered in their faith.

Like these our spiritual forefathers, may it be said of us that our faith is "the business of [our] lives."

WISDOM FOR TODAY

It is tempting, Father, to make our faith simply one aspect of our lives that we give attention to on specific days and at specific times. Help us make it an integral part of every area of our lives.

STRENGTHENING OUR NATION—
ONE CHILD AT A TIME

Teach [God's words] to your children, talking about them when you sit at home and when you walk along the road, when you lie down and when you get up.

DEUTERONOMY 11:19

Abraham Lincoln once said, "The strength of a nation lies in the people—in the homes of the people."

The home today is disintegrating. There is concern, deep concern, for what our children are being taught or not being taught, whether at home or at school or in the media. They are no longer being taught what is right and wrong—and they are floundering. They don't know which way to turn.

I don't believe that young people today can live clean, pure lives without the help of God. The peer pressure is too great, and the temptations they see in the movies and on television and what they hear in their music is too much. Only Christ can protect them. Only Christ can give them the power to say no.

Who in your home . . . in your neighborhood . . . in your life . . . would God have you prayerfully and carefully teach His truth and His way? Start today.

WISDOM FOR TODAY

We've been instructed, Father, to pass Your truths on to future generations. Help us be godly examples in word and deed to the children You've placed in our homes, churches, and communities so they will be able to discern what is right and wrong.

OUR GREATEST NEED

O LORD, revive thy work in the midst of the years.
HABAKKUK 3:2 KJV

I once asked a university professor what he thought our greatest need was. He said, "I may surprise you, because I'm not a religious man, but I believe that the greatest need that we have at this hour is a spiritual awakening that will restore individual and collective morals and integrity throughout the nation."

How do we achieve such a renewal? First, there must be prayer—the kind that springs from a deep-seated heart yearning for revival. We do not need pious platitudes and religious mouthings—but earnest, fervent prayer.

Second, we Christians must forsake our sins, both individually and corporately. We must forsake our pettiness, our peevishness, our littleness, and our conflicts—as well as our evil ways.

Third, God must become real to us. Let the Bible's truth soak deeply into your heart and mind every day. Then you will rediscover that God is holy, righteous, absolute, personal, loving, and merciful—and this reality will be transferred into action, and revival can come. It has worked before in history. It will work again.

WISDOM FOR TODAY

God, we have turned to our own ways and done what was right in our own eyes. Please send a spirit of revival across our land and turn our hearts back to You. We deeply desire Your power and presence in our lives.

PRAYING FOR YOUR NATION

"If my people . . . pray and seek my face . . . I will hear from heaven."

2 CHRONICLES 7:14

A great crisis in American history came at the Constitutional Convention called in Philadelphia to ratify a constitution for the new country that was being born. The delegates got angry with one another, and because they couldn't resolve their conflicts, they couldn't agree on a thing and picked up their hats and coats and started to leave. Suddenly Benjamin Franklin spoke up.

"What a minute, gentlemen," he is reported to have said. "This country was conceived in faith in God. Many of us here believe in prayer. Let us get upon our knees and pray to Almighty God and see whether God shall give to us the answer to our dilemma."

Upon their knees those men went, and out of that prayer meeting came the Constitution of the United States of America.

What dilemma in your nation—or in your life—is compelling you to get down on your knees and seek God's answer?

WISDOM FOR TODAY

Would You show us the way back to You, Father? Help us see one another as made in Your image. May we come together and pray for Your will in our lives and in our land.

THE BATTLE RAGES

Our struggle is not against flesh and blood, but against the rulers, against the authorities, against the powers of this dark world and against the spiritual forces of evil in the heavenly realms.

EPHESIANS 6:12

When we were in Romania, we visited the area known as Moldavia. What a beautiful part of Romania that is!

The bishop took us on a trip around Moldavia, and he showed us the famous churches with paintings from Scripture on them. In the past, before most people could read, they drew scenes from the Bible on the church walls and used those paintings to teach God's Word and His truth.

I will never forget one picture. It is of a stairway to heaven, and pilgrims are going up the ladder. Below them are devils trying to pull them down into the flames of hell. At the top of the picture, Jesus is standing, waiting in heaven for the faithful, and above the pilgrims are angels helping them along. That scene shows the great battle between good and evil, between God and Satan, that rages in the heavens and on this earth.

Today—and every day—put on the full armor of God to fight Satan's attacks so you can "be strong in the Lord" (Ephesians 6:10).

WISDOM FOR TODAY

Father, keep us mindful of the war that rages around us. The enemy would love for us to underestimate him and therefore fail to protect ourselves appropriately. We will face each day with the full armor You have provided.

VIRTUES FOR LIVING

Add to your faith goodness; and to goodness, knowledge; and to knowledge,
self-control; and to self-control, perseverance; and to perseverance, godliness;
and to godliness, brotherly kindness; and to brotherly kindness, love.

2 PETER 1:5–7

J esus summarized the whole of God's law with these words: "Love the Lord
your God with all your heart and with all your soul and with all your mind . .
. [and] love your neighbor as yourself" (Matthew 22:37, 39).

Yet, at the risk of sounding contradictory, love is not the whole of our spiritual
life, because it is only one of the virtues God wants us to have. If we ignore the
other virtues—such as joy, peace, patience, kindness, goodness, gentleness, and
self-control (Galatians 5:22–23)—our life will be unbalanced and incomplete.

Why are these virtues so important? Because they were part of Christ's
character—and God's will is that we would become more like Christ. As the
apostle Peter said, "If you possess these qualities in increasing measure, they
will keep you from being ineffective and unproductive" (2 Peter 1:8).

Ask God to show you if any of these virtues are missing in your life—and
then open your heart and mind to Christ's transforming power and love.

WISDOM FOR TODAY

Lord, we want to live lives that are effective and productive; we want our efforts to matter. We can't be good, kind, and loving on our own, so please fill
us with Your Spirit. Change us from the inside out.

A GOSPEL OF CRISIS

Multitudes, multitudes in the valley of decision! For the
day of the LORD is near in the valley of decision.
JOEL 3:14

C hristianity is a Gospel of crisis. It is the Gospel of Good News to be sure—
that God has a plan for your life, that God loves you, that He is a God of
mercy, that He will forgive you if you confess and forsake your sins and trust
Jesus Christ as your personal Savior and Lord.

But as far as the unbelieving world's understanding is concerned, Christianity
is a Gospel of crisis: it boldly proclaims that this world's days are numbered.
Every cemetery testifies that our days on this planet are indeed numbered. The
Bible teaches that life is only a vapor that appears for a moment and then van-
ishes (James 4:14).

There is another sense, however, in which the world's system will end: there
will be an end of history and the end of a world that has been dominated by
evil. Jesus will come again and set up His kingdom of righteousness and social
justice, and hatred, greed, jealousy, war, and death will no longer exist. Are you
ready for that day?

Join me in praying, "Come quickly, Lord Jesus!"

WISDOM FOR TODAY
Lord, we await the day when You return and evil is no more. Help us, in
the meantime, to take every opportunity to love others and share our faith,
knowing that we are not promised tomorrow.

Whom Will You Serve?

*"These people come near to me with their mouth and honor
me with their lips, but their hearts are far from me."*

ISAIAH 29:13

D o you serve God only with your lips? You profess God, you profess Christ, you go to church, you give to the church, perhaps you teach Sunday school or you serve on the church board. But deep in your heart are you totally surrendered and committed to Christ?

Outwardly the Israelites in Joshua's day were followers of God—but in their hearts they were idolaters. Joshua told them that this hypocrisy could not continue. They were to decide whether they wanted to serve the true and living God or serve their idols. It was Israel's day of decision. They were to go on record— either for God or against Him.

Likewise, we must decide whom we will serve. After all, a Christian should forsake everything false and turn wholeheartedly to Jesus.

Regardless of the decision his fellow Hebrews would make, Joshua declared, "As for me and my household, we will serve the LORD" (Joshua 24:15).

Will you decide to serve the true and living God? If so, what idols must you first forsake?

WISDOM FOR TODAY

We will live lives completely devoted to You, Lord. We will daily choose to honor You with our lips and our lives so there will be no question where our loyalty lies.

An Experience with God

I heard the voice of the Lord saying, "Whom shall I send? And who will go for us?"

And I said, "Here am I. Send me!"
ISAIAH 6:8–9

I think Isaiah 6 is one of the most unforgettable chapters in the Bible, for there we find Isaiah's intimate account of his experience with God.

First, Isaiah comprehended who God is. The ultimate experience of life is knowing God, and Isaiah came to know God in His righteousness and holiness.

Second, when Isaiah saw who God really is, his response was a deep conviction of his own sinfulness. Anyone who has genuinely seen God is deeply convicted of his or her own sin.

Isaiah's conviction about his sin led to confession, and then came cleansing as God touched a coal to Isaiah's lips, symbolizing the purging of his sin. Eight hundred years later, Jesus would die on the cross so our sins could be washed away by His cleansing blood.

Finally, the challenge: we who see God as He is are to see the world as He sees it—and then step out in faith to make a difference.

What part of Isaiah's experience do you stand in need of today?

Wisdom for Today

Help us live in constant communion with You, Father, so we will be listening when You give the command to go. Instill in us the courage to accept the challenge to go and share the Gospel wherever You send us.

PULLING OUT THE WEEDS

Let the word of Christ dwell in you richly.

COLOSSIANS 3:16

Have you ever had a weed in your yard that you chopped down and thought was gone—only to have it spring up again? Its roots, you discovered, were still alive, and they might even have spread.

Sinful thoughts can be like that. When we come to Christ, He begins to change our thinking, and new thoughts begin to take root in our minds—thoughts about God's love for us and His will for our lives. But those old thoughts haven't been completely killed, and sometimes they suddenly spring to the surface. When they do, Satan will try to deceive us into thinking that we aren't new creations in Jesus after all, because we have failed Him.

Don't be surprised when old ways of thinking crop up—but don't let them linger. When they come, immediately turn to God and ask Him to help you get rid of them—just as you pull weeds out of your garden.

Most of all, let the Word of God fill you and renew your mind every day. When our minds are on Christ, Satan has little room to maneuver.

WISDOM FOR TODAY

There isn't any doubt, Lord, that the enemy wants control of our minds. He wants to plant seeds of worry, doubt, and fear. Help us take every thought captive and make it obedient to Your truth.

BLESSED ASSURANCE

[God] has also set eternity in the hearts of men.

ECCLESIASTES 3:11

How do we know heaven even exists? How do we know it isn't just a myth—a product of our imaginations?

Let me give you two reasons we can know heaven exists (although I could give other reasons). First, I am convinced heaven exists because God has put the hope of heaven within our hearts. That hope is almost universal, and it is part of every religion. The Bible says that this hope comes from God: He wants us to know that death is not the end and that we were meant to live forever with Him. As the verse above says, God placed within our hearts a yearning for heaven.

The main reason I know heaven exists, however, is the death and resurrection of Jesus. When He died on the cross, He erased the only thing that can keep us out of heaven: our sin. When He rose from the dead, He guaranteed for all time that there is life after death and that heaven is real. Jesus said, "I am going there to prepare a place for you" (John 14:2).

By a simple prayer of faith ask Jesus to forgive your sins and come into your life. Then thank Him that someday you will go to be with Him in heaven forever.

WISDOM FOR TODAY

Thank You, Lord, for the reality of heaven and for placing a yearning for it within us. We were created by You to live with You forever, and You have made a way for that to happen through Your gift of salvation.

PRAY FOR THE PERSECUTED

*Remember those in prison as if you were their fellow prisoners, and
those who are mistreated as if you yourselves were suffering.*

HEBREWS 13:3

Few things touch my heart more than the news that some of my brothers and sisters in Christ are being persecuted, tortured, and killed for their love of Jesus.

It has been estimated that more Christians have been killed for their faith during the last one hundred years than in all the other centuries combined since the time of Christ. One reason is the great expansion of Christianity in the last few centuries—often into places of great unbelief and hostility. Another reason is the rise of militantly antireligious political systems.

Even where persecution isn't an issue, an upsurge in secularism and religious intolerance is apparent, and religion has been scorned and removed from public life. The Crucified One warned us: we who choose to follow Him would do so at the risk of rejection and persecution.

Thank God for whatever measure of religious freedom you enjoy—and pray today for those suffering for their faith in Christ.

WISDOM FOR TODAY

Give us true compassion for persecuted believers, Father, and help us not to take our religious freedoms for granted, knowing that we are at risk daily for persecution as well. It is our duty and privilege to pray for those suffering because of their faith.

WISDOM—OR SELF-CENTEREDNESS?

Greater love has no one than this that he lay down his life for his friends.
JOHN 15:13

H as an unbeliever ever accused you of being a hypocrite because you didn't show them Christian love? We need to take such accusations seriously, in case we have been at fault.

But not every accusation like this is justified; sometimes the accuser is just being selfish and demanding and unrealistic.

We aren't hypocritical just because we don't meet a person's every demand. Would we really be helping them if we met their every demand, no matter how selfish? Instead, we might just be encouraging greater self-centeredness on their part—and that is not God's will. Sometimes love says no, because that is what is best for the other person.

If you can fulfill someone's request, however, do so even if it involves sacrifice on your part. The Bible says, "Let us not love with words or tongue but with actions and in truth" (1 John 3:18). This is the kind of love God showed us when He sent His Son into the world to die for our sins.

May you always be an example to others of Jesus' selfless love—and may He grant you wisdom to know what that will mean in every situation.

WISDOM FOR TODAY
We truly need Your guidance, Lord, when it comes to loving others well. Help us make decisions based on Your will and their best interests and not from a desire for our own comfort or convenience.

MAKING US LIKE CHRIST

We also rejoice in our sufferings, because we know that suffering produces perseverance; perseverance, character; and character, hope.

ROMANS 5:3–4

God can take anything that happens to us—even bad things—and use it to shape us and make us into better, more Christ-like people—if we will let Him.

This doesn't mean God necessarily causes everything that happens to us; sometimes He only allows things to happen. Often, for instance, bad things happen to us because we made bad decisions—decisions that were the opposite of God's will for us. When that's the case, we can't blame God for the consequences.

Sometimes we don't know why God allows bad things to happen to us. Even then, however, God can use them to teach us and make us into better people. Disappointments and tragedies, for example, can teach us to turn in trust to God for the hope and comfort we need. These experiences can also teach us patience and make us more sensitive to others who are suffering.

Are you passing through a difficult time today? Ask God to use it to increase your faith and make you more like Christ.

WISDOM FOR TODAY

Whatever the reason for our current pain, Father, let it not be in vain. May it cause us to draw nearer to You, to seek out any sin or area of disobedience in our lives, and to look more like You.

TIME FOR A U-TURN?

There is a way that seems right to a man,
but in the end it leads to death.
PROVERBS 16:25

Are you walking on a path that you are realizing is not God's best for you? Do you even need to make a complete U-turn but are struggling to find the courage to do so? For example, is it time to end a wrong relationship, or cast off a habit that isn't healthy, or leave behind an undisciplined life that always seems to put God in second place?

Whatever situation has you feeling stuck, know that there is no shortcut or easy way out. You need to make the right decision—firmly and decisively—and then stick to it with God's help. You may need to get family members or friends to pray for you and support you.

There is no time like the present to begin building (or rebuilding) your life on the foundation of Christ and His will for you. He loves you, and He knows what is best for you. Don't be satisfied with anything less than His will for you—for His will is always best.

WISDOM FOR TODAY

It's difficult, Father, to admit when we've chosen our own will over Your will. Thank You that as long as there is breath in our bodies, it's not too late to make a change. Reveal any areas in our lives that need to be recommitted to You.

WHICH ROAD?

Small is the gate and narrow the road that leads to life, and only a few find it.
MATTHEW 7:14

You may not be old enough to remember July 16, 1969, but on that historic day American astronauts astonished the world with their spectacularly successful first visit to the moon. They were able to succeed because they steered the Apollo 11 craft along a very narrow trajectory through space. No deviation was permitted, and flight corrections were made periodically throughout the historic voyage.

Now suppose the NASA control center in Houston had received word from Apollo 11 that the astronauts were off course and had replied, "Oh, that's all right. A number of roads lead to the moon. Just keep on the way you are going." You and I know they would have kept going—but they never would have come back.

People today don't like the word *narrow*, but Jesus clearly said there are two roads to the future for all of us: the way to hell and destruction is broad, but the way to heaven is narrow. Which road are you on? Is a course correction necessary?

WISDOM FOR TODAY
We were made to be different and set apart, Lord. Give us the strength to stand firm in the truth and to stay on the narrow path, even if others don't understand or follow us.

GIVING WITH JOY

Each man should give what he has decided in his heart to give, not reluctantly or under compulsion, for God loves a cheerful giver.

2 CORINTHIANS 9:7

Why give to God's work? After all (perhaps you've said to yourself), "What good can my little amount do when the needs are so great? Why bother to give?"

But God looks at our finances differently. First, He knows that our giving is a measure of something far more important: the depth of our commitment to Jesus Christ. And it isn't just a question of how much we give, but what our attitude is as we give. Do we give reluctantly or under compulsion (perhaps to impress other people)? If so, it strongly suggests that we love ourselves more than we love Christ. Don't let this be true of you.

But God also is able to take what we give and use it in ways we never could imagine. That extra dollar might keep a starving child alive one more day, or bring the Gospel to someone who would otherwise never hear of Jesus. Give prayerfully . . . give joyfully . . . and ask God to use your gifts to help others in the name of Jesus.

WISDOM FOR TODAY

God, help us to always do the right thing, and help us have pure motives, which brings Your blessings. May our desire always be to obey the commands found in Scripture, to point others to You, and to further Your kingdom.

TRUSTING IN GOD'S LOVE

From everlasting to everlasting
the LORD's love is with those who fear him.
PSALM 103:17

Most of us are pretty good at worrying, aren't we?
When worries come, however, I've found it helpful to counter them with the Bible's promises about God's steadfast love. He loves us, and no matter what happens, He never abandons us. We know this because Jesus Christ demonstrated God's love for us by giving His life for our salvation.

Does this mean that things will never go wrong, or we'll never have any problems? Absolutely not! But it does mean that nothing we experience ever catches God by surprise or is too big for Him to handle. Even when our day seems dark, God never leaves us, nor does He allow anything to come our way that can overwhelm us.

Make it a practice to thank God every day for the blessings you have. Thank Him also each day that He loves you. Worries flee before a spirit of gratitude. Then, when problems do come, commit them in faith to God. Since God takes care of the smallest birds, Jesus said, can't we trust Him to take care of us? After all, "Are you not much more valuable than they?" (Matthew 6:26).

WISDOM FOR TODAY

Saturate our hearts and minds with Your truth, Father, so we know what we believe before the battle begins. We must determine what we know to be true of You so we may cling to it in the midst of the fight.

OUR PERFECT PARENT

*[Joseph] got up, took the child and his mother and went to the land
of Israel . . . and he went and lived in a town called Nazareth.*
MATTHEW 2:21, 23

I find it significant that God placed the young Jesus in a family. God knew that, with Mary and Joseph's love and guidance, His Son would grow "in wisdom and stature, and in favor with God and men" (Luke 2:52).

Twenty-one centuries later, this should happen in our families also. Parents are given the privilege—and responsibility—of teaching their children about God and helping them become wise in His ways. Yet we parents often fall short of God's design. When that happens, our children may grow angry and bitter, lashing out at us for the hurts we supposedly caused.

Did you allow anger and bitterness to poison your relationship with your parents—even over things that happened many years ago? Don't let your parents' failures—real or imagined—hold you in their grip any longer. Instead, ask God to help you forgive the past—and then ask Christ to change you into the person He wants you to be. And if you are a parent, ask God to help you be a loving and wise guide for your children and to build your family on Christ and His will.

WISDOM FOR TODAY

We will always be disappointed, Father, when we expect any human to meet all our expectations. Help us give grace to our parents where they may have failed us and point our own children to You.

LIFE-CHANGING LOVE

If you confess with your mouth, "Jesus is Lord," and believe in your heart that God raised him from the dead, you will be saved.

ROMANS 10:9

One heartbreaking question I'm sometimes asked goes like this: "I've asked Christ to come into my life dozens of times, but He hasn't. Does God hate me?" Perhaps you have felt like this.

But the Bible's teaching is clear: God does not hate you. God loves you, and He wants to be part of your life even more than you want Him to! From beginning to end, the Bible proclaims this simple truth: God loves you.

Why, then, hasn't God apparently come into your life? The key word is *apparently*. If you have confessed your sin and acknowledged that Jesus is your Lord, who died on the cross for you and rose again to give you eternal life, then God has promised to forgive you and save you. God does not lie, and He has promised that if we truly commit our lives to Christ, He will save us and come into our lives. Salvation is God's gift to you—a gift paid for by Christ's sacrifice of Himself for you. You may not feel any different, but you will be different because Christ now lives within you. Don't go by your feelings but by the fact of God's promises to you.

WISDOM FOR TODAY

Help us not mistake our feelings, which can be fickle and fleeting, for truth, Father. If our feelings ever contradict what Scripture has proclaimed, give us the wisdom to accept Your Word as truth.

MEETING THE CHALLENGE

How can a young man keep his way pure?
By living according to your word.
PSALM 119:9

Young men aren't the only ones who find it challenging to live a pure life. All believers are called to be holy in mind, body, and spirit (1 Peter 1:15)—but it certainly isn't easy. Advertisements and entertainment have become so saturated with sexual themes and images that it is difficult to avoid them. Greed, self-gratification, and the lust for power seem to drive our culture. We have become like the people of Jeremiah's day: "They have no shame at all; they do not even know how to blush" (Jeremiah 8:12).

If we are to be pure and holy, we must first commit ourselves—mind, body, and spirit—completely to Christ. We can't hold back any area of our life from Him. Second, we must avoid situations that might encourage impure thoughts or actions. And, third, we must fill our minds and hearts with Christ by feeding our souls on a daily diet of prayer and God's Word. With God's help we can keep our way pure by living according to His Word. Is this your goal?

WISDOM FOR TODAY
We live in a day, Father, when we must be proactive in our desire to remain pure. Help us protect our minds, eyes, and hearts by dwelling on things that are true, honorable, right, pure, lovely, admirable, and praiseworthy (Philippians 4:8).

SERVING GOD

Be very careful to . . . serve him with all your heart and all your soul.

JOSHUA 22:5

What comes to mind when you hear the phrase "serving God"?
Maybe you think of missionaries or pastors. Maybe you think of qualifications like seminary training, or a holy life, or a solid knowledge of God's Word. Or maybe you think of people who are younger and healthier than you, or older and more experienced than you, as those God can use most effectively.

But listen: God wants to use you right where you are. Every day you probably come in contact with people who will never enter a church, or talk with a pastor, or open a Bible—and God wants to use you to point them to Christ. You may be the "bridge" God would use to bring them to Himself.

Be alert for opportunities to share the Good News of Christ's love with others—even today. Never underestimate what God can do through even your smallest effort to reach out to others in the name of Jesus.

WISDOM FOR TODAY

Father, You have a purpose for every person alive today, whether they are young or old. Paul said that to remain in the body meant fruitful labor (Philippians 1:22). Let us continue being about Your business as long as there is breath in our bodies.

NOTHING IS TOO HARD!

Sovereign LORD, you have made the heavens and the earth
by your great power. . . . Nothing is too hard for you.
JEREMIAH 32:17

Are there some things God cannot do? The answer may surprise you: yes, there are some things that God can't do.

God cannot, for instance, tell a lie or go back on His promises. Neither can He do something evil or have an impure thought. Why? Because God cannot do anything that is contrary to His basic character. Remember: God is not some vague force like gravity or electricity. He is a person, and He is holy and perfect in His character.

But the Bible's focus is on what God can do. Not only is He perfect, but He is also absolutely sovereign and all-powerful. And because of that—as Jeremiah wrote—nothing is too hard for Him. If He could bring Jesus back from the dead, can't He also help you overcome whatever situation you are facing today?

Put whatever burden you are carrying into His hands—because He loves you, and nothing is too hard for Him.

WISDOM FOR TODAY

God, You created everything out of nothing. You have healed the sick, opened barren wombs, and robbed the grave of its power. You give joy in the midst of mourning and provide peace in the midst of chaos. Nothing is too difficult for You!

HOPE FOR TODAY, HOPE FOR ETERNITY

I desire to depart and be with Christ, which is better by far.

PHILIPPIANS 1:23

Her pain was more than physical. Over the years the crippling arthritis had taken its toll on her emotions as well, and now she was praying that God would take her to heaven. Was this prayer, she asked me timidly, wrong or even sinful?

First of all (I reminded her), it is not a sin to long for heaven. If we know Jesus, we know that in heaven all our burdens and pain will be lifted forever. It is, as the apostle Paul stated, "better by far" to be in heaven with Jesus than to be suffering on this sin-filled earth.

At the same time, though, God has a purpose in keeping us here until He finally takes us home. He has things to teach us about Himself, and He can still use us to bless others. Only eternity will reveal the powerful ways God used the prayers and the witness of men and women who could no longer do everything they once did but who still trusted God to use them.

Keep your eyes on eternity—but also seek Christ's will for you right now, no matter what you are facing.

WISDOM FOR TODAY

Every person who has trusted in You, Lord, desires to be in Your presence because we know it is far better. In the meantime, however, let us not be idle. Let us be passionately praying, pursuing holiness, and pointing others to You.

EASIER SAID THAN DONE

If it is possible, as far as it depends on you, live at peace with everyone.
ROMANS 12:18

God's will is for us to live at peace with everyone—but sometimes the door to a broken relationship seems closed forever. The marriage has died or the children are rejecting you. . . . Your father abandoned your family or your disapproving mother has cut off all contact. . . . A business partner has turned away in anger or a former friend wants nothing to do with you.

If someone rejects us and absolutely refuses to have anything to do with us, we can't force them to change. But we can—and should—do everything we can to keep the door open to a possible reconciliation. We shouldn't strike back or condemn; instead, we should let them know we still care and that we hope someday his or her attitude will change. And if we were at fault—even in small ways—we need to admit it and ask for forgiveness.

We also should pray. We can't change the person we're estranged from, but God can. Even when the door seems firmly closed, God is able to open it. Do all you can to restore that broken relationship—and trust God for the outcome.

WISDOM FOR TODAY
Some of our greatest hurts, Father, come from broken earthly relationships. Give us the humility to seek or extend forgiveness, the grace to live at peace with those who have wounded us, and the faith to never give up on the hope of reconciliation.

GOD'S HOUSEHOLD

[You are] fellow citizens with God's people and members of God's household.

EPHESIANS 2:19

Someone with a wry sense of humor once described a church as a group of porcupines in a snowstorm: we need each other to keep warm, but the closer we get, the more we poke each other—and the more uncomfortable we become.

But of course it shouldn't be that way. A church should be a place of warmth and fellowship, a place where even the newest member or latest visitor feels welcome and at home. Is this true in your church? Simply attending a worship service doesn't automatically mean closer relationships with others.

If you are an "old-timer" in your church, go out of your way to welcome visitors and new members. And if you are a visitor or new member, make a special effort to get to know people. Find out what activities the church offers for spiritual growth. What Bible classes are held? Does a group of people your age meet regularly? Don't depend only on one worship service a week to help you meet people or grow closer to Christ.

If this step sounds a little daunting, remember that your best Friend of all— Jesus Christ—will be with you each step of the way.

WISDOM FOR TODAY

Show us how we can begin growing closer to the people with whom we worship, God. Help us view them not as church members but as family members and fellow servants of Christ, and may we be quick to welcome new people into the fold.

Committing Your Life to Jesus

Salvation is found in no one else, for there is no other name under heaven given to men by which we must be saved.
Acts 4:12

Suppose you are riding down a road and you come to a deep gorge. The bridge has been washed away, and jumping across the gorge is not an option. Seemingly you have no hope of reaching your destination.

But then you notice another bridge some distance away. You watch people cross it to the other side. It certainly seems sturdy.

What would you have to do to get across? First, believe that the bridge will hold you. Then commit yourself to it: put your full weight on it and walk across it.

This illustrates what it means to commit your life to Jesus Christ. By His death and resurrection Jesus bridged the gap between us and God—a gap caused by sin. But simply believing intellectually that He has done this is not enough. Like that bridge across the gorge, we must trust Him and commit our lives to Him. And when we do, we will discover that He can be trusted to save us, because He truly is the bridge between us and God.

Have you committed your life in faith and trust to Jesus Christ as your "bridge" and your Savior?

Wisdom for Today

Let our faith be more than words, Lord. Someone viewing our lives should see us actively believing and following You. There should be a difference in the way we deal with grief, conflict, and disappointment that shows we are trusting You with our very lives.

WHEN GOD CALLS

[God] said to [Paul], "My grace is sufficient for you,
for my power is made perfect in weakness."

2 CORINTHIANS 12:9

God says the same thing to you when He calls you into service for His kingdom.

Perhaps you are asked to teach a Sunday school class. You feel inadequate, unsure that you know enough about the Bible. When an invitation like this comes, pray. Ask God if He wants you to accept this responsibility, even if you don't feel qualified or prepared. If God wants you to serve in this position, He will make it clear to you.

Once you accept the invitation to serve, know that as you turn to God and rely on Him, He will empower and guide you. Do all you need to do to be ready to serve in whatever capacity God calls you, and realize that the knowledge of God's Word is an essential tool for any aspect of kingdom work.

Don't be afraid to take a step of faith, to respond to God's call to serve. It is a wondrous thing to have God's power be made perfect in our weakness as He uses us for His eternal work.

WISDOM FOR TODAY

Help us, Lord, to always be prepared to serve when called on to do so. May we consider service to be a privilege and not a burden, and may it be for Your glory and not our own.

LOUDER THAN WORDS

I urge you to live a life worthy of the calling you have received.
EPHESIANS 4:1

Someone has wisely observed that the only Bible some people will ever read is the one they see demonstrated in the life of a Christian.

In other words, the way we live often speaks far louder than our words. People may tell us they don't believe the Bible—but they can't deny its power as they see it change our lives, guide our decisions, and influence how we live.

What do people see when they look at you? Do they see someone whose life reflects Christ? Do they see in you the Christlike traits of love, joy, peace, patience, kindness, goodness, faithfulness, gentleness, and self-control (Galatians 5:22–23)?

Ask God to rule in your heart and remake you from within into the person He wants you to be. Then ask Him to help you be sensitive to those around you who may be successful on the outside, but inwardly are empty and confused, so that by your life and by your words they may discover the joy and peace that come from knowing Christ.

WISDOM FOR TODAY

God, we can show others the power You have in our lives regardless of what we're going through. We can exhibit humility in our failings, peace in our trials, and love in our dealings with difficult people. Help us live in a way that draws people to You.

FULLY MAN—AND FULLY GOD

The Son is the radiance of God's glory and the exact representation of his being.

HEBREWS 1:3

The Bible's message is centered in Jesus Christ, God's one and only Son—who He is and what He has done for us by His death and resurrection. When we read its pages, we discover that Jesus was not only a great man, but He was God in human flesh, "the exact representation of [God's] being."

Why is this important? Because only a divine Savior can save us from our sins. We cannot save ourselves; even one sin, the Bible teaches, would be enough to keep us out of heaven. Nor can a Savior who is less than God save us, for only God can forgive sin and make us part of His family forever. This is why "salvation is found in no one else, for there is no other name under heaven given to men by which we must be saved" (Acts 4:12).

Today—even as you close this book—pause and thank God for coming to earth in the Person of Jesus Christ, His Son. And thank Him that because of Jesus we know God loves us, and that someday we will be with Him and see Him in all His glory.

WISDOM FOR TODAY

Thank You, Lord, for leaving all the beauty and glory of heaven to come to earth and put on flesh. You chose to experience hunger, temptation, sorrow, and suffering. You chose to experience the cross so that we, through Your sacrifice, could experience glory.

When Judgment Comes

It is time for judgment to begin with the family of God, and if it begins with us, what will the outcome be for those who do not obey the gospel of God?
1 Peter 4:17

Does God's judgment happen only after we die? Or does it take place now, before we die?

The answer is both. Someday we each will die and stand before God to give an account of our lives—and if we have ignored God and turned away from His offer of salvation, we can expect only His judgment. The Bible is clear: "Man is destined to die once, and after that to face judgment" (Hebrews 9:27). Those are sobering words that we ignore at our peril.

But the Bible warns us that God also brings judgment upon us in this life. The Bible says, "You may be sure that your sin will find you out" (Numbers 32:23). The headlines are filled with people who thought they could sin and get by with it—only to have it come out in the open and bring their lives crashing down.

Don't ever take God's judgment lightly—and don't ever take sin lightly. God doesn't take them lightly—and the proof is that they cost His dear Son His life.

Wisdom for Today

Help us take sin seriously, Father, and to constantly be seeking to remove it from our lives. May we follow the guidance of the Holy Spirit so we do not need to fear judgment either in this life or the one to come.

AUGUST

FREELY AND FULLY FORGIVEN

As far as the east is from the west,
so far has he removed our transgressions from us.
PSALM 103:12

If you could know beyond a shadow of a doubt that God had completely forgiven you, what reason would you have to keep feeling guilty? Absolutely none.

And God offers you exactly that: complete and total forgiveness, no matter what you have done. Jesus willingly took your sins and mine upon Himself, and He paid the penalty we deserved. The Bible puts it this way: "God made Christ, who never sinned, to be the offering for our sin, so that we could be made right with God through Christ" (2 Corinthians 5:21 NLT).

We don't need to wonder if we've been forgiven; we don't need to carry around a burden of guilt. If memories from the past return, immediately remind yourself of the truth of 1 John 1:9: "If we confess our sins, he is faithful and just and will forgive us our sins and purify us from all unrighteousness." Then thank God for forgiving you, freely and fully, because of Christ's sacrifice for you.

WISDOM FOR TODAY

Father, it is not humanly possible to forget the things we've done, and the enemy uses this human frailty against us. When Satan brings our former failings to mind, teach us to choose gratitude for the forgiveness we've received instead of guilt over the things we've done.

GROWING THROUGH FELLOWSHIP

We are members of [Christ's] body.

EPHESIANS 5:30

The only thing that counts as far as our salvation is concerned is our relationship to Jesus Christ. If you have acknowledged your sinfulness and truly trusted Christ to save you, then nothing can take away your salvation.

If we are committed to Jesus, however, God also wants us to become part of a fellowship of believers. God wants us to grow in our faith, and one of the ways we do this is through our fellowship with other believers. The Bible says, "As iron sharpens iron, so one man sharpens another" (Proverbs 27:17). It also says, "Let us not give up meeting together . . . but let us encourage one another" (Hebrews 10:25).

Ask God to lead you to a church—to a body of believers—where you can grow spiritually. God will use the preaching of His Word and the congregation's worship to encourage and strengthen you. Get involved also in other activities in your church—a Bible study, a prayer group, or a service project. God will use them to help you grow in your faith—and He also will use you to help others.

WISDOM FOR TODAY

Our moment of salvation, Father, should be the beginning of a life of devotion, service, and growth. Help us seek out opportunities to deepen our faith, learn from other believers, and learn more about You and Your will for our lives.

OUR SOVEREIGN GOD

Do you show contempt for the riches of his kindness, tolerance and patience,
not realizing that God's kindness leads you toward repentance?
ROMANS 2:4

Has it ever bothered you that some people who turn their backs on God seem to go through life without ever having anything bad happen to them? Life is so easy for them that they can't see any reason to bother with God.

But we don't know their hearts: deep inside they may actually be very insecure and fearful—although they may not be able to admit it to themselves.

God sees the whole picture, while we see only a little part. God knows what He is doing, and He can be trusted to do what is right according to His perfect plan.

Sadly, these people will one day die and face God. His goodness to them should have caused them to turn to Him in thankfulness and trust—but instead they ignored His blessings and lived only for themselves. How tragic to enter eternity unprepared. Don't let this happen to you!

Ask God to use you to point others to Christ—even those who seemingly have no interest in Him. And be grateful for God's goodness to you, and walk with Him in gratitude and faith.

WISDOM FOR TODAY

Teach us not to judge others, Lord, based on what worldly possessions or prestige they may have accumulated. May we minister to and witness to them, knowing they are just as in need of Your grace as the rest of us.

SATAN'S PERSISTENCE

Thrown into the lake of burning sulfur . . . [and]
tormented day and night for ever and ever.
REVELATION 20:10

God—who cannot lie—assures us that this is what awaits Satan. So why doesn't he just give up and stop bothering us?

Perhaps he still expects to win. After all, Satan totally rejects everything about God—including His promises. Even in the garden of Eden, Satan rejected God's Word and branded God a liar (Genesis 3:1–4). Perhaps Satan still rejects everything God says, even about his own destiny.

But Satan also persists because he has one main goal: to block God's work in any way he can. As long as he is active, people will be deceived into following his way instead of God's way. Even believers can be diverted from God's plan for their life and be content with a lukewarm faith that makes little impact on others.

Yes, someday Satan will be defeated—but in the meantime we must be on our guard, because he "prowls around like a roaring lion looking for someone to devour" (1 Peter 5:8). Don't be his next victim!

WISDOM FOR TODAY

Father, help us not grow complacent in our faith and, by doing so, diminish our effectiveness. May we remain alert to the schemes of the enemy so we are not led astray and tricked into leading unfruitful lives.

A CHILD'S FAITH

"Let the little children come to me, and do not hinder them,
for the kingdom of God belongs to such as these."
MARK 10:14

Young children can ask the most amazing questions about God and heaven! And when they do, we shouldn't ignore them or act like their questions aren't important—because they are.

When children ask you about God, do your best to answer simply and honestly in terms they can understand. Of course they don't need deep and complicated answers, but just because they can't understand everything about God doesn't mean they can't understand something about Him. I don't understand electricity, but that doesn't mean I can't turn on a light switch.

Ask God to give you patience also; children have a way of asking questions until we adults run out of answers! Be thankful for their interest in spiritual things, and do all you can to let them know that God is important to you. They can begin to sense Jesus' love for them through your love and your words.

Jesus told His disciples to let the children come to Him, and He continues to open His arms to them twenty-one centuries later. So should we.

WISDOM FOR TODAY

Father, You are patient and loving toward us, Your children. Help us to display that same gentleness toward the children You've placed in our lives. May they know Your love through the way we love them.

MAKING GODLY DECISIONS

In all your ways acknowledge [God],
and he will make your paths straight.

PROVERBS 3:6

Are you facing a significant decision? Then look again at these words in Proverbs 3:6. Implicit in this verse is the truth that God knows what is best for us and that He wants to guide us so we will make right, God-honoring decisions.

When you face a decision about your future, seek God's will above all else. Make your decision a matter of prayer, and ask Him to guide you. If we are truly open to His will, He will direct us.

Does this mean we should just wait around until God gives us some kind of miraculous sign or deep inner conviction? No, not necessarily. God wants us to be practical. Do research if you need to; understand yourself and your gifts; seek the advice of others. Make your decision in light of God's Word also; God never leads us to do anything that is contrary to the Bible.

Remember, too, that God often guides us only one step at a time—but that is all we need to know. So don't be anxious. Trust God to guide you, and He will.

WISDOM FOR TODAY

Help us to remember to pause and pray, Lord, before making big decisions. We can also study Scripture and seek counsel from the godly people You have placed in our lives. Most of all, remind us that You are in control of it all.

A GLIMPSE OF HEAVEN

Though the doors were locked, Jesus came and stood among them.
JOHN 20:26

There is much about heaven we don't know; God hasn't chosen to reveal everything to us. But we do know heaven will be far more glorious than anything we can imagine.

One truth God has revealed to us, however, is one we sometimes overlook: in heaven we will have new bodies—bodies that will be free from the pain and death of this present world. They will be like Christ's body after His resurrection—somewhat like our present bodies, yet free from the limitations we now experience. Someday, the Bible says, Christ "will transform our lowly bodies so that they will be like his glorious body" (Philippians 3:21).

Can you imagine this? I can't—not fully. But it reminds us that God cares about our physical bodies—and so should we. It tells us, too, that someday all evil and sin will be destroyed, and we will be part of "a new heaven and a new earth, the home of righteousness" (2 Peter 3:13). Is your hope in Christ and in the glorious future He has prepared for us?

WISDOM FOR TODAY

We look forward to the day, Lord, when we are able to worship You unhindered by any physical limitations. We will finally be able to fully express our praise in ways not possible here on earth. Lord, hasten the day.

SOVEREIGN OVER ALL

It is God who works in you to will and to act according to his good purpose.

PHILIPPIANS 2:13

I s everything that happens to us already determined by God? Or do we have the ability to carry out plans on our own, regardless of what God hoped would happen? You have probably wondered about this question yourself.

Theologians have disagreed about this for centuries—some stressing God's absolute control over everything, others emphasizing our freedom to act on our own. And the reason they haven't agreed is because the Bible teaches both God's sovereignty and our human responsibility. To us this sounds like a contradiction—and one I don't believe we'll fully understand until we get to heaven. Until that day we need to hold firmly to both truths: God is in control of everything, but we also are responsible for our actions.

Why is this important? In the verse above Paul stresses that God is working behind the scenes to accomplish His purposes. What if He weren't? What if it were all left up to us? What hope would we have then? But God is at work—even if we can't fully understand it now. Be comforted by this truth today.

WISDOM FOR TODAY

Give us the wisdom, Lord, to be okay not knowing what we can't know. We know You are sovereign over all and at work in all things. We also believe that we are responsible for and will be held accountable for the choices we make.

OUR FURIOUS FOE

But mark this: There will be terrible times in the last days . . . evil men and imposters will go from bad to worse, deceiving and being deceived.
2 TIMOTHY 3:1, 13

Is the world getting worse? Is the devil working more furiously today than ever before?

To many observers this certainly seems to be the case. Take the record of the last century: two world wars and other conflicts that killed more people than all previous wars combined; six million Jews mercilessly killed in the Holocaust; millions more innocent civilians slaughtered by evil atheistic despots; more Christians martyred for their faith than at any other time in history.

Paul in the verse above called the final days before Jesus' return "terrible times"; Jesus Himself declared that we "will hear of wars and rumors of wars. . . . Nation will rise against nation" (Matthew 24:6–7).

Why will it be like this? The reason, the Bible says, is because Satan will lash out in one final burst of fury, seeking with all his might to block Christ's victory.

Does this alarm you? Don't let it—because Christ, not Satan, will be victorious. In the meantime, "be joyful in hope, patient in affliction, faithful in prayer" (Romans 12:12).

WISDOM FOR TODAY

Help us, Father, to remain alert and aware of world events without giving in to despair or fear. You've told us that these things must happen but that You have overcome the world and will be returning to make all things new.

THE PROMISE OF BLESSING

Blessed are they whose ways are blameless,
who walk according to the law of the LORD.
PSALM 119:1

These words from the Psalmist's pen present a view of life that is the exact opposite of what the world around us promotes—through advertising, the media, entertainment, even the lifestyles of the rich and famous. "Live for yourself," the world proclaims. "Have a good time; indulge your senses; pursue every pleasure; strive for success. And if you do," these voices add, "then you'll be happy and blessed."

But God calls us to another way—His way. Blessing, He says, comes only from following Him. Every other way promises what it cannot deliver—and delivers exactly the opposite of what it promises. Some of the most miserable people I have ever known were highly successful in the eyes of the world. But down inside they were restless and spiritually empty.

Have you fallen into the world's trap, following its self-indulgent goals and driven by its self-centered motives? It can happen without you even being aware of it. Make sure Christ is first in your life, and make it your goal to live according to His Word.

WISDOM FOR TODAY

Give us a desire for the joy that is found only in following You, Lord. Let us not be swayed by the false idols of this world that promise things they can never provide.

SWIMMING AGAINST THE STREAM

Everyone who wants to live a godly life in Christ Jesus will be persecuted.
2 TIMOTHY 3:12

The apostle Paul knew what it meant to be persecuted; even a quick survey of Acts reveals that he and his companions encountered opposition almost everywhere they went. His brief notes in 2 Corinthians 11:23–33 catalog an even larger number of persecutions.

Millions of Christians experience the same reality every day.

Faithfulness to Christ for them can mean rejection by their families, loss of their jobs, social ostracism, injustice, violence, even imprisonment or death. You may never meet them this side of eternity—but their commitment and courage should challenge and inspire us all. Pray for them, and learn from their example.

We may not face the same situation they do—but every believer knows what it is to swim against the stream of an unbelieving world. The friend or relative who mocks you . . . the business associate who scorns your integrity . . . the indifference of those around you to moral and spiritual values. But don't let them sway you. Be faithful to Christ, who for your sake "endured the cross, scorning its shame" (Hebrews 12:2).

WISDOM FOR TODAY

Thank You, Lord, for Your example of faithfulness in the face of adversity. Please give us the strength to stand firm for what we know to be true and to faithfully pray for fellow Christ followers around the world.

THE DEEPER PROBLEM

From within, out of men's hearts, come evil thoughts, sexual immorality, theft, murder, adultery, greed, malice, deceit, lewdness, envy, slander, arrogance and folly.

MARK 7:21–22

Few words of Jesus were more blunt—and few were less likely to win Him the affection and praise of those who opposed Him. They saw themselves as holy and pure, but Jesus cut through their veneer of "righteousness" to reveal the inner pride and evil that actually motivated them—and not only them but every human being.

Why, more than twenty centuries later, is our world still filled with conflict and war, turmoil, and insecurity? Jesus said the basic problem is in our hearts—and the reason is because we are alienated from our Creator. Instead of giving God His rightful place at the center of our lives, we have substituted the "god" of Self. Only Christ can change our hearts—and through us begin to change our world.

Does this mean we can never make any progress against the massive problems that assail us—poverty, war, injustice, famine, sickness, disease? No, of course not; God wants us to fight evil wherever it is found. But our greatest need is for repentance and spiritual renewal.

Pray that this may happen—beginning with you.

WISDOM FOR TODAY

There is much that is alarming in our world, Father, and a great deal that we desire to see changed. Let revival begin in the hearts of Your people.

THE ONLY SIN THAT CAN'T BE FORGIVEN

*"I tell you the truth, all the sins and blasphemies of men will be
forgiven them. But whoever blasphemes against the Holy Spirit
will never be forgiven; he is guilty of an eternal sin."*
MARK 3:28–29

I suppose I've been asked it almost more than any other question over the years: What is the unforgivable sin? Very often the person who is asking is convinced they have committed it.

But notice what Jesus first said: "All the sins and blasphemies of men will be forgiven them." Think of just a few of the people Jesus forgave during His ministry: the woman caught in adultery; the murderer who was executed with Him. Or think of Saul of Tarsus, who violently attacked Christians and determined to stamp out the Church. If God could forgive them, can't He forgive anyone, no matter what they have done? Can't He even forgive you?

There is only one exception: the person who deliberately rejects the Holy Spirit's witness that Jesus is the Savior, sent from heaven to save us from our sins. The only sin God cannot forgive is the sin of rejecting Christ. Turn to Him in repentance and faith—and He will forgive.

WISDOM FOR TODAY

Father, You are so faithful to forgive us of our sins. Help us not to listen to the lies of the enemy who would have us believe that our sins are too many or too great for Your forgiveness.

THE ONE WHO MADE IT ALL

In the beginning God created the heavens and the earth.

GENESIS 1:1

What image (if any) comes into your mind when you think of God? A kindly old grandfather? A stern policeman or harsh judge? Or even a vague, impersonal power or force?

Look again at that first sentence in the Bible: "In the beginning God created the heavens and the earth." Can you even begin to comprehend the power it took to bring into being the billions of stars that astronomers are still discovering with their telescopes? Can you even begin to comprehend the wisdom it took to develop the complex laws that would govern the whole creation and give it order—from the smallest subatomic particle to the swirling galaxies of outer space? As the Bible says, "Since the creation of the world God's invisible qualities—his eternal power and divine nature—have been clearly seen, being understood from what has been made" (Romans 1:20).

Don't ever underestimate God's power—and don't ever underestimate His love. And because of His power and love, He is worthy of our trust and our worship.

WISDOM FOR TODAY

God, we are in awe of Your power, wisdom, and love, and we trust in You. You created everything with only a word and remain in complete control of all You created.

THE HARDEST COMMANDMENT?

"Love your neighbor as yourself."
LEVITICUS 19:18

Why is it easier to see someone else's faults than to see our own? I can think of several reasons—but one of the strongest is because we naturally love ourselves more than we love other people. And because we love ourselves, we don't like to criticize ourselves or admit our faults—because that can be painful, and we don't like pain.

But the Bible tells us to love others just as much as we love ourselves. Jesus, in fact, taught that this commandment—along with the commandment to love God above all else—summarizes God's Law (Luke 10:27).

How can we truly love others? First, ask God to help you see them through His eyes. He knows their faults far more than you do—but He still loves them, just as He loves you, in spite of your faults. Then ask God to replace your selfishness with His love—the self-giving love that sent His Son to the cross for you. Finally, demonstrate your love with a kind word, a helping hand, a prayer for their salvation.

WISDOM FOR TODAY

Help us, Father, to honor You by obeying Your Word, knowing that it will lead us to love others. Give us the hearts and humility necessary to see people as You see them, to serve them selflessly, and to seek their interests more than our own.

THE CURE FOR LONELINESS

The LORD God said, "It is not good for the man to be alone."

My husband died two years ago," her letter said, "and I'm so lonely I don't care if I die. It's like a searing pain that just won't go away." Her letter reflects something we all know: loneliness is one of the most painful experiences many of us will ever face.

The Bible says we weren't meant to be alone. Even in the garden of Eden—long before sin entered the world—God knew that Adam needed someone with whom he could share his life, and so He created Eve.

When loneliness afflicts you, remember two truths. First, we are never alone when we know Christ. You can't see Him—but He is more real than the chair you are sitting in, and He is with you. Take comfort in His promise: "Never will I leave you; never will I forsake you" (Hebrews 13:5).

Second, learn to reach out to others. All around you are people who are lonely. Ask God to help you be a friend to someone who is going through hard times. Whom will you reach out to today?

WISDOM FOR TODAY

Reveal to us, Lord, the people in our lives who struggle with loneliness. Give us opportunities to love them so they feel the peace and presence of the One who loves them most of all.

Two Paths—Two Destinations

*"Wide is the gate and broad is the road that leads to
destruction, and many enter through it."*
MATTHEW 7:13

Advertisers know we're more likely to buy a product if they can convince us that everyone else uses it. "If everyone else is using it, then it must be good, and I ought to buy it"—or so they hope we'll say to ourselves.

But on a far more serious matter, this is what Satan hopes you will say to yourself. "Look at the way most people are living," he whispers in our ear. "They're having a good time—enjoying life, living for themselves, absorbed in the moment, not bothering about God or eternity. Follow them—that's the path to real life!" But it is a lie. Jesus warned that it will lead only to destruction and hell.

Jesus calls us to take another path—His path. Yes, it may be harder, and far fewer take it. But it alone offers us true peace and joy—the kind that can come only from knowing God. And it alone leads to eternal life and heaven. On which path are you? Don't let another day go by without Christ.

WISDOM FOR TODAY

It takes boldness and faith, Lord, to choose the narrow and less-traveled path.
But we do just that because we believe that You are the only way, and we trust
that Your Word is truth. Help us remain faithful to the path we've chosen.

DAILY LIVING BY FAITH

This righteousness from God comes through faith
in Jesus Christ to all who believe.

ROMANS 3:22

Have you ever stopped to think about all the things you accept by faith every day? By faith we assume the other driver will stop at his red light. By faith we assume the pharmacist filled the prescription correctly. By faith you assumed that when you put your feet on the floor this morning it wouldn't collapse. Faith is a much greater part of life than most of us realize.

A skeptic may protest that these are things we can see and touch, whereas God is not. But look at the world around you, with all of its beauty and complexity. Isn't it more logical to believe that behind it is an all-powerful and all-wise Creator than to think it happened by chance?

But the real foundation for our faith is Jesus Christ. The Bible says He was God in human flesh—and He proved it by dying and then coming back from the grave. Do you want to know not only if God exists but what He is like? Look at Jesus Christ—and then put your faith and confidence in Him.

WISDOM FOR TODAY

Jesus, we believe that You are the Son of God and that You left heaven and came to earth as the man who was born of a virgin, was resurrected, and now sits at the right hand of the Father.

THE MAN WHO WAS GOD

*The gospel he promised beforehand through his prophets in the Holy Scriptures
regarding his Son . . . who through the Spirit of holiness was declared with power
to be the Son of God by his resurrection from the dead: Jesus Christ our Lord.*
ROMANS 1:2–4

Most people will readily admit that Jesus was a great man. But why have
Christians always insisted that He was more than a man—that He was
also divine?

One reason is because Jesus Himself claimed He was divine: "I and the
Father are one" (John 10:30). His miracles backed up His claim, as did His asser-
tion that He could forgive sins—something only God can do (Luke 5:20–25).

In addition, repeatedly the Gospel writers pointed out the way He fulfilled
the Old Testament's prophecies concerning the Messiah, who was to be called
"Immanuel—which means, 'God with us'" (Matthew 1:23). But Jesus' divinity
was demonstrated most of all by His resurrection from the dead and His ascen-
sion into heaven—events that were witnessed by hundreds.

What difference does it make? Only a sinless, divine Savior could save us,
for only He could become the perfect and final sacrifice for our sins. Pause right
now and thank Him for leaving heaven's glory and coming to earth for you.

WISDOM FOR TODAY

Thank You, Jesus, for leaving all the glories of heaven behind to walk the
dusty ground of earth. Thank You for leaving the praises of heavenly beings
for the pain of the cross. You did it all out of love for us.

JUST A BUNCH OF HYPOCRITES

"If you love me, you will obey what I command."

JOHN 14:15

You know it as well as I do: the most common charge leveled against the Christian faith is that Christians are "just a bunch of hypocrites."

Sadly, those who make such a charge often have someone in mind who claimed to be a Christian but didn't act like it.

What they may not know, however, is that some of Jesus' strongest words were reserved for hypocrites—for people who claimed to believe in God and follow His laws but in reality lived only for themselves. He compared them to "whitewashed tombs, which look beautiful on the outside but inside are full of dead men's bones and everything unclean" (Matthew 23:27).

None of us is perfect; even the most dedicated Christian falls short.

When we do, we need to confess it and seek God's help to live more consistently. But hypocrisy—living a deliberate lie—is another matter. Be on guard; don't let hypocrisy take root in your soul. Instead, make sure of your commitment to Christ, and walk close to Him every day.

WISDOM FOR TODAY

Father, help us live in such a way that others are drawn to You. While we can never be perfect, we will seek to be genuine and consistent in the way we love others and live out our faith.

SHINING IN A DARK WORLD

*[Be] blameless and pure, children of God without fault in a
crooked and depraved generation, in which you shine like
stars in the universe as you hold out the word of life.*
PHILIPPIANS 2:15–16

I have enough problems of my own," a man said to me once. "I'm a Christian, but I just haven't got the time or the energy to worry about anyone else's problems."

I could understand his attitude; when we have problems, they have a way of blocking out everything (and everyone) else. And it's not necessarily wrong to give attention to our own problems and—with God's help—to overcome them if we can. But when our problems deafen us to the hurts of others—when they make us fail to reach out to someone we could help—then we have become part of the darkness instead of shining like stars and holding out the Word of Life as we should.

Do you remember the Good Samaritan? No doubt he was preoccupied with his journey—but he still stopped and took care of the man who had been left for dead (Luke 10:25–37). Ask God to free you from whatever preoccupies you today so you can be a light for Christ in the midst of this dark world.

WISDOM FOR TODAY
It's tempting to think of only ourselves in times of trouble. Help us instead, Lord, to open our eyes to the needs of others. May we be sources of comfort to the suffering and blessings to the brokenhearted.

HIDDEN WEAKNESS

Blessed is he who has regard for the weak.
PSALM 41:1

Weakness in others takes all kinds of forms—and some of them are easy to overlook.

Sometimes, of course, a person's weakness is obvious: a chronic illness, a physical disability, a destructive habit or addiction. Sometimes it is less obvious (but no less real): a tendency to make bad decisions, a personality trait that alienates others, a destructive habit no one knows about. And then there are the weaknesses we may never detect because the person has successfully hidden them from others—and even from themselves. Often those who seem to be the strongest on the outside are the weakest on the inside.

But God sees our weaknesses, and He sees the weaknesses in others as well. And just as He wants to help us deal with our own weaknesses, so He wants to use us to help others deal with theirs. Ask God to make you sensitive to those around you who are weak—whatever their weakness may be—and to help them, both in practical ways and by pointing them to Christ and His transforming power and love.

WISDOM FOR TODAY

We who are strong have an obligation to bear with the failings of the weak (Romans 15:1). Help us to obey this command, Lord, and to recognize those who may be trying to disguise their weaknesses.

245

OUR SURE FOUNDATION

"My Father, who has given them to me, is greater than all;
no one can snatch them out of my Father's hand."
JOHN 10:29

If you asked many Christians if they knew beyond a shadow of doubt they would go to heaven when they die, they would admit they weren't sure. And yet God wants us to be sure—and we can be, once we understand what Jesus Christ did for us.

The problem is that down inside many of us still feel our salvation must be up to us, and we can go to heaven only if we are good enough. But how do you know when you are good enough? The answer is—you don't. And that's why many Christians lack assurance of their salvation.

The key is to understand that Christ took away all our sins—not part of them, but all of them. No matter how good we are, we can't save ourselves—because God's standard is perfection. But Christ—who was without sin—did for us what we could never do for ourselves: He took all our sins upon Himself, and He took the death and hell we deserve. Depend solely on Christ for your salvation. He paid the price—and now you owe nothing!

WISDOM FOR TODAY

We are so grateful, Father, that our salvation doesn't depend on our righteousness or ability to be good enough. It's all because of Jesus. The work He has done can't be undone, and our places in heaven are secure.

TURNING IT ASIDE

A gentle answer turns away wrath,
but a harsh word stirs up anger.
PROVERBS 15:1

What a different world this would be if we only learned to heed this advice! Behind these words in Proverbs is a profound truth: our tongues have enormous power—both for good and for evil. The apostle James put it this way: "The tongue also is a fire, a world of evil among the parts of the body. . . . With the tongue we praise our Lord and Father, and with it we curse men, who have been made in God's likeness" (James 3:6, 9).

Commit your tongue to God. Beyond that, commit your whole inner being to Christ, and ask Him to cleanse you of anger and hate and fill you instead with His love and patience. After all, our words are an expression of our inner hearts and minds—and only Christ can change those. And when someone tries to provoke you to anger or deals with you in a way that makes you want to strike back, don't take the bait. Instead, immediately ask God to remind you that "a gentle answer turns away wrath."

WISDOM FOR TODAY
Lord, hearts are wounded and time is wasted when we allow anger to control our tongues. May we be so filled with Your Spirit that our first response is one of gentleness that is a blessing to the hearer.

A TOUGH TRUTH

Do not be deceived. . . . A man reaps what he sows.
GALATIANS 6:7

One of life's hardest lessons is that we cannot turn back the clock and change something we've already done. When we make a wrong decision or act foolishly, we have to live with the consequences, bitter as they may be. In biblical terms, we must reap what we have sown.

Then why bother to ask for God's forgiveness? If nothing is going to change—if we still must face the consequences of our sin—why seek God's forgiveness?

One reason is because it is the only way to deal with our guilt. Down inside we feel unclean and ashamed for what we've done—but when we turn to Christ and seek His forgiveness, that burden of guilt is lifted. When we seek His forgiveness, the Bible says, "the blood of Jesus, his Son, purifies us from all sin" (1 John 1:7).

But we need God's forgiveness also to keep from becoming spiritually hardened. Unconfessed sin leads inevitably to spiritual coldness. Does any sin in your life need to be brought to God for forgiveness?

WISDOM FOR TODAY

Thank You, Lord, that we can have peace with God even in the midst of the earthly consequences for our sin. Help us repent quickly so we can experience the freedom of knowing that we are forgiven.

NEEDED: GODLY LEADERSHIP

Righteousness exalts a nation,
but sin is a disgrace to any people.
PROVERBS 14:34

I don't intend to vote this year," his letter to me stated. "I don't have much use for politicians, and anyway, my vote won't make any difference."

I can understand his attitude; it's easy to become cynical about government or feel that our vote is insignificant. But what would happen (I reminded him) if everyone had his attitude? What kind of leadership would we likely get then? We need leaders who are men and women of integrity and wisdom, and we should thank God that we live in a country where we have the privilege of choosing our leaders. We must never take that responsibility lightly.

The Bible tells us to pray for "all those in authority, that we may live peaceful and quiet lives in all godliness and holiness" (1 Timothy 2:2). Pray as you vote, and pray regularly for all those who are in positions of political leadership. And if God leads you to become involved in politics in some way, take your responsibilities seriously and seek His wisdom in all you do.

WISDOM FOR TODAY

It's easy to be critical of those in authority over us, Father, but we are instructed to pray for them. Please give our leaders hearts that seek Your will and wisdom as they make decisions that affect a nation.

He Has Always Known You

"Before I formed you in the womb I knew you,
before you were born I set you apart;
I appointed you as a prophet to the nations."
Jeremiah 1:5

Think of it: God not only knows what is going on in your life right now, but He knew all about you even before you were born. In fact, He gave you life and put you on this earth. You are not here by accident; you are here by His design!

The same is true of every human being; every person on this earth (even those not yet born) is important in the eyes of God. Don't ever scorn someone because they are different from you or ignore them when they suffer. God calls them valuable—so valuable that His Son gave His life for them. Human life is sacred, and we must never lose sight of that fact.

But look again at what God said to Jeremiah. Not only did God know him and put him on earth—but He put him here for a purpose: "I set you apart; I appointed you as a prophet." The same is true of you. Have you asked God to show you His purpose in putting you here—and are you seeking to fulfill it?

Wisdom for Today

We believe, God, that every person is created with a purpose and for a purpose. Help us to encourage one another and spur one another on to good works. Reveal to us Your will for our lives.

IN HIS HANDS

No man has power over the wind to contain it;
so no one has power over the day of his death.

ECCLESIASTES 8:8

Ultimately our lives are in God's hands; even the next breath you take is a gift from Him. If He were to withdraw His hand from you, your life would end—despite the most strenuous efforts of your doctors. The Psalmist said it well: "When you take away their breath, they die and return to the dust" (Psalm 104:29).

What difference should this make? First, it should remind us of our dependence on God. All too often we assume that our lives and our futures are in our hands. But they aren't; they are in His hands. He gave us life, and someday He will bring our time on earth to an end.

But this should also remind us that each day is a gift from God—a gift to be used wisely, joyfully, and for His glory. And it should remind us as well of an even greater gift—the gift of eternal life in Christ. Thank God for the gift of today—and the gift of eternal life that awaits us in heaven.

WISDOM FOR TODAY

You know the number of our days, Lord. Teach us to number them as well and to live each day to Your glory. May we not waste a single moment in anger or bitterness but instead embrace every opportunity to love others.

WHEN FAITH IS TESTED

Consider it pure joy, my brothers, whenever you face trials of many kinds, because you know that the testing of your faith develops perseverance.
JAMES 1:2–3

James reminds us here that difficulties and trials can take many different forms. It may be a soured relationship, a financial reversal, an unexpected illness or disability, or the death of a loved one. For others it may take the form of mockery or even persecution for their faith.

It's natural for us to shrink back from any kind of trial; we all wish we could be free of problems and instead live a life of peace and serenity all our days. But life isn't like this, and we all know that it can radically change even in a matter of seconds. The real question is how we will react. Will we react in anger or despair? Will we lash out in hatred or revenge? Or will we turn to God in faith and seek His help?

Trials will either make you turn you away from God, or they will drive you toward Him. When we choose the latter, James says, our faith will grow stronger—and we will be better equipped to meet the next challenge that comes our way.

WISDOM FOR TODAY

When trials come, Father, we will run to You. You are our shelter and our strong tower. You are a place of protection and defense. Let us be found faithful when we encounter times of suffering.

WHEN OTHERS HURT US

They sharpen their tongues like swords
and aim their words like deadly arrows.
PSALM 64:3

We've all been hurt by the words of others. Often—perhaps more often than we realize—what was said was simply spoken thoughtlessly or carelessly. But sometimes it wasn't; those words were meant to sting—and they did.

Either way, when others criticize us or say something hurtful or insensitive, our first reaction should be to ask ourselves if there is any truth in what they say. If so, we need to be honest with ourselves and ask God to help us correct it. But even if those words were spoken maliciously, we need to turn our hurts over to God and ask Him to help us respond with forgiveness and grace.

In addition, if we're honest we have to admit that we sometimes hurt others by our words. Don't excuse it or ignore it, but admit it and seek forgiveness—both from God and from the person you've hurt. Then make the Psalmist's prayer yours: "Set a guard over my mouth, O LORD; keep watch over the door of my lips" (Psalm 141:3).

WISDOM FOR TODAY

We've all said words that we wish we could take back. Help us be quick to apologize and repent, Lord, when we have used our words carelessly and to forgive when we are the ones wounded.

OUR WAY OR GOD'S WAY?

We all, like sheep, have gone astray,
each of us has turned to his own way.
ISAIAH 53:6

L ife is full of decisions. Some of them are minor and relatively insignificant—but others are major (even if we don't realize it at the time), and they can have enormous consequences.

Does God care about the decisions we make? Of course He does—and the reason is because He loves us, and He wants what is best for us. When we go down a wrong path in life, God grieves over our foolishness because He knows we are only hurting ourselves. He also knows that this is our natural tendency, because we—like sheep—easily wander and stray from the only Shepherd who can guide us and keep us safe.

What decisions are you facing? Don't rely only on your own wisdom, or even on the wisdom of others. Instead, seek God's will, and ask Him to guide you and show you His will. Remember: His way is always best—always. God's promise is for you: "I will instruct you and teach you in the way you should go" (Psalm 32:8).

WISDOM FOR TODAY

Your Word tells us that we all go astray, Father. None of us is exempt from foolish or selfish choices. May we seek Your will in the decisions we face and allow You to guide us on the good and godly way.

SEPTEMBER

USING OUR SKILLS

*"Every skilled person to whom the LORD has given skill and ability . . .
[is] to do the work just as the LORD has commanded."*
EXODUS 36:1

We sometimes forget that during most of His life Jesus was a carpenter, working with His hands among His neighbors in the town of Nazareth. "Isn't this the carpenter?" some of His critics asked scornfully, implying that no mere carpenter could possibly be the promised Messiah (Mark 6:3).

Do you tend to downplay the work you do? "I'm only a housewife . . . I'm just a plumber . . . I simply teach school . . . I'm merely a clerk in a grocery store . . . I make my living as an accountant." But if God gave you that skill, and you are where He wants you to be, then your work is valuable and significant in His sight.

One other thought for you to ponder: What kind of a carpenter do you suppose Jesus was? Did the doors fall off His cabinets? Do you suppose He took shortcuts or did just barely enough to get by? No, of course not. The Bible says, "Whatever you do, work at it with all your heart, as working for the Lord, not for men" (Colossians 3:23).

WISDOM FOR TODAY

There are no insignificant roles in Your kingdom, Father. Help us take pride in the positions You've placed us in, recognize the value in other positions, and do all we do in honor of You.

UNDER THE SPOTLIGHT

Search me, O God, and know my heart;
test me and know my anxious thoughts.
See if there is any offensive way in me.
PSALM 139:23–24

Have you ever stopped to think how difficult it must have been for David to pray this prayer? We don't know if he penned these words before or after his terrible sin with Bathsheba (2 Samuel 11–12). But either way, David knew he was capable of terrible sin—and that often his first impulse when he had sinned was to deny it or try to hide it from God. To ask God to search out the darkest, most secret corners of our minds and hearts takes courage.

And yet what happens if we aren't willing to do this? Then the sins we know about remain unconfessed, and our fellowship with God remains cold and distant. Perhaps more important, the hidden sins we may not even realize we have—sins like pride, suppressed anger, lack of love, jealousy, a secret yearning for recognition—remain firmly in place, manipulating us and eventually destroying us.

Have the courage to pray this prayer. And whatever God reveals, confess it, repent of it, and ask Christ to replace it with His purity and love.

WISDOM FOR TODAY

We don't want anything to hinder our intimacy with You, Father. Show us any areas of disobedience in our hearts so we may enjoy complete fellowship with You and the many blessings of being in Your presence.

FACING THE FUTURE WITH PEACE

They sang [to Jesus] a new song: "You are worthy . . . because
you were slain, and with your blood you purchased men for God
from every tribe and language and people and nation."
REVELATION 5:9

Never forget: Jesus Christ died to save people from even the most remote corner of the world—people you and I will never know during our lifetimes but people we will be with in heaven forever. "For God so loved the world that he gave his one and only Son" (John 3:16). God's plan is universal! No tribe, no language group, no nation is beyond the scope of His love.

The same should be true of us. Jesus' words to His disciples have never been rescinded: "You will receive power when the Holy Spirit comes on you; and you will be my witnesses . . . to the ends of the earth" (Acts 1:8).

Not everyone is called of God to be a missionary or evangelist. But if you know Christ, you are a partner in His "grand design" to call men and women from every part of the world to Himself. By your prayers, your giving, your faithful witness, and your service, you can have an impact for the Gospel far beyond your homeland. How will you respond?

WISDOM FOR TODAY

We are called to speak the truth of the Gospel to all people, Lord. Give us the willingness to get out of our comfort zones and to reach people from all walks of life with the message of hope found only in You.

BACK FROM THE BRINK

Remember this: Whoever turns a sinner from the error of his way
will save him from death and cover over a multitude of sins.

JAMES 5:20

How do you react when you see someone whose lifestyle is inevitably going to destroy them? Do you shake your head in disgust? Or simply ignore them? Or secretly congratulate yourself that you aren't as bad off as they are?

Or do you ask God to use you to help them?

Think of all the people Jesus dealt with during His ministry. Some were society's rejects—the woman caught in adultery, lepers, despised Samaritans, the criminals on the cross. Others were powerful and sophisticated—Nicodemus, Pilate, the Pharisees. They covered the whole social spectrum—but they all needed the Savior; they all were headed toward death and eternity; they all were the objects of His love.

Not everyone Jesus tried to turn back from the brink of destruction responded—nor will they with us. But that didn't keep Jesus from trying—nor must it us. Whom would God have you reach out and try to help in the name of Christ today?

WISDOM FOR TODAY

Give us such a love for people, Lord, that we are simply unable to stand by and watch them continue on the path to destruction. Help us speak the truth in love, knowing that we were once also far from You.

SHAPING THE FUTURE

Impress [these commandments] on your children. Talk about them when you sit at home and when you walk along the road, when you lie down and when you get up.
DEUTERONOMY 6:7

P arenting may be the hardest job you will ever undertake. If your parenting days are ahead of you—brace yourself! And if they are mostly behind you, then you know what I mean. (I say "mostly" because they are never completely finished.)

One of your goals as a parent is to work yourself out of a job. Someday your children will leave home—and a major part of your responsibility is to prepare them for that day. From learning to brush their teeth and tie their shoes to helping with their homework and teaching them to make wise decisions, your goal is to prepare them for the day when you won't be there.

But what about their spiritual foundations? Have they learned from you what it means to walk with Christ every day? Have you taught them to pray and to love the Bible and live by its truths? Have you encouraged them to give their lives to Jesus Christ? Don't leave it until it's too late, but begin now to help them build the moral and spiritual foundations they need for life.

WISDOM FOR TODAY

It is the greatest joy of any parent or parental figure, Father, to see our children place their hope in You and seek to follow You all their days. May they see something in us that points them to You.

STRENGTH IN WEAKNESS

When I am weak, then I am strong.
2 CORINTHIANS 12:10

Look carefully at these words written by the apostle Paul. Don't they seem like a contradiction? After all, how can you be strong if you are weak?

But it isn't a contradiction—not in God's eyes. Paul was stating a very important truth: when we attempt to do God's work in our own strength instead of God's strength, we will fail. Only when we acknowledge our weakness and look to the Holy Spirit for the wisdom and strength we need will God bless our efforts.

Perhaps you teach a class of young people in your church . . . or someone has come to you with a problem . . . or you are thinking of volunteering for a summer mission project . . . or your children are beginning to ask questions about God. How will you do what needs to be done? Yes, you'll study and work diligently; trusting God for the outcome doesn't mean we sit back and do nothing. But only God can work in the hearts of those you are seeking to help. Confess your weakness to Him and trust Him to work through you—today and always.

WISDOM FOR TODAY

The real work of salvation is done by You, Lord, and we can do nothing of eternal value without You. Even so, we will pray fervently and be in Your Word daily so we will be prepared to be a part of the work You are doing.

PERFECTION . . . SOMEDAY

Not that I have already obtained all this, or have already been made perfect,
but I press on to take hold of that for which Christ Jesus took hold of me.
Brothers, I do not consider myself yet to have taken hold of it. But one thing
I do: Forgetting what is behind and straining toward what is ahead.
PHILIPPIANS 3:12–14

We will never be completely free from sin in this life. Although Jesus Christ came to live within us by His Spirit when we gave our lives to Him, our old sinful nature still resides within us, and as long as we live it will keep trying to assert itself.

But that must not keep us from pursuing perfection! To put it another way, that must not keep us from battling sin and embracing righteousness. God's will is that we would become more and more like Christ—more like Him in our purity, our love, our service. The Bible says, "Do not conform any longer to the pattern of this world, but be transformed by the renewing of your mind" (Romans 12:2).

Someday we will enter God's presence forever—and when we do, not even a hint of sin will remain. But until that day, make it your goal to become more like Christ by refusing to let sin have its way, and pursuing instead that which is pure and good in the sight of God.

WISDOM FOR TODAY

Let us not grow weary, Father, in fighting the sin that constantly seeks to entangle us. Instead, let us continually seek to have the attitudes and actions that cause us to resemble Christ. May all who see us know we belong to You.

A FIRM PLACE

I waited patiently for the Lord;
he turned to me and heard my cry.
He lifted me out of the slimy pit,
out of the mud and mire;
he set my feet on a rock.

PSALM 40:1–2

We don't know exactly what "slimy pit" David had been experiencing before he wrote this psalm—but it doesn't really matter, because life for any of us has its share of "slimy pits." For many it's the "mud and mire" of sin—of a life that has no place for God and desperately pursues happiness in ways that can never satisfy. Or we may find ourselves mired in the "pit" of a broken marriage, or a lost job, or sickness, or a thousand other "pits" of confusion or despair.

David said he "waited patiently" for God to act—and sometimes that's hard for us to do. But in time God did answer, and God lifted him out of the mire and put his feet on a rock—a picture of what happens when we give our lives to Jesus Christ. He alone is the solid, unshakeable rock on which to build our lives (1 Peter 2:6–8).

If you're in a "pit" right now, don't give up. Instead, turn to Christ and find in Him the solid foundation you need.

WISDOM FOR TODAY

Because of Your power, Father, no pit in our lives is permanent. You are able to reach into the deepest, darkest pit and rescue the godly from their trials.

WHILE HE IS NEAR

Seek the LORD while he may be found;
call on him while he is near.
ISAIAH 55:6

Some people claim to be disappointed with God: "If He really cared about me I wouldn't have so many problems. But since He doesn't do anything about them, why should I bother with Him?" As a result they go through life without ever knowing God or giving Him His rightful place.

What is the problem? Almost always, I've discovered, they have made no effort to seek God or find His answer to their problems. Instead of actively seeking Him, they passively expect Him to come to their aid without any effort on their part. They ignore Jesus' words: "Ask and it will be given to you; seek and you will find" (Matthew 7:7).

If you have never trusted Christ for your salvation, don't sit back and wait for a better time to accept Him; it may never come. And if you do know Christ but are struggling with some problem or decision, don't try to solve it on your own. Commit it to God and seek His will without delay.

WISDOM FOR TODAY

We don't have to go through our problems alone, Lord. You invite us to come to You when we are weary, to ask when we have needs, and to exchange our heavy burdens for Your light one.

RENEWING POWER

He who was seated on the throne said, "I am making everything new!"
REVELATION 21:5

Think of all the advancements in medicine, communications, and technology the human race has made in the last century or so. We should be grateful that God has given us the ability to make this kind of progress.

But now also think of the tragic fact that these same centuries have seen the most devastating wars in human history. In spite of our accomplishments, we humans are still a painful mixture of good and bad, love and hate, joy and sorrow. We have the ability to reach the moon, but we can also destroy millions with the touch of a button.

Even those of us who have committed our lives to Jesus Christ often do things we don't want to do, and we don't do the things we ought to do (see Romans 7:19–20). That's why we need to open our hearts continually to Christ and allow Him to take away our sin and self-centeredness. Only He can make us new; only He can change our hearts and make us more like Himself.

Don't be satisfied to remain the same person you have always been, but open your heart and life to Christ's transforming power.

WISDOM FOR TODAY

Thank You, Father, that we don't have to be who we have been in the past. You make us more than repurposed versions of our old selves; You make us brand-new individuals with hearts of flesh instead of stone.

IN LIFE'S DARK HOURS

God is our refuge and strength,
an ever-present help in trouble.
Therefore we will not fear, though the earth give way
and the mountains fall into the heart of the sea.
PSALM 46:1–2

The horror of what took place on September 11, 2001, will remain stamped on our memories for generations to come. Who can ever forget the sight of those hijacked airplanes slamming into the twin towers of the World Trade Center and the side of the Pentagon? Who can forget the courageous men and women who stopped another plane from reaching its destination, and the hundreds of brave emergency personnel who lost their lives in the line of duty?

I have asked myself hundreds of times why God sometimes allows evil to flourish—and I don't have the full answer. Evil is real, however, and we ignore it at our peril. Evil is so real that it cost God's Son His life.

But I do know this: even in life's darkest hours, "God is our refuge and our strength." Not money, not military might, not diplomacy, not human cleverness—but God. As you reflect on what happened on that September 11, is God your refuge and strength? He can be as you open your heart and life to Jesus Christ.

WISDOM FOR TODAY
We place our trust in You, Lord. You don't weaken in age, cower in the face of evil, or worry about the days to come. While we believe in the reality of evil, we also believe that You have overcome the world.

WHEN TROUBLES COME

Is any one of you in trouble? He should pray. . . . The prayer of a righteous man is powerful and effective.

JAMES 5:13, 16

You've probably had your doctor take a little rubber hammer and tap you on the knees—and if your reflexes are good, your lower leg responded with a gentle kick. That reflexive action occurs automatically, and it's the same every time that nerve gets hit.

But how do you respond when troubles hit you? What is your automatic reflexive action then? Panic? Anger? Depression? Confusion? All of these?

James in these verses reminds us what our reflexive action should be: turning to God in prayer. Why? For one thing, prayer is an acknowledgment of our helplessness. You will never pray if you think you can solve everything on your own or if you are too proud to ask God for help. Pride leads to prayerlessness.

But prayer also is an acknowledgment of God's power and love. We aren't trying to manipulate God when we pray—but we are looking to Him to bless us and help us according to His perfect will. When troubles come may prayer be your automatic response.

WISDOM FOR TODAY

What we really believe, Lord, becomes evident when we encounter times of trial. May our attitudes and actions in those seasons show a watching world that we truly believe the promises given to us in Scripture.

CHOOSING THE BEST

As we have opportunity, let us do good to all people.
GALATIANS 6:10

D o you sometimes feel frustrated because you can't solve all the problems you see around you? It's easy to feel helpless when you read about a famine or natural disaster in some foreign land that threatens the lives of millions; it's easy to feel helpless when you read about the dropout rate in your local school system or the number of people who are homeless or hungry in your community.

No, you can't solve everything—but don't let that keep you from obeying the Bible's injunction to do good to everyone you can, as God gives you opportunity. It may be by supporting the work your church is doing in your community, or by sending money to an international Christian humanitarian aid organization. Or it may be through helping a single parent who lives near you . . . or tutoring in a local school . . . or simply being a friend to someone who is going through hard times.

Jesus said, "Whatever you did for one of the least of these brothers of mine, you did for me" (Matthew 25:40).

WISDOM FOR TODAY
Lord, help us to have the mind of Christ, which means to look for ways to exhibit Your compassion and extend a helping hand to others in Your mighty name.

WHEN HOPE SEEMS IMPOSSIBLE

Why are you downcast, O my soul?
Why so disturbed within me?
Put your hope in God.
PSALM 42:5

How can we have hope when there isn't any reason to have hope? Some people, I've found, are just naturally optimistic; no matter what happens to them, they almost always react with a brave smile and a positive outlook. "We must keep up our hopes," they say—even when they have no reason to hope. Unfortunately, their hope is little more than wishful thinking.

But this isn't the kind of hope the Bible urges us to have. It tells us to find our hope in God—not in our circumstances, or our natural optimism (or pessimism), or our family or friends—but from God.

How is this possible? It happens only when we realize how much God loves us—a love so deep that His Son was willing to give His life for us. It happens, too, when we realize that this life is not all there is, but ahead of us is heaven if we know Christ. Is your hope in Him—both for this life and the life to come?

WISDOM FOR TODAY
We need more than wishful thinking, Lord, to make it through this life. Our faith is firmly placed in Your Word and Your work on the cross. Because of You we have hope in this life and the next.

SEEING THROUGH GOD'S EYES

From now on we regard no one from a worldly point of view.
2 CORINTHIANS 5:16

When we first glimpse the apostle Paul in the Bible, he was called Saul—and his mission in life was to stamp out the Christian faith: "Meanwhile, Saul was still breathing out murderous threats against the Lord's disciples" (Acts 9:1). But all that changed when he met the risen Lord Jesus Christ on the road to Damascus. From that moment on the persecutor became the proclaimer, fearlessly taking the Gospel throughout the Roman Empire.

What made him change? First, he became absolutely convinced that the Gospel was true. Jesus Christ was no imposter; He was the risen Son of God, sent from heaven to save us from our sins. How could Paul remain silent in the face of this profound truth?

But there was another reason for Paul's change: he began to see people the way God sees them. He now saw them in their lostness and confusion—and also as those for whom Christ died. What difference does the truth of the Gospel make to you? And are you asking God to help you see others through His eyes?

WISDOM FOR TODAY

Everything changes when we begin seeing people through Your eyes, Father. You came to seek and save the lost and not to shun them. May we always remember that we, too, were once lost and without hope.

SHAPING THE NEXT GENERATION

Fathers, do not embitter your children, or they will become discouraged.

COLOSSIANS 3:21

His marriage is over, and now, after years of tension and coldness between the young man and his parents, he is back living with them while he tries to sort out his future. "I'm glad he came home," his father said to a friend of mine. "I'm afraid we didn't treat him the way we should have when he was a boy, and it's hurt him."

As they grow older our children become responsible for the decisions they make in life; parents shouldn't take upon themselves all the blame if those decisions are bad. But our failures do have an impact on them, making them more open to foolish or evil ways. Harsh, unreasonable discipline . . . neglect . . . favoritism . . . failure to express love . . . being too busy to give them any attention . . . failing to teach them the difference between right and wrong . . . all these and more can "embitter your children" so that "they will become discouraged."

Don't let this happen in your family. And if it has, ask God to forgive you and help you reverse it as much as possible.

WISDOM FOR TODAY

Father, our children are a gift we are entrusted with, and they only remain under our roofs for a short time. Help us to train them in the ways of holiness, encourage them with truths from Scripture, and live a godly example before them.

BEAUTY OUT OF ASHES

The LORD has anointed me . . .
to bestow on them a crown of beauty
instead of ashes.
ISAIAH 61:1, 3

One of the Bible's greatest truths is that our lives can be different. No matter what our past has been, Christ stands ready to forgive and cleanse us—and then to make us new. "Therefore," the Bible says, "if anyone is in Christ, he is a new creation; the old has gone, the new has come!" (2 Corinthians 5:17).

When Isaiah wrote these picturesque words about beauty from ashes, he was probably thinking first of Jerusalem, the once-proud city now shattered and burned at the hand of a brutal enemy. Some seven hundred years later, Jesus applied this passage from Isaiah to the ministry God had given Him.

Only Christ can bring hope to lives that have been turned into ashes by the assaults of our enemy, Satan. And He doesn't just restore us to what we once were; He gives us "a crown of beauty"—the beauty of forgiveness and the beauty of hope and joy and peace. Who around you is experiencing the ashes of a shattered life? Pray for them, and ask God to use you to point them to Christ.

WISDOM FOR TODAY

You promise us that, though sorrow may last through the night, joy will come in the morning. We believe that to be true, Lord, and we cling to that promise in the midst of suffering, and we will share that truth with those around us.

THE FINAL PROOF

*This is how God showed his love among us: He sent his one and
only Son into the world that we might live through him.*

1 JOHN 4:9

L ove isn't just a feeling; love must be expressed in action. If it isn't, we won't
have any reason to believe it even exists in someone's life, no matter how
much they claim it does.

Nor is God's love just a vague feeling or sentimental emotion hidden in His
heart. God's love is real—and we know it because He demonstrated it to us. He
put His love into action! Do you want to know if God loves you? Here is the proof:
Jesus Christ left heaven's glory and came down to this sin-infested earth to die
for you. Paul put it this way: "Very rarely will anyone die for a righteous man,
though for a good man someone might possibly dare to die. But God demonstrates his own love for us in this: While we were still sinners, Christ died for
us" (Romans 5:7–8).

Have you been tempted to doubt God's love for you? Don't doubt it any
longer, but look instead at Christ and His cross. There you see God's love poured
out for you.

WISDOM FOR TODAY

The cross is the symbol of love for those of us who have put our faith in God.
The Father gave His Son, and the Son gave His life, forever proving their
love for us.

WHY, GOD? WHY?

If only my anguish could be weighed
and all my misery be placed on the scales!
It would surely outweigh the sand of the seas.
JOB 6:2–3

Have you ever cried out as Job did here, weighed down beyond measure with heartache and grief and anger, and demanding to know why God let it happen—but not receiving an answer?

If so, let me assure you first of all that God isn't upset or angry at you; He understands your heartaches and weaknesses. As the Psalmist said, "He knows how we are formed, he remembers that we are dust" (Psalm 103:14).

In reality, however, we often don't know why God permits certain things to happen to us. We do know that evil is real, and we live in a world that is ravaged by sickness and death and sorrow—a world that isn't the way God intended it to be. Someday Christ's victory will be complete and all this will be changed—but not yet. In the meantime, put your faith and hope in Christ. He knows what it is to suffer; He went to the cross for us. And because He did, we have hope even in the midst of life's darkest hours.

WISDOM FOR TODAY

There will be times, Lord, when we don't understand why we must suffer. In those moments, help us focus less on why and more on who is always at work behind the scenes. We trust in Your love for us even in times of grief.

LIKE THE TOSSING SEA

The wicked are like the tossing sea,
which cannot rest,
whose waves cast up mire and mud.
"There is no peace," says my God, "for the wicked."
ISAIAH 57:20–21

You probably know people who are like this; you may have been one of them yourself. They have no stability in their lives and are constantly pursuing one goal after another, one relationship after another, one pleasure after another. Yet they never find the happiness they seek.

The reason? They have left God out of their lives—and without Him they have no purpose or direction and no ultimate sense of right and wrong. A life without God is like a boat without an anchor.

But God didn't intend for our lives to be this way. And when we come to know Christ, He brings calm to our chaos and direction to our drifting. It doesn't necessarily happen overnight—but as we learn to live by the principles He has given us in His Word, we leave the past behind and discover the peace He alone can give. Thank God for doing this in your life—and pray for your friends who do not yet know Christ, that they may find in Him the stability and peace they seek.

WISDOM FOR TODAY

No amount of worldly power or prestige can bring about the peace we desperately seek, Lord. True peace is found only through a relationship with You and knowing that, by placing our faith in You, our future is secure.

ADOPTED INTO HIS FAMILY

He chose us in him before the creation of the world. . . . to be adopted as his
sons through Jesus Christ, in accordance with his pleasure and will.
EPHESIANS 1:4–5

From time to time someone writes me who was adopted as a child and is now haunted by the idea that they had been rejected by both of their birth parents, and therefore they must have been unloved and unlovable. Those feelings have oppressed them most of their lives.

What they have forgotten—and what I always try to point out to them—is that they weren't unloved and unwanted by their adoptive parents—not at all. That couple had a choice in the matter—and they deliberately chose to bring this child into their family. If anything, their adoption proves that their feelings are lying to them. The truth is, they are loved, and they are wanted.

In an even greater way, God loves us so much that He chose to make us part of His family. Jesus' death and resurrection accomplished many things for us— our forgiveness, our new life, even our eternal destiny. But something else took place when you accepted Christ: you were adopted into His family forever. God loves you that much!

WISDOM FOR TODAY

Regardless of our family situations here on earth, Father, Your Word has made it clear that You have chosen us to be a part of Your heavenly household. Thank You for adopting us into Your family and offering us a seat at the table.

FAITH VS. FEELINGS

Faith is being sure of what we hope for and certain of what we do not see.
HEBREWS 11:1

This verse introduces one of the Bible's great chapters—what someone has called "The Bible's Hall of Fame." Beginning in Genesis—with Abel, Enoch, Noah, and Abraham—and continuing through the Old Testament, the author spotlights those spiritual heroes who stayed faithful to God in the face of almost overwhelming odds.

Why did they remain faithful? One reason is because their faith was in God and His promises, and not in their feelings. These great men and women of faith faced discouragement and doubt the same way we do. But their trust was in God, not their emotions—and the same should be true of us.

Emotions aren't wrong; God gave them to us, and they are an important part of life. But our feelings go up and down—and if our faith is based merely on our feelings, it, too, will go up and down. Only when we build our lives on Christ will our faith be stable and strong. Don't let your feelings mislead you, but base your faith solely on Christ and what He did for us through His death and resurrection.

WISDOM FOR TODAY

Thank You, Lord, for the examples of so many saints and martyrs who lived lives of faith believing that You would do what You promised. Help us to always view our feelings through the lens of Scripture so we are not deceived.

JESUS AS LORD

"Why do you call me 'Lord, Lord,' and do not do what I say?"
LUKE 6:46

Jesus demands to be Master and Lord of every part of your life.

Is He Lord of your mind, of what you think, read, and believe? Of what you dream about, meditate on, and entertain yourself with?

Is Jesus the Master and Lord of your body? Are you presenting it to Christ as a living sacrifice? Do your eyes belong to Christ? What about your ears? Your mouth? Your hands? Your feet? Your sexual urges? Our eyes can be covetous and never satisfied. Our tongue can do unspeakable harm. Our hands can do the work of the devil. Our feet can take us where we shouldn't go. And our sexuality can get us in trouble before we know it.

Is Jesus also the Master and Lord of your social life—your friendships, your relationships, your amusements? Always ask yourself these questions about your plans: "Can I ask God's blessing on it? Can I do this to the glory of God? Or will this be a stumbling block to me or someone else?"

Are you calling Jesus "Lord" but not doing what He wants?

WISDOM FOR TODAY

No area of our lives is off limits to Your rule and authority, Lord. We will seek to obey and honor You in our work, entertainment, relationships, and worship. Help us submit to Your authority in our lives.

WHICH WING?

What good is it, my brothers, if a man claims to have faith but has no deeds? . . . Faith by itself, if it is not accompanied by action, is dead.

JAMES 2:14, 17

Which wing of an airplane is more important? Obviously both are equally necessary, and therefore both are equally important.

Which is more important: what we believe about God or what kind of life we live? Again, both are equally necessary, and therefore both are equally important.

In fact, the Bible says that if we claim to believe in Christ but it doesn't make any difference in the way we live, then our faith isn't really genuine. That is the exact point James was making in the verses above. This doesn't mean we must be perfect (because we never will be this side of eternity)—but it does warn us about the dangers of a shallow belief in Christ that isn't honest or real. Don't let this be true of you.

At the same time don't lose sight of the fact that we are saved solely by our faith in Christ, not by our good deeds. Only Christ can save us, for only He was the sinless Son of God who took all our sins upon Himself when He died on the cross for us. As the Bible says, "By grace you have been saved, through faith" (Ephesians 2:8). What difference will Christ make in your life today?

WISDOM FOR TODAY

Let us not deceive ourselves, Lord, by being hearers of the Word without doing what it is we've been told to do (James 1:22).

GOD IN HUMAN FLESH!

[Jesus] is the image of the invisible God.
COLOSSIANS 1:15

The Incarnation—God's taking upon Himself our humanity and becoming a man—is an amazing truth—and one that gives us a solid foundation for our faith.

Both Jesus and the very first Christians clearly asserted that He was fully divine, and over the centuries this truth has remained central to the Christian faith. Long before Jesus' miraculous birth, the Old Testament foretold that God would enter this world in human form: "'The virgin will be with child and will give birth to a son, and they will call him Immanuel'—which means, 'God with us'" (Matthew 1:23). When confronted by those who questioned His divinity, Jesus responded, "I and the Father are one" (John 10:30). The consistent witness of the apostles was that "the Son is the radiance of God's glory and the exact representation of his being" (Hebrews 1:3). When Thomas—unconvinced at first that Jesus had been raised from the dead—met the risen Savior, he immediately exclaimed, "My Lord and my God!" (John 20:28).

Spend a few minutes marveling over this wondrous truth—and thank God for demonstrating His great love for us by taking upon Himself our human flesh.

WISDOM FOR TODAY

You knew, God, that we could never make our way to You, and so You became like one of us. What love You displayed by coming down and bridging the great divide our sin has caused.

WHOM DO WE BLAME?

Each one is tempted when, by his own evil desire, he is dragged away
and enticed. Then, after desire has conceived, it gives birth to sin.
JAMES 1:14–15

I s Satan always to blame when things go wrong in our lives? Or are we sometimes responsible?

On one hand, the Bible makes it clear that Satan is real and that he is ultimately behind all the evil that goes on in the world. Before he rebelled against God (long before the human race was created), the world was perfect; sin and evil didn't exist. But now we live in a fallen, twisted, sin-infested world—and Satan is the reason.

But on the other hand, Satan is not all-powerful, nor does he directly cause every bad thing that happens to us. Sometimes we don't know the cause—but often we alone are responsible, because we have turned our backs on God and deliberately followed our own sinful desires instead of His will. When we do, we pay the consequences; as the Bible warns, "God cannot be mocked. A man reaps what he sows" (Galatians 6:7).

But remember: by His death and resurrection, Jesus triumphed over all the forces of evil—those in our heart and those in the world. Turn to Him for the strength you need to resist temptation and follow Him.

WISDOM FOR TODAY

You are well acquainted with Satan's tempting ways, Lord. You are familiar with the false promises he makes and have seen him twist Scripture for his own purposes. Strengthen us so that we resist the devil and cause him to flee.

FREE OF PRIDE

Patience is better than pride.

ECCLESIASTES 7:8

He had dropped out of church when he didn't agree with a building project that was being planned. After his wife died, however, he found himself wishing he had never left; his loneliness was almost more than he could bear. But would he have the courage to swallow his pride and go back to church? Finally he did, and his only regret was that he hadn't done it sooner.

Maybe this reminds you of a situation in your life. Do you need to swallow your pride? Do you need to apologize or admit you were wrong about something? Do you need to work to restore your relationship with a brother or sister in Christ—especially if you were the one at fault? Or, like this person, do you need to get back into a fellowship of believers?

If so, confess your pride and seek God's wisdom and strength for the future. Let go of your pride—and then patiently wait to see how God will work to restore and change your heart and your life.

WISDOM FOR TODAY

So much time is wasted due to pride, Lord, and regret is a hard burden to bear. Help us to apologize, forgive, reconcile, or return—whatever it is that our pride has prevented us from doing or enjoying.

SPIRITUAL FOOD

Your word is a lamp to my feet
and a light for my path.
PSALM 119:105

I recently heard from a dear woman in the Lord. Listen to what she wrote: "I am eighty-four, and almost all my life I read the Bible every day. But now my vision is getting very bad and the doctor says I'll probably be blind soon. I miss seeing the way I once did, but most of all I miss reading my Bible. Please tell people to read the Bible while they can, because it truly does give light for my path."

She had learned a vital lesson: nothing will help us grow spiritually more than spending time alone with God every day, reading His Word, and praying. I know our lives are busy today, but time alone with God is essential to our spiritual welfare. Most of us wouldn't think of missing a meal, yet we miss our spiritual "meals" when we neglect God's Word—and we end up spiritually weak.

Many years ago I heard a speaker say something I have never forgotten: "Either sin will keep you from God's Word, or God's Word will keep you from sin." Even five minutes alone with God each day can renew and strengthen your soul.

WISDOM FOR TODAY

May we not take for granted the gift of Your Word, Father. It is what guides, sustains, and comforts us. Through reading and studying Scripture, we learn who You are and who we are in relation to You.

PURE SPIRITUAL MILK

Like newborn babies, crave pure spiritual milk, so that
by it you may grow up in your salvation.
1 PETER 2:2

Birth is only the beginning for a newborn baby; that child isn't meant to be a baby forever but to grow and become strong and eventually reach adulthood. The same is true for us. When we first come to Christ we are "spiritual newborns"—but we aren't meant to remain that way. God's plan is for us to grow strong in our faith and become mature in our understanding of God's will.

How does it happen? First, we must be convinced that spiritual growth is God's will for us. Then we must take steps to grow spiritually strong—and we do this by consuming the "pure spiritual milk" God has provided for us. What is that "milk"? First, God has given us the Bible; through it we learn about Him and His will for our lives. God also has given us the privilege of prayer and fellowship with other believers. If any of those—God's Word, prayer, fellowship—is missing, our growth will be stunted.

Are you growing in your faith? If not, why not? Make God's "pure spiritual milk" part of your soul's diet every day.

WISDOM FOR TODAY

Just like with our physical bodies, Lord, we sometimes neglect the things necessary to have a healthy spiritual life. Give us the desire and discipline to do the things necessary to grow in our faith and to deepen our relationship with You.

PERFECTION LOST

God saw all that he had made, and it was very good.

GENESIS 1:31

I could hear the puzzlement in her question: "Why would God say the world is good, when so much of it is obviously imperfect or even evil?"

After God created the world, He said it was perfect, because He had made it exactly the way He had wanted it to be. But notice: He pronounced His creation "very good" before Satan tempted Adam and Eve and before the world was invaded by sin.

The world was indeed a perfect place—before Adam and Eve chose to believe Satan's lies instead of God's truth. Adam and Eve had everything they needed, and they walked in perfect harmony with God—until they turned their backs on Him. Suddenly sin—like a deadly cancer—took root in the human heart, and even the plants and animals became ravaged by sin and death.

The Bible tells us, however, that this sin-sick, fallen world won't last forever. At the end of time God will intervene, and the new heaven and new earth He will create will be free from all evil and pain. Come quickly, Lord Jesus!

WISDOM FOR TODAY

We look forward to the day, God, when this earth passes away and the new earth and new heaven are revealed. At that time we will enjoy Your presence and experience the perfection that You created us to enjoy.

OCTOBER

LEARNING FROM THEIR EXAMPLE

These things occurred as examples to keep us from
setting our hearts on evil things as they did.

1 CORINTHIANS 10:6

Sometimes people ask me why they should bother reading the Old Testament. After all, they say, didn't Christ by His death replace all the detailed sacrificial laws we find there? And anyway, what can we possibly learn from people who lived so long ago?

But the Old Testament is just as much God's Word as the New Testament, and God has much to teach us through its pages. "All scripture is given by inspiration of God, and is profitable" (2 Timothy 3:16 KJV). And one of the most important things God wants to teach us from the Old Testament is how not to live.

Let me explain. The Old Testament tells us about some of God's greatest servants—Joseph, Moses, Jeremiah, and so forth—and God has much to teach us from their example. But the Old Testament also is filled with the accounts of men and women who failed God. How did it happen? What were the consequences? They, too, are examples, warning us of what happens when we turn aside from following Christ. Learn from them how not to live.

WISDOM FOR TODAY

Give us insight, Lord, as we read and study the pages of Scripture. If You inspired the words to be written, there is something for us to learn about You, ourselves, and the world around us.

Opened Eyes

God opened [Hagar's] eyes and she saw a well of water . . .
[and] God was with the boy as he grew up.
Genesis 21:19–20

Hagar was a single parent, and she almost gave in to despair. Perhaps you are in that situation also, or you may know of someone who is.

Hagar was Sarah's handmaiden (or personal attendant), and after Sarah mistakenly tried to fulfill God's promise of a son by giving Hagar to her husband, Abraham, Hagar became the mother of Ishmael. Forced to flee into the desert with her son, Hagar ran out of water and felt the end had come. But God had not abandoned her, and we read that He helped her see a well of water He had provided. It had been there all along, but Hagar saw it only with God's help.

Being a single parent is very difficult. But God knows your situation just as He knew Hagar's, and perhaps He wants to show you a "well" He has already prepared—something or someone to refresh and help you.

Don't give in to despair or self-pity, but look to Jesus Christ every day for the hope and strength you need. He loves you and your children, and He will not abandon you.

Wisdom for Today

Teach us to expect Your presence, protection, and provision, Lord. Give us eyes that watch expectantly for You to show up. Reveal ways that we can be a source of provision and refreshment to someone else.

THE GOSPEL IS COMPLETE

*Dear friends . . . [I] urge you to contend for the faith
that was once for all entrusted to the saints.*
JUDE 3

I s the Gospel of Jesus Christ complete? Or do we need something else in addition to what the Bible tells us?

Perhaps you've had someone come to your door asking to speak to you about the beliefs of their particular religious group. If you invited them in, however, it wasn't long before you realized they were convinced that their group—and only their group—had the full truth about God and salvation. And if you probed further, you discovered that they were convinced the Bible's message of salvation through faith in Christ was not enough; the message in the books "discovered" or written by their founder was also necessary.

But Jesus Christ is all we need—and the reason is because He alone was the Son of God, sent from heaven as God's final sacrifice for our sins. Cults deny this—but the Bible is clear: "Salvation is found in no one else, for there is no other name under heaven given to men by which we must be saved" (Acts 4:12). Thank God for this truth!

WISDOM FOR TODAY
Your Word is all-sufficient, God. All we need to know in order to receive salvation and live a godly life is found within its pages. May we not be led astray or deceived by individuals promoting anything else as Your truth.

ANGER'S CRUEL HARVEST

As churning the milk produces butter,
and as twisting the nose produces blood,
so stirring up anger produces strife.
PROVERBS 30:33

Have you ever asked yourself why God takes anger so seriously and urges us to cast it out of our lives?

One reason is because of what it does to other people. When we lash out at someone in anger, we hurt them and create conflict with them—and that is wrong. God loves them just as much as He loves us, and when our anger hurts someone, we are harming someone God loves.

God also hates our anger because of what it does to us. Anger cuts us off from others; no one likes to be around someone who may explode at any moment. Anger also hurts us by turning us into resentful, bitter, unloving people. Most of all, anger cuts us off from God, because it makes us preoccupied with our own problems rather than God's will for our lives.

Commit your anger to God and seek His forgiveness. Then ask Him to fill you with His patience and love. "The fruit of the Spirit is . . . patience" (Galatians 5:22).

WISDOM FOR TODAY

Anger can become such a habit, Lord, that we don't even realize the power we've given it in our lives. Open our eyes to its poisonous ways. Help us rid it from our hearts and replace it with grace and gentleness.

291

We Will Be Whole

The body that is sown [in death] is perishable, it is raised imperishable; it is sown in dishonor, it is raised in glory; it is sown in weakness, it is raised in power.
1 Corinthians 15:42–43

Almost nothing is more painful than losing someone we deeply love.

"We were convinced God was going to heal my husband of his cancer, but He didn't," a woman wrote me recently. "Why didn't God answer us?"

I had to confess to her that I didn't know why God hadn't restored her husband to health. I assured her, however, that God knew what she was going through, and He still loved her and was with her. He truly is the One "who comforts the downcast" (2 Corinthians 7:6).

But I also pointed out that even if God didn't answer her prayers the way she hoped He would, He did not ignore them. In fact, He answered her prayers in a far greater way than she realized—because now her husband is in heaven, and all his sickness and pain are over. He has been healed! In the midst of our tears there still can be joy, because we know that those who die in the Lord are now with Christ, "which is better by far" (Philippians 1:23).

Wisdom for Today

One day, Father, we will be with You and we will never again experience the pain of loss. Help us trust You when physical healing doesn't happen here on earth, knowing that to live is Christ and to die is gain.

RETURNING TO GOD

This is what the LORD Almighty says: "Return to me," declares the LORD Almighty, "and I will return to you."

ZECHARIAH 1:3

We don't use the word *backsliding* as much as we used to—but the reality is still with us: a seemingly sincere Christian begins to "slide backward" in their faith, returning to their old ways and acting as if Jesus no longer means anything to them.

Why does it happen? Sometimes their faith wasn't real; they had never committed their lives to Jesus Christ in the first place. The writer of Hebrews warned, "See to it, brothers, that none of you has a sinful, unbelieving heart that turns away from the living God" (3:12).

But it also happens to believers—and when it does, Satan rejoices. Perhaps old habits overwhelm them; perhaps they cave in to the pressure of the crowd; perhaps temptation lures them into sin. Whatever the reason, a backsliding Christian compromises their faith and causes unbelievers to mock the Gospel.

The good news is that God loves even the backslider and stands ready to forgive. Guard against sliding backward in your faith—but if you do, don't stay that way. Return to God—and He will return to you.

WISDOM FOR TODAY

Keep us faithful in the spiritual disciplines of prayer, Bible study, and worship so we guard our hearts against the attacks of the enemy. When we do backslide, Lord, give us the humility to return to You quickly so our fellowship is restored.

YES AND NO

Love the brotherhood of believers.
1 PETER 2:17

Someone has wisely observed that if we ever found a perfect church, it would be imperfect the minute we joined it! We Christians aren't perfect, and we don't become perfect when we join together in a church.

That truth, however, doesn't excuse lovelessness or wrongdoing in any fellowship of believers. In God's plan, churches should reflect Jesus Christ, and when church leaders or church members do wrong, they bring dishonor to His name.

Can a person be a Christian without going to church? Is a walk through the woods or a relaxing game of golf as spiritually uplifting as a service of worship? The answer is . . . both yes and no. Yes, when you come to Christ, commit your life to Him, God accepts you as an individual, just as you are. And sometimes He draws us closer to Himself when we reflect on His beauty or enjoy His good gifts.

But when you come to Christ, you also become part of His family. Every true Christian is now your brother and sister—and you need each other. Don't use your church's imperfections as an excuse to stay away, but ask God to use the preaching of His Word and your fellowship with others to make you more like Christ.

WISDOM FOR TODAY
Our church families are made up of imperfect people just like our earthly ones, Father. Help us love one another in Your name.

ALWAYS RELEVANT

Prophecy never had its origin in the will of man, but men spoke
from God as they were carried along by the Holy Spirit.

2 PETER 1:21

The Bible is a remarkable book for many reasons—but the most important of all is that it is God's Word. It isn't just an ancient collection of human wisdom; it was written by people who were "carried along by the Holy Spirit." God gave it to us so we could come to know Him and His will for our lives.

Don't dismiss the Bible because it was written thousands of years ago. God has not changed . . . human nature has not changed . . . and neither has our need for Christ and His salvation. From Genesis through Revelation, the Bible points us to Jesus Christ, who was God in human flesh, sent from heaven to save us from our sins. It also points us to God's perfect will for our lives.

Let the Bible's truth become part of your life every day.

WISDOM FOR TODAY

Your instructions for the way we are to live and Your love for Your people haven't changed since the first Words of Scripture were penned. Help us to learn from the trials and triumphs of those who have gone before us by the study of Your Word.

GOD'S CONSTANT LOVE AND COMPASSION

Because of the LORD's great love we are not consumed,
for his compassions never fail.

LAMENTATIONS 3:22

Have you ever had someone you loved do something that embarrassed or hurt you? Probably. But did you stop loving that person? No! You might have been disappointed, but you kept on loving them.

In a far greater way, God still loves us—even when we disappoint Him or do something wrong. He loves us in the good times, but He also loves us when things aren't going our way and we begin to doubt Him. God's love for us is constant—in the good times and the bad. "His compassions never fail."

Think about Peter for a moment. He was one of Jesus' closest disciples, yet after Jesus was arrested, Peter denied even knowing Him (see Luke 22:54–62). But Jesus forgave Peter when he repented and returned to Him, and Peter became one of the most powerful preachers of the Gospel in that generation.

Difficult times come to us all—but how will you react? Will they drive you away from God—or will they draw you closer to Him in trust and faith? The time to decide is now.

WISDOM FOR TODAY

Thank You, Father, that You don't stop loving us when we fail or disappoint You. Help us remember this truth and repent quickly when we have sinned against You in times of weakness.

ANGELS WATCHING OVER US

Are not all angels ministering spirits sent to serve those who will inherit salvation?

HEBREWS 1:14

Her car accident was serious; she felt she had been almost miraculously delivered from death. "It's almost as if an angel intervened to protect me." She wrote, "Do angels still do things like that?"

The answer is yes; angels are just as active today as they were in Bible times. Angels are spiritual beings that seldom assume physical form, which is why we don't see them and are largely unaware of their presence. But I am convinced that when we get to heaven, we will be amazed to discover how often God's angels intervened to help or protect us. The Bible says that God "will command his angels concerning you to guard you in all your ways" (Psalm 91:11).

If you have ever had an experience similar to this woman's, I hope you didn't consider it merely a "lucky" escape—because it wasn't. God protected and preserved you. Don't miss whatever lessons He wants to teach you from that experience. And thank Him for both His protection and His lessons!

WISDOM FOR TODAY

We may never know, Father, all the many ways You have intervened to protect us from harm during our time here on earth. But one day we will worship You with the very angels who helped preserve our lives.

UNITY'S WITNESS

May they be brought to complete unity to let the world know that
you sent me and have loved them even as you have loved me.
JOHN 17:23

I t is unfortunate when Christians can't get along or even refuse to have anything to do with one another. Not only does this harm our witness to an
unbelieving world, but it turns us away from God's priorities for us.

No church has cornered the market on God's truth, and in my travels around
the world I have found sincere believers in virtually every church and denomination imaginable. I know the issues are complex and won't be solved this side
of eternity, but that is no excuse for lovelessness and conflict.

Shortly before His death on the cross, Jesus prayed for unity among those
who would come to believe in Him. When the world sees Christians fighting,
they wonder if the Gospel is really true. Only Satan wins when sincere Christians
reject one another.

Do what you can to live at peace with your fellow believers—and join your
Lord in praying for the unity of Christ's people so "that the world may believe"
(John 17:21).

WISDOM FOR TODAY

Discord among Your people, Lord, is a tool of the enemy to distract us from
the mission of the Church. Help us live in unity with other believers so Your
name is honored and unbelievers do not turn away because of what they see
in us.

A SPIRITUAL VIRUS

What kind of people ought you to be? You ought to live holy and godly lives.

2 PETER 3:11

Do you remember the last time you had the flu? You probably felt terrible—and with good reason. That flu virus had invaded your whole body, and it made you weak all over. That is what sin is like. Sin is like a spiritual virus that has invaded our lives, making us morally and spiritually weak, and we will never be completely free of it this side of eternity. The only sinless person who ever lived was Jesus Christ.

Why is this? Why can't we be sinless in this life? Why can't we become perfect? One reason is because sin has weakened us so much that we don't have the strength to overcome its power. Sin is like a deadly disease that infects every part of us: our bodies, our minds, our emotions, our relationships, our motives—everything.

But when we come to Christ, another spiritual power takes up residence within us: the Holy Spirit. Learn to take sin seriously—be on guard against it, resist its tug, fight its power. But most of all, learn to take the Holy Spirit seriously, calling on Him to help you overcome sin's power and live a holy and godly life.

WISDOM FOR TODAY

We would not willingly expose ourselves to illnesses like the flu, Lord, and we take precautions against them. Help us be even more adamant in protecting our hearts and minds from sin through consistent prayer and Bible study.

REVERSE MAGNETISM?

Flee the evil desires of youth, and pursue righteousness, faith, love and peace.
2 TIMOTHY 2:22

Did you ever play with magnets when you were a child? If you had two of them, you probably remember that the closer they got to each other, the harder it was to pull them apart.

Temptation is something like that. The more you dwell on it and the closer you get to it, the stronger its attraction becomes. In fact, if you don't look out, it will become almost impossible for you to pull away from it. Don't let that happen.

Why do I mention this? Because the first step you need to take to gain victory over sin is to flee from whatever is tempting you. Don't play with it or toy with it in your mind; get as far from it as possible. I have known of people who had to change jobs to keep away from something (or someone) that was tempting them to do wrong! But it was the only way to win.

What step do you need to take to overcome temptation in your life?

WISDOM FOR TODAY

Give us a realistic view of our weaknesses, Father, and give us the wisdom to do whatever is necessary to protect ourselves from them. Help us confess our temptations to You and seek Your will. Most of all, like a magnet, draw us close to You.

FAITH BUILDING

I pray that out of his glorious riches he may strengthen you.
EPHESIANS 3:16

How can your faith become stronger? Let me point out three ways.

First, be sure of your commitment to Christ. Have you acknowledged your sins to God and put your faith and trust in Jesus Christ as your Savior and Lord? Sometimes a person's faith is weak because he or she has never clearly taken this step of commitment. If you haven't done this—or if you aren't sure—ask Christ to come into your life today—and He will.

Second, build your faith on the truths of God's Word. The Bible is spiritual "food" given to us by God to strengthen our faith. In it, we learn of God's love for us, and also how He wants us to live. Without a firm knowledge of God's Word, our faith will always be vague and uncertain.

Finally, draw strength from other believers. You need to hear His Word as it is preached and taught. Bible studies, prayer groups, and other programs also can help you grow stronger in your faith.

Don't stand still in your faith, but make use of the resources God has given you to move forward in confidence and joy.

WISDOM FOR TODAY

It is Your desire, Lord, that we constantly be growing and deepening our relationship with You. We do not want to grow stagnant in our spiritual lives. Help us to have the mind of Christ (1 Corinthians 2:16).

WHEN TEMPTATION KNOCKS

Jesus said to him, "Away from me, Satan! For it is written: 'Worship the Lord your God, and serve him only.'" Then the devil left him.
MATTHEW 4:10–11

How do you know if the devil is tempting you to do something wrong, or if it's only your own desires?

In truth, we don't always know when the devil is tempting us directly or when he is only working in the background. In reality it doesn't matter, because the basic issue is the same: we are being tempted to turn our backs on God.

Ultimately, the Bible says, the devil is the source of all temptation; he is called "the tempter" in Matthew 4:3. But he is able to succeed only because we let him—and we let him succeed because of our own weakness.

This is one reason why we need Christ. Only He can forgive us when we sin, and only He can give us the strength, by the power of His Spirit, to resist temptation. And in His encounter with the devil at the beginning of His ministry He pointed the way to victory: using the truth of God's Word to counteract Satan's lies. Three times Satan attacked Him with almost-overwhelming temptations—and three times Jesus replied with Scripture.

A friend of mine says, "When the devil comes knocking, I just send Jesus to the door." Try that next time!

WISDOM FOR TODAY
The Word of God is our weapon against the attacks of Satan. May we be quick and confident in wielding the Sword.

PRAY WITH CONFIDENCE

This is the confidence we have in approaching God: that if
we ask anything according to his will, he hears us.

1 JOHN 5:14

The frustration and discouragement in his letter were unmistakable: "I know I ought to pray, but sometimes I feel like my prayers aren't getting above the ceiling. Is there a secret to praying?"

Prayer is not something mysterious or secret; prayer is simply talking to God. And God wants you to talk to Him! He loves you, and He has promised to hear you when you pray.

Prayer is possible because Jesus Christ removed the barrier between God and us, a barrier caused by our sins. Sin separates us from God, and because of that, we have no right to come to Him in prayer. But Jesus removed that barrier when He died on the cross for us. When we commit our lives to Christ, God gives us the privilege of approaching the "throne of grace with confidence, so that we may receive mercy and find grace to help us in our time of need" (Hebrews 4:16).

If you find prayer awkward or intimidating, remember this: God promises to hear you—and He cannot lie. Trust that promise and learn to bring every concern to Him in prayer.

WISDOM FOR TODAY
Remind us, Father, that when we pray we are speaking to the One who loves us deeply, knows us completely, and hears us when we call.

THE RICHES OF THE OLD TESTAMENT

Turn my heart toward your statutes and not toward selfish gain. Turn my eyes away from worthless things; preserve my life according to your word.
PSALM 119:36–37

Sadly, many people find the Old Testament confusing and hard to understand. Some even wonder if it has any value to those of us living on this side of the cross. But the Old Testament is God's Word just as much as the New Testament, and He wants to teach and encourage us through it. For example, we learn that God made the world—including you and me. We also learn how sin entered the world and why Jesus Christ had to die on the cross for our salvation.

The Old Testament also helps us understand how we should live. For example, we can learn much from studying the lives of its main characters—including their failures.

Don't worry about the parts you don't understand. Instead, ask God to help you learn from the parts you can understand. If you have never really studied the Old Testament, begin with the book of Psalms—the hymnbook of the Old Testament—or Proverbs, the Old Testament's guide to practical living.

Thank God for the entire Bible—and make it part of your life every day.

WISDOM FOR TODAY
Lord, open our minds to understand the Scriptures from beginning to end, for "the etirety of Your word is truth" (Psalm 119:160).

BLACK SHEEP

"I have loved you with an everlasting love."
JEREMIAH 31:3

Did your family have a black sheep—someone who disgraced the family or behaved in a disreputable way? Were you even considered at one time your family's black sheep? Being labeled a black sheep is a heavy burden to carry through life.

But the Bible tells us that God loves black sheep! Think of Jacob, for example—cheating his brother, Esau, out of his rightful inheritance and his father's blessing. Or remember Manasseh, rebelling against his godly father King Hezekiah and doing everything in his power to stamp out his father's heritage. And yet in time God humbled both Jacob and Manasseh, and they became His servants.

No matter who we are or what we have done (or haven't done), God still loves us, and He yearns to welcome every one of us home—even the black sheep. And although it may startle you, all of us who call earth our home are black sheep in God's eyes, for we all have sinned and rebelled against God, but He has not rejected us—even if we have rejected Him.

Never doubt the depths of God's love—for you or for the worst black sheep you know. Even if you were the only black sheep, Jesus Christ still would have died for you. Let Him welcome you home today.

WISDOM FOR TODAY

Father, the beautiful truth of the Gospel is that we could never be bad enough to be turned away from Your love if we only repent and believe.

Speak the Truth—Always

Each of you must put off falsehood and speak truthfully to his neighbor.
Ephesians 4:25

Why is it wrong to tell a lie, even if it doesn't seem to hurt anyone? One reason—and one that we should take very seriously—is because God commands us to tell the truth. One of the Ten Commandments states clearly, "You shall not give false testimony against your neighbor" (Exodus 20:16).

But another reason is because a lie always—without exception—hurts someone. How do you know, for instance, what impact your untruthful words might have on someone's reputation? The answer is, you don't. Or do you honestly want your children to grow up thinking it doesn't matter whether or not they tell the truth? Do you honestly want your unbelieving friends to conclude that Christ doesn't mean anything to you?

Most of all, a lie always hurts the one who tells it. It makes them less concerned about God's truth. In addition, others will eventually realize that they can't be trusted.

Don't compromise on the truth. Instead, commit every part of your life to Christ, including your speech.

Wisdom for Today

We often label it in less offensive ways: half-truths and white lies. The reality is, Father, that any falsehood is offensive to You. Help us to live lives of honesty and integrity so we are pleasing in Your sight and do nothing to dishonor Your name.

THE PURPOSE OF THE STARS

The heavens declare the glory of God; the skies proclaim the work of his hands.
PSALM 19:1

I f God created the stars," she wrote me, "isn't it reasonable to believe that He wants to send us messages through them? Why shouldn't Christians practice astrology, since millions of people do?"

One reason Christians shouldn't practice astrology is, quite simply, because the Bible tells us not to. Astrology and other forms of fortune-telling were very common in the ancient world, but the Bible writers called them "detestable practices" (Deuteronomy 18:12).

Why? Because God did not create the stars to give us insights into the future, but to witness His power and glory. "The heavens declare the glory of God," the Psalmist wrote (Psalm 19:1).

Second, Christians don't follow astrology because we don't need to. God has given us everything we need to know about the future in His Word. Of course, the Bible doesn't tell us what will happen next week or next year; if it did, we would never learn to trust God or seek His guidance. But the Bible does tell us all we need to know: the future is in God's hands, and someday Christ will come again. Trust Him for your tomorrows—and for eternity.

WISDOM FOR TODAY

You are a good Father to us, God, and You warn against things that are harmful to us. You have given us all we need to know concerning our futures. Teach us to trust You and not seek to know things that are not ours to know.

HEART CONDITIONS

The heart is deceitful above all things and beyond cure. Who can understand it?
JEREMIAH 17:9

That judgment may seem harsh, but our Creator knows what He's talking about.

Our hearts are sinful. All the things happening in the world that discourage us and cause despair come from the human heart.

Our hearts, Jesus said, are a storehouse of evil (Mark 7:21). Fornications, murders, thefts, covetousness, wickedness, deceit, blasphemy, pride—all these come from the heart.

Our hearts are far from God (Matthew 15:8). Many of us go to church and outwardly live good lives, but our hearts are far from God. We are living for ourselves instead of Christ. Even hearts redeemed by Christ's love can be unbelieving, blind, proud, rebellious, idolatrous, and cold toward God.

Jesus died on the cross to show us the seriousness of our heart condition. He came to cleanse our hearts, to give us a heart-softening picture of God's divine and infinite love, and to woo us to Himself when the world tempts us to stray. Turn to the Great Physician for healing—whatever your current heart condition.

WISDOM FOR TODAY

Show us, Father, the conditions of our hearts. Reveal any hidden sins or areas of our lives that we are attempting to withhold from You. We lay our hearts bare before You, Lord, so that You can heal us from within.

THE GOD OF THE BIBLE

Jesus Christ is the same yesterday and today and forever.
HEBREWS 13:8

Too many people talk about God being a God of wrath in the Old Testament and a God of love and peace in the New Testament. But God is the same throughout the Bible.

It is true that the Old Testament tells us God is holy and pure, and He punishes those who rebel against Him. But the New Testament tells us the same thing. In fact, some of the strongest warnings about judgment in the Bible come from the lips of Jesus (see Matthew 7:14).

In the same way, the New Testament certainly stresses God's love and mercy. In fact, it gives us the greatest proof that God loves us: Jesus laid down His life for our salvation (1 John 3:16). But the Old Testament also tells us repeatedly about God's love for us: "I have loved you with an everlasting love; I have drawn you with loving kindness" (Jeremiah 31:3).

Still not convinced? Then consider this an invitation to open the pages of the Bible for yourself. You'll be blessed as you get to know God more fully—in all of His righteousness and love.

WISDOM FOR TODAY
We know, Father, that You are a God who doesn't change. We take great comfort in knowing that who You are is who You have always been, and Your character is consistent throughout all the pages of Scripture.

HERE FOR A REASON

*"Seek the peace and prosperity of the city to which I
have carried you. . . . Pray to the LORD for it."*
JEREMIAH 29:7

God does not lead us contrary to His Word. He will lead us out of situations that may cause us to stumble, and He may keep us in a dark place for a while to teach us important truths.

Jeremiah and his fellow countrymen had every reason not to seek the peace and prosperity of the places where they were living. They were no longer in their homeland; a vicious enemy had conquered their nation and forcibly taken them away into exile. Why help an enemy prosper there? And yet that is what God ordered them to do.

This world is not our final home; because of what Christ has done for us, we have "an inheritance that can never perish, spoil or fade . . . kept in heaven for you" (1 Peter 1:4). But in the meantime God calls us to be instruments of His love and justice in an unbelieving world. Ask God to use you for His glory right where He has placed you.

WISDOM FOR TODAY

It's easy to see the problems in the places we live, especially if it isn't our ideal home. Help us pray for and seek opportunities to love those You put in our pathways.

WHO IS BOSS?

Whatever you do, work at it with all your heart,
as working for the Lord, not for men.

COLOSSIANS 3:23

E ven the most interesting job has its moments of routine or drudgery; even the most fascinating and fulfilling position requires contact with difficult and demanding people. No job is perfect, and no position can insulate us completely from life's tensions and conflicts. With some jobs the stress is almost constant—and after a time it takes its toll.

The Bible tells us two important truths about our work. First, it acknowledges that work . . . is work! After Adam and Eve sinned, God cast them out of Eden and declared that "by the sweat of your brow you will eat your food" (Genesis 3:19). But the Bible also tells us that God has given our work to us, and it has dignity and importance in His eyes. It should in our eyes as well.

Whatever your job—no matter how difficult or enjoyable it is—"work at it with all your heart, as working for the Lord, not for men." It will make all the difference—in your attitude and your output.

WISDOM FOR TODAY

To have work to do is a gift from You, Lord, and there is purpose in it. May we give our best efforts in the tasks we've been entrusted with, knowing that any work can be used for our sanctification and for Your glory.

FIT FOR THE BATTLE

Put on the full armor of God so that you can take
your stand against the devil's schemes.
EPHESIANS 6:11

Don't doubt for a moment the devil's existence, and don't doubt for a moment that he is your enemy. Forget the cute cartoon images of an impish figure with a pitchfork and a red suit; he is absolutely malicious and evil, and he has great influence over this world. The Bible says, "Your enemy the devil prowls around like a roaring lion looking for someone to devour" (1 Peter 5:8). He is strong, and he is determined to make you stumble. He also is clever and scheming, bent on deceiving and outmaneuvering us at every turn.

But we are not defenseless! God has provided us with all the armor we need—armor so strong that Satan and his servants cannot penetrate it. Truth, righteousness, peace, faith, salvation, the Word of God, prayer—every one of these has its part in defeating our adversary. (You can read Paul's full description in Ephesians 6:10–18.)

What parts of God's armor are missing in your life? Don't let another day go by without "the full armor of God."

WISDOM FOR TODAY

The enemy loves for us to underestimate him or, even better, completely doubt his existence. After all, we won't defend against what we don't believe even exists. May we live with an awareness of Satan's presence, Lord, and actively guard against his attacks.

How to Grow Your Faith

*Faith comes from hearing the message, and the message
is heard through the word of Christ.*

ROMANS 10:17

Would you like to grow weak? It's not difficult, you know; all you have to do is stop eating and exercising. And yet no one in their right mind would willingly do this.

Why, then, do we fail to see the connection between the weakness of our faith and our lack of spiritual food and exercise? Faith doesn't grow automatically; it requires spiritual "food" for its nourishment. It also requires exercise—seeing God work as we put it into action. And if we don't feed and exercise our souls, we shouldn't be surprised when our faith grows weaker and weaker. But it doesn't need to be this way—and it mustn't be this way. Christ's work is too important and too demanding for it to be carried out by spiritual weaklings.

What is the main "food" God has given to strengthen us? It is the Bible, the Word of God. Jesus prayed, "Sanctify them by the truth; your word is truth" (John 17:17). Read it . . . study it . . . meditate on it . . . listen to it preached and taught. And then watch your faith grow.

WISDOM FOR TODAY

The Bible, not breakfast, is the most important meal of the day. Give us the desire to feed on Your Word as often as possible, Lord, that we may have the strength to do the work You have called us to do.

LOVING WITH GOD'S LOVE

Love is patient, love is kind. . . . It is not rude, it is not self-seeking,
it is not easily angered, it keeps no record of wrongs.
1 CORINTHIANS 13:4–5

I can't live with him, but I can't seem to live without him either," her letter said. She added that she had moved out of their house three times but still kept coming back. With minor variations, her story could be repeated thousands of times every day.

Each marriage is different, and we mustn't oversimplify or overlook the uniqueness of every relationship. But what is the problem? Why can't spouses seem to get along?

Let me answer by asking another question: What is the opposite of love?

It isn't hate (although it may take that form). The opposite of love is selfishness. When a husband and wife are concerned only about their own individual desires, the stage is set for conflict.

The Bible gives us another way—the way of Christ. True love, it says, is self-giving, not self-seeking. True love puts the needs of others first. This is what Christ did when He left heaven's glory and came down to earth for us. Begin a new page in your marriage by asking Christ to become the center of your life—and your marriage.

WISDOM FOR TODAY

What would change in our marriages if we truly made Christ the center of our relationships? What attitudes would change? What offenses would be overlooked? Do a mighty work in our homes, Lord!

COMING IN GLORY

*"At that time men will see the Son of Man coming
in clouds with great power and glory."*

MARK 13:26

Jesus' first coming passed almost unnoticed: born in a small out-of-the-way town and laid in a manger with only animals and humble shepherds to greet Him on that first night. Even at the height of His ministry He could say, "Foxes have holes and birds of the air have nests, but the Son of Man has no place to lay his head" (Luke 9:58).

How different His second coming will be! Then "every eye will see him" (Revelation 1:7), and He will come with glory and power to establish His kingdom of perfect justice and righteousness. No one will dismiss Him as insignificant or unimportant; all will acknowledge Him as King of kings and Lord of lords.

Does the thought of His return fill you with concern, or even terror?

It shouldn't—not if you have trusted Him as your Lord and Savior and put your life into His hands. Instead, His return should fill you with expectancy and joy and worship. Make sure you are ready, and then pray for His quick return.

WISDOM FOR TODAY

We wait with great anticipation, Jesus, for the day You return and we all behold You with our very own eyes. We will see the One in whom we have believed, and our faith will finally be sight.

THE SEEDS OF DOUBT

[Satan] said to the woman, "Did God really say, 'You must not eat from any tree in the garden'?"
GENESIS 3:1

The devil is a master at making us question God and His Word. God's command to Adam and Eve had been crystal clear: they could eat of every tree in the garden—except one. If they ate of it, death would come upon them. But now Satan raises the question: "Did God really say . . . ?" It is the first question in the Bible, and it's significant that it comes from the mouth of the one whose primary goal is to turn us away from God.

But notice: Satan misquoted God! This wasn't what God had told them—as Eve points out in her reply. Twisting Scripture . . . taking a verse out of context . . . deceiving us into thinking God is mean-spirited—these are some of Satan's favorite tricks.

Eve's mistake was in prolonging the conversation—and eventually being deceived by the Deceiver. His promise—that she would become like God if she ate from the forbidden tree—was a lie. Don't let Satan sow the seeds of doubt in your soul, but always stand firmly on the truth of God's Word.

WISDOM FOR TODAY

Satan's tactic with Eve was to question her certainty regarding God's Word, and he uses the same trick today. We can't be satisfied with Christian clichés or a secondhand knowledge of Scripture. Give us a hunger, Lord, to know truth for ourselves.

SATAN'S PROMISES

You belong to your father, the devil . . . he is a liar and the father of lies.
JOHN 8:44

Although many prisoners find hope in Jesus, this letter was from one who was still skeptical: "Can you give me even one reason to give my life to Jesus? It won't get me out of prison any quicker, and no one here would believe me anyway if I said I gave my life to God."

The best reason (I replied) to give your life to Jesus Christ is because you need Him. You need Him for this life, and you need Him for the life to come. So far in life—whether you realize it or not—you have been following the devil. He promised to give you happiness and peace. But has he kept his promise? No, not at all—nor will he ever keep it. He also promises that you don't need to worry about what will happen to you when you die—which is another lie.

But Christ does not lie—neither to this prisoner nor to you. You can depend on His promises—and the greatest promise of all is God's promise of new life in Christ. No matter what you have done, God can forgive you and give you the power to start life again. Begin today by committing your life and your future to Jesus Christ.

WISDOM FOR TODAY
We can all look to choices we've made, Lord, that didn't provide the outcome we expected. Unlike the empty promises of the enemy, we can trust You to be true to Your Word. You are a promise keeper.

Stand Strong!

Submit yourselves, then, to God. Resist the devil, and he will flee from you. Come near to God and he will come near to you.
James 4:7–8

Satan is certainly active today—but he has always been active, because his goal has not changed: to block God's work. Whenever God is at work, you can be sure Satan will counterattack and try to stop whatever God is doing.

The Bible doesn't tell us in detail about Satan and how he works. After all, our focus should be on God, not on Satan. (If we concentrate mainly on Satan, we'll become either overly fearful or overly fascinated—and both are wrong.)

But the Bible does tell us two important truths about Satan (whose name means "adversary"). First, he is real, and he will do everything he can to draw us away from Christ. He tempts us to do wrong, but most of all he tempts us to turn away from God. Second, Satan is a defeated foe. By His death and resurrection, Jesus conquered Satan, so by the power of His Holy Spirit in us, we can stand against him.

Don't be deceived by Satan and his lies. Instead, stay close to Christ—because the closer you are to Him, the farther away you are from the devil.

Wisdom for Today

What is the key to making the devil flee? According to Scripture, we must actively resist him. This means being filled with Your Word, Father, and standing firm in what we know to be true and right.

NOVEMBER

NOW IS THE TIME

Man is destined to die once, and after that to face judgment.
HEBREWS 9:27

Many today find the idea of reincarnation attractive—the belief that after we die we come back to earth again and again. Some of them have been influenced by other religions; others simply like the thought of enjoying life's pleasures indefinitely.

The Bible, however, is clear: reincarnation is not true, and the life we are leading now is the only one we will ever live. Once we die, we go into eternity—either to heaven to be with God forever or to that place the Bible calls hell, where we will be eternally separated from God and His blessings.

What difference should this make? First, it gives urgency to our lives right now. If you are ever going to trust Christ for your salvation . . . if you are ever going to live for Him . . . the time is now. The Bible says, "Now is the time of God's favor, now is the day of salvation" (2 Corinthians 6:2).

Second, it should give us a greater burden for those who don't know Christ. With whom should you be sharing Christ today?

WISDOM FOR TODAY

There are no do-overs or second chances, Father. One life is all we are given, and it will be over in the blink of an eye. May we not miss a single opportunity to share the Gospel with a lost and dying world.

LIVING BY GOD'S STANDARDS

I tell you the truth, until heaven and earth disappear, not the smallest letter,
not the least stroke of a pen, will by any means disappear from the Law.
MATTHEW 5:18

God's moral standards do not change. What He decreed in the Ten Commandments thousands of years ago is still in force and will be to the end of time. Not murdering, committing adultery, stealing, lying, coveting—His commandments have not changed (Exodus 20:1–17).

Why don't God's standards change according to the fashions and whims of the times? One reason is because God is absolutely pure—and these standards are a reflection of His righteous character. And because His character does not change, neither do His moral standards. "I the LORD do not change" (Malachi 3:6).

But God has given us these standards for another reason: He loves us, and He wants what is best for us. What happens when an individual or society ignores these basic moral laws? What happens when lying and stealing and immorality and murder become the norm? The result can be summarized in one word: *chaos.* Thank God that He cares about us so much that He has told us how to live. And ask Him to help you follow His will in everything.

WISDOM FOR TODAY

Thank You, Father, for loving us enough to give us guidelines on how we are to live. There is security and comfort in knowing what is expected of us as well as the consequences for disobedience.

BEING HONEST WITH GOD

I loathe my very life;
therefore I will give free rein to my complaint
and speak out in the bitterness of my soul.
JOB 10:1

You can understand Job's bitterness; he had lost everything—family, possessions, health, even his friends. But the hardest blow of all was that he couldn't understand why the God he had worshiped and served so faithfully had done this to him.

Have you ever felt this way toward God? Life can be hard, and sometimes it leaves us confused, or even angry and bitter. And like Job, you may have told God exactly how you felt. And why not? He already knew your mind and heart, and He doesn't want us to pretend that everything is all right when it isn't. He didn't chastise Job for his honesty; He understood his heartache, just as He understands ours—and He still loved Job, just as He still loves us.

But Job didn't just keep complaining (as we're prone to do). Instead, he turned toward God in faith, and in time, God gave him comfort and peace. Not all his questions were answered—but he realized that God can be trusted, even when we don't understand. May this be true of you.

WISDOM FOR TODAY

Thank You, God, that we can come to You with our hurt and confusion when life is difficult. Your Word promises that, when we come to You weary and heavy-laden, You will allow us to experience rest.

TRUE BELIEF

You believe that there is one God. Good! Even the
demons believe that—and shudder.

JAMES 2:19

I t's true: the devil and his demons really do believe in God—and why wouldn't they? They understand that they are engaged in a cosmic battle of titanic proportions, and they know they are up against the Creator of the universe—a truth that makes them shudder. There are no atheists in hell!

But their belief is a far cry from the kind of belief you and I are called to have. They believe God exists; they even believe in the facts of Jesus' birth, life, death, and resurrection. But their belief is not a saving belief—and the reason is because it has not led them to turn to God in repentance and trust Christ alone for their salvation.

True belief—saving belief—involves not only an intellectual acceptance of certain facts about God and about Jesus. It also involves trust and commitment— trust in Christ as our Savior and commitment to Him as Lord. Is your belief a saving belief? Make sure by trusting Christ and committing your life without reserve to Him.

WISDOM FOR TODAY

Father, we do far more than acknowledge Your existence. We submit to Your lordship in our lives, and we believe that, through Christ and His work on the cross, we will be in Your presence when we die.

GOD'S AMAZING LOVE

God demonstrates his own love for us in this: While
we were still sinners, Christ died for us.
ROMANS 5:8

Have you ever asked yourself what you would do with the human race if you were in God's shoes? How would you treat them in light of their rebellion and neglect and mockery toward you?

We can't really put ourselves in God's shoes, of course; He is far greater than we are. But if you were God, wouldn't you be tempted to wipe out the human race and blot them from your memory? Why would you even try to do anything good for them, knowing they'd probably reject it?

But this isn't God's way—and the proof is Jesus Christ. You've heard the old statement that God hates the sin but loves the sinner. When Adam and Eve rebelled against God, He punished them by sending death on the human race. But He also refused to stamp them out, and even promised an eventual way of salvation. That way is Jesus Christ, who loved us so much that He gave His life for us. Thank God today for His grace to you—grace that is greater than all your sin.

WISDOM FOR TODAY

We're so grateful, Father, that Your love is vastly superior to human love. You loved us while we were deep in our sin and incapable of returning it in kind. May we never doubt the depth of Your love.

EVERY MOMENT OF THE DAY

On my bed I remember you; I think of you through the watches of the night.

PSALM 63:6

One of the habits I have always urged new Christians to develop is the discipline of spending time alone with God every day—reading the Bible, meditating on its truth, and turning to God in prayer. Even if it's only a few minutes at first, nothing can calm our souls more or better prepare us for life's challenges than time spent alone with God.

But the Bible also urges us to walk with God every waking moment.

"Pray continually," Paul urged the Thessalonian Christians (1 Thessalonians 5:17). "Night and day I constantly remember you in my prayers," he told Timothy (2 Timothy 1:3).

The Psalmist noted that the righteous person takes delight in God's Word, and on His law he meditates "day and night" (Psalm 1:2). Often when I'm speaking to someone or preaching to a crowd, I find myself praying for them in my heart.

Jesus promised, "I am with you always" (Matthew 28:20). Ask God to help you be aware of His constant presence and to turn your heart and mind toward Him.

WISDOM FOR TODAY

We want to live with a continual awareness of Your presence, Lord. May we find ourselves throughout the day meditating on Your Word and spending time with You in prayer.

RESPECTING AND ENCOURAGING

Respect those who work hard among you, who are over you in the Lord.
1 THESSALONIANS 5:12

H ave you ever noticed? Often when a new pastor takes up his responsibilities, almost without fail people first begin looking for his faults. How sad!

No pastor is perfect, of course; the apostle Paul admitted to the Christians in Corinth that "when I came to you, brothers, I did not come with eloquence or superior wisdom" (1 Corinthians 2:1). His young pastor friend Timothy was apparently somewhat shy (1 Timothy 4:12).

If you are a pastor or church worker or teach a class in your church, be honest about your weaknesses and ask God to help you overcome them so you can serve Christ more effectively.

Instead of criticizing your pastor and others who have leadership in your church, show respect for them; God gave them their gifts and their responsibilities. Pray for them also—regularly and sincerely. Encourage them as well, thanking them for what they're doing and expressing appreciation for their service. And encourage and pray for their families; they, too, are part of your church's ministry.

WISDOM FOR TODAY

Let us be a source of support and encouragement, Lord, to those who lead and teach within our churches. Show us how we can best show our appreciation for their work and, where possible, help bear the load of ministry.

WHEN ANGER GOES UNCHECKED

An angry man stirs up dissension,
and a hot-tempered one commits many sins.
PROVERBS 29:22

We all know what it is to be angry, and we all know the damage it can cause. Anger makes us do things we ordinarily wouldn't do, and even when we think we have it under control, it can build up within us until it bursts forth in all kinds of hurtful ways. Anger damages everyone it touches and opens the door to many other sins.

No wonder God wants to help us deal with our anger! How can this happen? First, we must admit our anger, and then hand it over to God. We can't deal with it by ourselves—not fully and finally. We need God's help, and the first step is to ask Him for it.

Then ask God to help you see others the way He sees them, and love them as He does. Their wrongdoing may have caused your anger—but God still loves them. Ask Him to fill you with His love, because anger and love can't coexist. The Bible says, "Above all, love each other deeply, because love covers over a multitude of sins" (1 Peter 4:8).

WISDOM FOR TODAY
Fill us with the fruit of the Spirit, Lord, so there won't be room for anger. When tempted to respond in anger, help us choose love, joy, peace, patience, gentleness, kindness, faith, and self-control.

EXCUSING OUR SIN

Woe to those who call evil good and good evil, who put darkness for light and light for darkness.
ISAIAH 5:20

I s God behind everything that happens to us?

This isn't an easy question to answer. On one hand, God is sovereign, and in ways we can only dimly understand this side of eternity, He is at work behind the scenes. The Psalmist wrote, "He guides me in paths of righteousness for his name's sake" (Psalm 23:3).

But on the other hand, the Bible warns us against assuming that everything that comes our way is from God. Recently a woman wrote me about a man she had fallen in love with, and she said they were now living together. "God brought us together," she stated—in spite of the fact they both were already married. But she was wrong; God never leads us to do anything that is contrary to what He has told us in His Word. This woman was excusing her sin by claiming it must be God's will.

Don't be deceived; don't ever "call evil good and good evil." Sin is serious—so serious it sent Jesus Christ to the cross. Flee from it, and stay close to Christ.

WISDOM FOR TODAY

You never change, Father. What You call good will always be good, and evil will always be evil. Give us the wisdom to avoid the trap of believing that what makes us happy must be Your will.

REFUSING THE REMEDY

As Paul discoursed on righteousness, self-control and the judgment
to come, Felix was afraid and said, "That's enough for now! You
may leave. When I find it convenient, I will send for you."

ACTS 24:25

Paul was under arrest, and the Roman governor Felix had full authority either to release him or keep him in jail. Rather than flatter Felix or try to win his favor, however, Paul instead spoke openly to him about Christ. Finally Felix had had enough; he ordered Paul to leave, promising to listen more fully "when I find it convenient."

Hoping for a bribe (which Paul wouldn't give), Felix did send for him repeatedly—but two years later Paul was still in jail, and Felix was still an unbeliever. Like a patient who consults his doctor and yet refuses to take his prescription, Felix listened to Paul but refused to repent of his sins and commit his life to Christ. The cost was too high; he wasn't willing to give up his sins and begin following Jesus. He was curious . . . he knew what the Gospel was—but that wasn't enough.

Don't wait until a more convenient time to give your life to Christ; the devil will make sure it never happens. Instead, commit your life to Jesus—beginning today.

WISDOM FOR TODAY

Father, give us an urgency to place our faith in You and to encourage others to do the same.

DEPENDING ON THE TRUTH

This is the testimony: God has given us eternal life, and
this life is in his Son. He who has the Son has life.
1 JOHN 5:11–12

I magine that you had a wealthy relative, and one day her attorney called to tell you she had died and left you a million dollars. The money, he added, was now deposited in a bank in your name, and you could draw on it at any time.

What would you do? Would you say, "Oh, well, it can't be true; I'll just forget about his call"? I doubt it. Instead, you'd act on it, accepting by faith that what the attorney had told you was true, and you were now a millionaire. And what a difference it would make!

In a far greater way God offers us a gift—the gift of salvation in Jesus Christ. Christ has done everything possible to provide it for you; all you must do is receive it. Have you taken that step and by faith received Christ into your life?

But God's generosity doesn't end there. God wants you to draw upon His riches every day—the riches of His wisdom, strength, truth, and presence. Don't live like a spiritual pauper any longer!

WISDOM FOR TODAY

There are many, Lord, who have placed their faith in You for salvation and yet are missing out on the blessings available to them in the here and now. Thank You that our hope is not just for eternal life but for our present life as well.

HONORING OUR PARENTS

"Honor your father and your mother, as the LORD your God has commanded you."
DEUTERONOMY 5:16

One of the signs of the latter days before Christ returns, the Bible says, is that "people will be . . . disobedient to their parents" (2 Timothy 3:2). Instead of obeying the commandment to "honor your father and your mother," they'll bring dishonor to them.

Does this command become irrelevant as we grow older? Is it meant only for young children? No, not at all. As long as our parents are alive, we are to honor and respect them. They weren't perfect—but they were the ones God gave you, and you should honor them because of that.

If your parents are still living, ask God to help you let them know you love them, and you honor them for the sacrifices they made for you. I'm saddened whenever I visit a nursing home and the staff begs me to visit some of the residents "because their children have just dumped them here and never come to visit." And if your parents are no longer living, ask God to help you befriend an older person who feels lonely and forgotten.

WISDOM FOR TODAY

We all have different experiences with our parents, Lord, and You are aware of all the details of the relationships. Please reveal to us, in our unique situations, what it would look like for us to honor our mothers and fathers.

THE COST OF DISCIPLESHIP

*"If anyone would come after me, he must deny himself
and take up his cross daily and follow me."*
LUKE 9:23

These are sobering words; Jesus was warning His disciples that it would be costly for them to follow Him. It would be costly because they would have to give up their own plans and goals; it would be costly also because they must share in His rejection and death. No wonder "many of his disciples turned back and no longer followed him" (John 6:66).

The cost of following Jesus has not changed. We want to cling to our plans—but He says they must go. We want to live for ourselves—but He says we must live for Him. We want to live a life of pleasure and ease—but He says we must follow Him to the cross.

But why not be His disciple? Why not follow the King of kings and the Lord of lords? Someday your life will be over, and all the things you accumulated will vanish. Don't waste your life, but give everything you have and everything you are to Christ, for He alone is "the way and the truth and the life" (John 14:6).

WISDOM FOR TODAY

Following You will always cost us something, Lord. But we know that, whatever the price or sacrifice, You are worthy. When we are experiencing paradise in Your presence, we will not regret choosing the cross over our comfort.

OVERCOMING DISCOURAGEMENT

[Elijah] came to a broom tree, sat down under it and prayed
that he might die. "I have had enough, LORD," he said.

1 KINGS 19:4

We all experience discouragement, and sometimes it can be almost overwhelming. Look at Elijah. He had been one of God's most faithful servants, never wavering in the face of disaster and King Ahab's threats. Then, in one of the most dramatic confrontations in the Bible, God used Elijah to overcome the pagan prophets of Baal and demonstrate to all the nation that God alone was worthy of their worship.

But now, only days later, discouragement and depression had almost overwhelmed him. Fearing Queen Jezebel's rage and convinced the people's hearts were unchanged, Elijah fled into the desert and concluded he was a failure: "I have had enough, Lord."

How did God answer? First, He provided him with rest and food; Elijah had neglected to take care of himself, and it affected his emotions. Second, God showed Him His glory, reminding Elijah of the greatness of the God he served. Finally, God assured him that He still had work for him to do. When discouragement comes and you wonder if you can go on, remember Elijah—and be encouraged.

WISDOM FOR TODAY

Discouragement, Father, is not a surprise to You. Help us recognize the signs of despair and to turn to You before it overwhelms us.

LIFE'S HARD REALITY

The length of our days is seventy years . . .
yet their span is but trouble and sorrow.
PSALM 90:10

There it is in black and white: life is hard, and our years on earth are marked by "trouble and sorrow." As someone has said, there is no false advertising in the Bible!

We wish it weren't so, of course; maybe that's why we're so quick to believe the advertisements that promise happiness if we'll only use their product. And sometimes life can bring us a measure of happiness; the Bible says, "The LORD bestows favor and honor; no good thing does he withhold from those whose walk is blameless" (Psalm 84:11). But I've never met a person who didn't have problems of some kind. We live in a world that is broken because of sin, and we share in its brokenness.

What difference should this make? First, it should give us greater compassion for others. All around you are people whose lives are filled with trouble and sorrow, and they need your compassion and encouragement. Second, it should make us yearn for heaven. There our troubles and sorrows will cease, and we will be safely with Christ forever.

WISDOM FOR TODAY

Life is difficult for everyone, and no one makes it through unscathed, Lord. Help us to assume the best in others, to err on the side of grace, and to make compassion our default response.

LIFE'S TOUGHEST JOB

Train a child in the way he should go,
and when he is old he will not turn from it.
PROVERBS 22:6

I'm president of a large corporation," he said to me, "but the hardest job I've ever tried to do is be a good parent." Then he added, "If my home was as successful as my company, I'd be elated." Being a parent is hard; every child is different, and every day brings fresh challenges. It's especially hard if one parent is missing; being a single parent is surely one of the most difficult responsibilities imaginable.

But sometimes we overlook some basic truths about parenting that we need to keep before us (or, if we're older, pass on to others). Let me mention three for you to ponder.

First, see your children as a gift from God. He entrusted them to you; take them as a gift (and responsibility) from His hands. Second, let them know you love them. Show affection for them; teach them right and wrong; spend time with them. Third, be an example of faith. Pray with them, read the Bible to them, and let them see that Christ is important to you. With God's help, you can be the kind of parent they need.

WISDOM FOR TODAY

Father, teaching our children about You and Your Word is our life's greatest work, and we long to do it well. May they see in us a genuine love for You, a desire to follow Your will, and a faith that stands firm in all the seasons of life.

THE BODY OF CHRIST

Christ is the head of the church, his body, of which he is the Savior.
EPHESIANS 5:23

When we come to Christ we come as individuals. We alone repent of our sins; we alone believe Christ's death on the cross will save us; we alone decide to become His follower.

But once we come to Christ we are no longer just individuals. We are now members of His family—what the Bible here calls "the church, his body." We are now part of that vast group of people throughout the ages who have trusted Christ and are our brothers and sisters in His family. Although we'll never meet most of them this side of eternity, we're still united spiritually with them. This transcends any local church or denomination; it includes all who truly belong to Christ.

Christian fellowship is one of God's greatest gifts to us. Are you sharing in it—worshipping with others and growing closer to Christ through their fellowship? No local church is perfect, of course—but don't use that as an excuse to avoid fellowship with others. The Bible tells us to "encourage one another and build each other up" (1 Thessalonians 5:11).

WISDOM FOR TODAY
You've said from the beginning, God, that it is not good for man to be alone. Thank You for the gift of Christian fellowship that provides a source of encouragement, accountability, and wisdom.

FAITH AND REASON

Since the creation of the world God's invisible qualities—
his eternal power and divine nature—have been clearly
seen, being understood from what has been made.

ROMANS 1:20

I s faith illogical?

If you listen to some people, the answer would appear to be yes.

Every year books hit the best-seller lists announcing that faith in God is dead; every year college students write me wondering why their professors reject God; every year talk show hosts promote the latest self-help gurus claiming to solve all our problems.

Is faith illogical, as some would have you believe? No, not at all.

Some of the most brilliant people I have ever known were also men and women of deep faith in Christ, and without exception they said they believed in the Gospel because it made sense. Believing our intricate world happened by accident, they said, takes more faith than believing in God!

But there was another reason for their faith: they were convinced Jesus Christ was who He claimed to be: God in human flesh, sent to save us from our sins. Don't be misled, but rejoice that in Christ "are hidden all the treasures of wisdom and knowledge" (Colossians 2:3).

WISDOM FOR TODAY

Scripture tells us that all of creation points to a Creator and, God, we believe it to be true. We believe that the claims and promises made in Your Word are true, and we know in whom we have believed.

STILL SERVING

Now Barzillai was a very old man, eighty years of age. He had provided for the king during his stay in Mahanaim.
2 SAMUEL 19:32

You've probably never heard of Barzillai. He lived in an obscure, isolated village, and virtually his whole life was behind him when we meet him in the Bible. Even then, his story occupies only a few verses.

But without Barzillai the history of God's people might have been vastly different. In one of the saddest events in the Bible, King David's son Absalom revolted against his father and attempted to take the throne by force. David and his men had to flee for their lives, and by the time they reached the vicinity of Barzillai's home they were out of supplies and in danger of starvation. But Barzillai came to their aid and David's army was saved. Absalom's rebellion collapsed and David—Jesus' ancestor—was restored to the throne.

Barzillai was eighty when this happened, and he easily could have said, "I'm too old to do anything" or "It's too risky; what if Absalom wins?" But he didn't. Are you older, perhaps retired or nearing retirement? Don't waste those years, but ask God to use you—just as He did Barzillai.

WISDOM FOR TODAY

As long as there's breath in our bodies, God, You have kingdom work for us to do. Let us not grow weary of doing good but continue, at any age, to seek ways to serve You and to further the Gospel message.

THE BIBLE'S CENTER

These are written that you may believe that Jesus is the Christ, the
Son of God, and that by believing you may have life in his name.

JOHN 20:31

Jesus Christ is the Bible's central message. The Old Testament looks forward to His coming; the New Testament recounts His coming. Without Christ the Bible is only another book of ancient history—but beyond that it has little relevance. But Christ gives the Bible its value, because before time began God planned to send Him into the world for our salvation (Ephesians 1:4).

But Jesus Christ isn't just the center of the Bible; He is the center of our lives. By believing in Him, John says, we "have life in his name." What does this mean? First, it means eternal life. Without Christ we have no hope of heaven; as the Bible says, "The wages of sin is death" (Romans 6:23). But when we yield our lives to Christ and trust Him alone for our salvation, we know we will be with Him through all eternity.

But Jesus Christ also gives us life right now—not the artificial, unstable life the world offers but a life of purpose and peace and joy. Is Christ the center of your life?

WISDOM FOR TODAY

When we read any page of Scripture, Lord, we should ask, "What does this tell me about Jesus?" You are there in every page. Likewise, every aspect of our lives should reveal You and point others to faith in You.

HOW DO YOU DEFINE SUCCESS?

Therefore, holy brothers, who share in the heavenly calling, fix your thoughts on Jesus. . . . He was faithful to the one who appointed him.
HEBREWS 3:1–2

Recently a friend of mine went on the website of one of the major booksellers and searched for books with the word *success* in their titles. After a few minutes he gave up; literally thousands were listed. Our world is obsessed with success.

What is success? The world has its measures: financial success, athletic success, business success, professional success, social success—the list is almost as endless as my friend's website search. And most people spend their lives pursuing at least one of these.

But how does God define success? His measure is very different from the world's measure, and it can be summed up in one sentence: success in God's eyes is faithfulness to His calling. Paul was a failure in the world's eyes—but not to God. Even Jesus was a failure as far as most people were concerned, but "he was faithful to the one who appointed him"—and that is all that mattered.

What is your definition of success? Is it the same as God's—and are you pursuing it?

WISDOM FOR TODAY

Help us pursue the things that make us successful in Your eyes, Father, even when the world mocks or misunderstands us. May we seek to be faithful in the small things and to walk humbly with our God.

The Spirit of Gratitude

Give thanks to the Lord, for he is good;
his love endures forever.
PSALM 107:1

One day when Jesus was on His way to Jerusalem, ten lepers approached Him and pleaded for Him to heal them. In an instant they were restored to perfect health, but only one, "when he saw he was healed, came back, praising God in a loud voice. He threw himself at Jesus' feet and thanked him" (Luke 17:15–16). All the others left without a single word of thanks. They were preoccupied with themselves and gripped by a spirit of ingratitude.

Such ingratitude and thanklessness are far too common in our world. Children forget to thank their parents for all they do. Common courtesy is scorned. People take for granted the way others help them. And, above all, we fail to thank God for His blessings. Such an ungrateful heart is cold toward God and indifferent to His mercy and love. It is a heart that has forgotten how dependent we are on God for everything.

Be like that one leper: take time to give thanks—and mean it. It brings glory to God, warmth to relationships, and a special awareness of God's love and grace toward you.

Wisdom for Today

Gratitude guards our hearts against bitterness and selfishness, Lord. When we recognize that every good and perfect gift comes from Your hand, we realize just how much You have blessed us.

Make It a Habit!

I have learned the secret of being content in any and every situation,
whether well fed or hungry, whether living in plenty or in want.
Philippians 4:12

The next footsteps, he knew, might be those of the guards taking him away to his execution. His bed was the cold, stone floor of the dank, cramped prison cell. There was never any relief from the constant irritation of the chains and the pain of the iron manacles cutting into his wrists and ankles.

Separated from friends, unjustly accused, brutally treated—if any man had a right to complain, it was this man, languishing almost forgotten in a harsh Roman prison. But instead of complaints, his lips rang with words of praise and thanksgiving!

This was the apostle Paul, a man who had learned to give thanks even in the midst of great adversity. Look carefully at what he wrote during his prison experience: "Sing and make music in your heart to the Lord, always giving thanks to God the Father for everything, in the name of our Lord Jesus Christ" (Ephesians 5:19–20).

For Paul, giving thanks was a regular habit that made him joyful in every situation. It can do the same for you. Start developing that habit today!

Wisdom for Today

Gratitude does not come naturally, Lord. Help us to be intentional in the practice of praising You for all the good things in our lives. We can be content in every situation because we are confident in Your love and care for us.

THE RIGHT ATTITUDE

Now, our God, we give you thanks, and praise your glorious name.

1 CHRONICLES 29:13

The Pilgrim Fathers who landed at Plymouth to settle in what became the United States of America can teach us an important lesson about giving thanks.

During that first long winter, seven times as many graves were made for the dead as homes were made for the living. Seed, imported from England, failed to grow, and a ship that was to bring food and relief brought instead thirty-five more mouths to feed, but no provisions. Some Pilgrims caught fish, and others hunted wild fowl and deer. They had a little English flour and some Indian corn.

Yet William Brewster, rising from a scanty dinner of clams and water, gave thanks to God "for the abundance of the sea and the treasure hid in the sand."

According to today's standards, the Pilgrims had almost nothing, but they possessed a profound and heartfelt gratitude to God for His love and mercy. Gratitude is one of the greatest Christian virtues; ingratitude, one of the most vicious sins.

Our English words *thank* and *think* come from the same word. If we'll stop to think, we'll be more thankful.

WISDOM FOR TODAY

It's easy to think of things we wish we had or to become overly interested in the blessings that someone else is enjoying. Help us instead, Father, to see all that we've been given as gifts and to see You as the giver of all good things.

343

GRATITUDE FOR HIS GIFTS

Thanks be to God for his indescribable gift!
2 CORINTHIANS 9:15

The apostle Paul warned that the time would come when "people will be lovers of themselves . . . ungrateful" (2 Timothy 3:2). What a description of our own times! Rather than being grateful, we get wrapped up in ourselves and take for granted what others do for us. Of course, it shouldn't be this way, but it often is.

I know of a couple without children of their own who—at great sacrifice— helped put their two nieces through college—without ever hearing a single "thank you." If something like that happens to you, I hope you will find satisfaction in knowing that you made a difference in someone's life—and that someday they will appreciate what you did and perhaps even see the Lord's hand in it.

While we're thinking about gratitude, though, I find myself thinking about how ungrateful we often are to God. He has given us everything we have—but are we truly thankful? Most of all, God sent Jesus into the world to die for us. Have we responded by thanking Him for His love and giving our lives to Him?

WISDOM FOR TODAY

If asked, Lord, we would certainly say that we are grateful for Your many gifts. Help us to be faithful, however, about expressing that gratitude to You with our words and not take any gift for granted.

GIVE THANKS!

Enter [God's] gates with thanksgiving and his courts with
praise; give thanks to him and praise his name.
PSALM 100:4

Throughout the Bible we are commanded to be thankful. A spirit of thanksgiving is one of the most distinctive marks of a Christian whose heart is attuned to the Lord.

First, we are to be thankful for the material blessings God gives us. Some people are never satisfied with what they have, but what a difference it makes when we realize that everything we have has been given to us by God!

Second, thank God for the people in your life. It is so easy to take them for granted or to complain or become angry because they don't meet our every wish. But we need to give thanks for our spouse, our children, our relatives, and our friends. Most of all, thank God for Christ and His love for you.

Third, thank God in the midst of trials and even persecution. We draw back from difficulties, but not one of us is exempt from trouble. Yet in the midst of trials we can thank God because we know He has promised to be with us and help us.

For the Christian, every day is Thanksgiving Day!

WISDOM FOR TODAY

If we were to literally count our blessings, Father, we would be amazed at the gifts we've overlooked or taken for granted. Instill in us the discipline of recognizing the gifts You've bestowed and taking the time to express gratitude.

GRATITUDE IN WORD AND DEED

If anyone has material possessions and sees his brother in need but has no pity on him, how can the love of God be in him?
1 JOHN 3:17

Whenever we sit down for a meal, let us not forget that at least half the world goes to bed hungry. When we enjoy the comfort of our home, let us not forget that millions have no home to go to. As we ride in our car, let us not forget that many people in the world cannot afford even a bicycle.

Whenever we go to church to thank God for our material and spiritual blessings, let us remember that millions have never heard the Gospel, the Good News of salvation in Christ. Let us remember as well those who follow Jesus but risk their lives by owning a Bible or attending a worship service. Let us also remember that missionaries in many parts of the world are suffering in order to take the Gospel to those who have yet to hear about Jesus.

And let us always be grateful not only in word but in deed. May our gratitude find expression in our prayers, our service for others, and in our commitment to live wholly for Christ.

WISDOM FOR TODAY

As we count our blessings, Lord, let us make it our practice to pray for those who don't have the very things for which we are expressing gratitude. Show us opportunities to use our gifts to meet the needs of others.

THANKING GOD IN EVERYTHING

He has shown kindness by giving you rain from heaven and crops in their seasons; he provides you with plenty of food and fills your hearts with joy.

ACTS 14:17

God delights in giving—even to His enemies. He gives people food—but they give Him rebellion. God gives people wisdom—but they serve the devil with it. He gives them strength—but they waste it in evil pursuits.

All of God's giving, however, should drive us to thanksgiving. Whatever material things we enjoy come from God, and He gives them to us to remind us of His goodness. Some people ask, "Why should those who have plenty pray, 'Give us our daily bread'? We can understand why a poor person would pray such a prayer, but why should a rich person pray it?" The reason is clear: to remind us all of our constant dependence on God. The bread is in our hand, yet both the bread and the blessing are from God's hand.

No matter what we receive from Him, it should drive us to give humble thanks to God, from whom all blessings flow.

WISDOM FOR TODAY

May we express our gratitude daily for Your many gifts, Father, being mindful that it all comes from Your hand. Whether in a season of want or plenty, we trust You for our protection and provision.

THE HOPE-FILLED TRUTH

"Surely I am with you always, to the very end of the age."
MATTHEW 28:20

On the purely human level, there is little hope in the world. Immorality and lawlessness seem to be increasing. Wrong seems to be winning and right seems to be losing the battle for the minds and hearts of people.

Many of us have put our faith in money, jobs, status, gadgets, pleasures, and thrills. Many of us—and society as a whole—have tried to bypass God, and now we are paying the inevitable price. We are in trouble because we have left God out; we have left the Ten Commandments out; we have left the Sermon on the Mount out. Now we as individuals and as a culture are reaping the tragic results.

But the living Christ can bring glorious hope to us and to our world. After His resurrection, Jesus promised, "I am with you always." There is the encouragement for the discouraged. There is the hope for the hopeless. There is the help for the helpless. There is purpose and guidance and peace and power.

Turn to Jesus. He is with you . . . always.

WISDOM FOR TODAY

There is nothing of worldly value that is guaranteed to be with us always. Jobs, prestige, health, wealth, and family can all be gone in an instant. That's what makes Jesus' promise to be with us always and everywhere a source of comfort to all believers.

THE FAITH OF A CHILD

He called a little child and had him stand among them. . . .
And he said . . . "whoever humbles himself like this little
child is the greatest in the kingdom of heaven."
MATTHEW 18:2–4

Is it of any use to talk to young children about God and encourage them to give their lives to Jesus? Perhaps you are a parent, or you've taught a children's class in your church, and you've asked yourself this question. Or perhaps you made a decision for Jesus when you were a child, and you wonder if it really counted for anything.

But Jesus welcomed the children who flocked around Him: "Let the little children come to me, and do not hinder them, for the kingdom of heaven belongs to such as these" (Matthew 19:14). Their openness, their enthusiasm, their trust—all these delighted Jesus.

A young child may not understand everything about God—but he or she can understand something. A young child understands love and also understands what it means to obey someone. They—like us—can confess Jesus as their Lord and believe that Jesus came back to life for them. Don't ignore the children God brings across your path, but by your words and by your example tell them about Jesus.

WISDOM FOR TODAY
We must never underestimate a child's ability to understand and accept the Gospel. Let us never miss an opportunity, Father, to tell a young person about You.

DECEMBER

THE SECRET OF HIS STRENGTH

When you pray, go into your room, close the door and pray to your Father, who is unseen. Then your Father, who sees what is done in secret, will reward you.
MATTHEW 6:6

Recently I heard about the owner of a small factory who was greatly respected by his employees—not only for his business skills but for his integrity and his concern for his employees. They knew he went out of his way to be fair to them and that more than once during hard times he sacrificed the company's profits to keep his workers employed.

After his death one of his longtime employees was showing the man's grandson around the factory. "Do you want to know the secret of your grandfather's success?" he asked. "Certainly," the grandson replied, wondering what gems of wisdom he might learn. Wordlessly the employee led him to the rear of the factory, and then in one corner opened the door to what looked like a small storage closet. "This was the secret of his success," he said. "Every morning he slipped in here before anyone else arrived and spent at least half an hour in prayer. Prayer was the foundation of his life."

What is the foundation of your life?

WISDOM FOR TODAY

Lord, You modeled for Your followers a powerful and consistent prayer life. You prayed with Your disciples, and You often slipped away alone to spend time with the Father. May we also be known as people who make prayer a priority in our lives.

WE SHALL BE CHANGED

We know that when he appears, we shall be like him, for we shall see him as he is.

1 JOHN 3:2

I t's natural to wonder what heaven must be like. Are the streets really paved with gold? Will we know each other? What will we do with our time?

These and a hundred other questions crowd our minds—and to be honest, the Bible doesn't answer all our questions about heaven. Heaven is so glorious, and our hearts and minds are so limited, that we can only dimly perceive its grandeur. I often think of the apostle Paul's statement: "Now we see but a poor reflection as in a mirror; then we shall see face to face" (1 Corinthians 13:12).

But one truth about heaven is absolutely clear: we will be safely in God's presence forever. All the fears and insecurities and sorrows and disappointments that afflict us here will be banished. So, too, will all the weaknesses and sins and failures that mark our lives right now. We will be changed—for we will be like Christ! When life weighs you down, turn your heart to Christ—for someday you will see Him, and all life's burdens will be over.

WISDOM FOR TODAY

Whatever tragedy or loss we experience here below, Father, You've promised that it will dim in comparison with the glories that await us, and we believe Your Word to be true. We trust You to make all things new.

AN OPEN DOOR

What he opens no one can shut, and what he shuts no one can open. . . .
See, I have placed before you an open door that no one can shut.
REVELATION 3:7–8

When God opens a door, what possible excuse can we have for not going through it?

All over the world God is opening doors of opportunity today, making it possible for us to take the Gospel to millions who have never heard of Christ. Some live in lands that have been freed in recent years from the grip of atheism; others are immersed in a rising tide of secularism or religious oppression. But in spite of the barriers—and they are real—God is opening doors today in unexpected ways for the preaching of the Gospel. Will we fail to go through them?

God may not call you to be a preacher or missionary (although He may). But what will you do to help the Church of Jesus Christ move through those open doors? Will you pray? Will you give? Will you go on a short-term mission project? Jesus said, "The harvest is plentiful, but the workers are few. Ask the Lord of the harvest, therefore, to send out workers into his harvest field" (Matthew 9:37–38).

WISDOM FOR TODAY

Reveal to us, Father, the part You would have us play in the spread of the Gospel. Show us how we can use our gifts and abilities to make Your name known around the globe.

THE EXACT IMAGE OF GOD

"Anyone who has seen me has seen the Father."
JOHN 14:9

Many respect Jesus' moral teachings; they may even respect Him for His impact on civilization. But one part of His teachings shocked and offended many of His hearers, and do so to this day.

The offending teaching? It was His teaching about Himself. Repeatedly Jesus made the most startling claim imaginable: He was God in human flesh. He wasn't just a man (although He was that); He was also God. Think of it: the great and powerful God of the universe came down to earth and took upon Himself human flesh!

But His teaching about Himself didn't stop there. He went on to say that because He was divine, He was without sin—and because He was without sin, He could become the sin-bearer for the human race. All our sins would be placed on Him, and He would take upon Himself the death and hell we deserve. And this is what happened.

Don't ever lose sight of who Jesus was: God in human flesh. And don't ever lose sight of what He did: He died for you, because He loves you.

WISDOM FOR TODAY

You stepped down from Your throne, Lord, and came to earth knowing that the cross awaited You. May we never forget the price You paid and never question the magnitude of Your love.

DANGER ZONE

In them is fulfilled the prophecy of Isaiah:
"You will be ever hearing but never understanding;
you will be ever seeing but never perceiving."
MATTHEW 13:14

The person who is in the most danger spiritually is the one who doesn't see any need for God. They may enjoy life; they may be successful and looked up to by others. They may be moral and honest and even be outwardly religious (although only outwardly, because it hasn't touched their hearts).

But they live only for the moment, giving no real thought to eternity or the place God should have in their lives. They may give a fleeting thought to such things when they have to attend a friend's funeral—but for practical purposes, they are like the hard ground in Jesus' parable on which the Word of God falls, but "the devil comes and takes away the word from their hearts" (Luke 8:12).

Do you know people like this—even in your own family? Only God can break through the barrier of a heart that has no place for Him. That is why the most important thing you can do is to pray for them. Don't give up; God is able to do what we cannot do.

WISDOM FOR TODAY

No one is beyond Your reach, Father. We will not give up on seeing our un-saved loved ones come to know You. Open their blinded eyes, Lord, and draw them to You before it's too late.

DON'T CHEAPEN GOD'S GRACE

What shall we say then? Shall we go on sinning so that grace may increase?
By no means! We died to sin; how can we live in it any longer?

ROMANS 6:1–2

If God will forgive us when we sin—no matter what we do—then why bother trying to be good? All we need to do is ask for forgiveness, and He'll grant it, won't He? So why try to avoid sin?

But the Bible tells us that this kind of thinking makes a mockery of God's forgiveness and grace. It makes a mockery, too, of Jesus' death on the cross, for Christ died not just to forgive us but to free us from sin. The Bible says, "Sin shall not be your master" (Romans 6:14). When we keep on sinning without ever attempting to turn from it or restrain it, it is because we are still sin's slaves.

Never forget that sin is God's enemy—and Satan's friend. Sin is so serious that it caused Jesus Christ to leave heaven's glory and come into the world to die as the final and complete sacrifice for sin. Don't take sin lightly. Repent of it when it rears its ugly head, and with God's help cast it out of your life.

WISDOM FOR TODAY

Reveal to us, Lord, any sins that continue to have a hold in our lives. May we repent of them and turn to You so we can experience the forgiveness and freedom available to us.

357

SERVING WITH A PURE HEART

Delight yourself in the LORD
and he will give you the desires of your heart.
PSALM 37:4

How do you draw the line between your own desires and God's will for you? It isn't always easy.

Take, for example, someone who loves to sing. They are good at it, they enjoy it, they love being around people who like to sing also. Would it be wrong for them to join the church choir? Would they be doing it just because they enjoyed it . . . or even because they liked to show off their talent and have others praise them? Or because they were sincerely seeking to serve God?

This may not be your problem; you may be like me and hardly able to carry a tune! But the question of our motives—why we do what we do—is always with us.

It's not wrong to enjoy something, as long as it's good and honorable.

God may even have gifted you in certain ways, and it would be wrong to deny those gifts. But always commit your motives to Christ and seek His will in everything—even in things you enjoy.

WISDOM FOR TODAY

Whether we are fasting, praying, giving, or serving, our motives matter to You, Lord. You do not take pleasure in things done for our own glory. Help us make much of You in all we do.

THE BREVITY OF LIFE

Show me, O LORD, my life's end
and the number of my days;
let me know how fleeting my life is.
PSALM 39:4

I was speaking at a university, and afterward the students were invited to ask questions. I'll never forget the question one student asked: "What has been the biggest surprise of your life?" Almost without thinking I replied, "The brevity of life."

It's true; life is short, and the older you get, the more you realize it. Events that happened thirty years ago seem like they took place just yesterday—but when your mind turns to the future, you realize just how short life is. None of us knows how much more time we'll have, but even if God gives us a long life by most standards, our time is still brief. In the Psalmist's words, "Each man's life is but a breath" (Psalm 39:5).

Don't waste your life on things that have no eternal value. Draw closer to Christ, and make each day count for Him. See each day as a gift from His hand, and use it for His glory. The Bible says, "Teach us to number our days aright, that we may gain a heart of wisdom" (Psalm 90:12).

WISDOM FOR TODAY

We all want our lives to matter, Father. We know that tomorrow isn't promised to us, so help us take every opportunity to love others better, to serve You more, and to live out examples of godliness.

WHERE IS HIS PEACE?

Glory to God in the highest,
and on earth peace to men on whom his favor rests.
LUKE 2:14

On that memorable night in the Judean hills of Bethlehem two thousand years ago, this was the song of the angels. Though the centuries have rolled by, still the world longs for and looks for the peace that the angels announced. Where is this peace?

Clearly it is not evident in the world, with its constant fighting and conflicts. This peace abides instead in the hearts of all those who have trusted in God's grace. In the same proportion that the world has trusted Christ, it has peace. There can be no lasting peace until Christ has come to the hearts of all people and brought them His peace.

There is no discord in heaven, and there is no strife in heaven, for Christ reigns supreme there. Similarly, in the heart where Christ abides and reigns, His words become a reality: "Peace I leave with you" (John 14:27). The truth of these words has been proven in human experience over and over again. Thank your heavenly Father today for the times they have proven true for you.

WISDOM FOR TODAY

Thank You, Father, for the times we have experienced Your peace in the midst of pain. No diagnosis, news headline, or earthly loss can remove Your peace from the heart that trusts in You.

FOLLOW—NOW!

Another disciple said to him, "Lord, first let me go and bury my father."

But Jesus told him, "Follow me, and let the dead bury their own dead."
MATTHEW 8:21–22

At first Jesus' words here sound harsh and insensitive. After all, if this man's father has died, wouldn't it be compassionate to let him go and arrange for his burial?

But in all likelihood this man's father was still alive (although infirm), and what he was saying was that someday in the future—maybe months or even years later—he would be willing to follow Jesus. (Burial in those days was usually carried out within hours of a person's death, and if the father had already died his son probably wouldn't be away from home listening to Jesus.) But Jesus told him that nothing—absolutely nothing—must stand in the way of being His disciple.

Many people are willing to have Jesus as part of their lives—as long as it doesn't cost them anything. They may even profess faith in Jesus and join a church. But Jesus to them is almost like an insurance policy—something they obtain and then forget about until they die. But Jesus calls us to follow Him every day. What keeps you from being His disciple?

WISDOM FOR TODAY

You are our first love, Jesus, and we will follow You all of our days. We will not choose the gifts we've been given—be it family, careers, or pleasures—over You. Help us to keep You first in our lives.

THE CHRISTMAS CRUNCH

When they saw the star, they were overjoyed. On coming to the house, they saw the child with his mother Mary, and they bowed down and worshiped him.
MATTHEW 2:10–11

I t may sound like Scrooge—but do you almost hate to see Christmas coming? It's such a busy time, and our spending easily gets out of control. Instead of a season of peace and goodwill, it becomes a season of exhaustion and resentment.

Of course Christmas shouldn't be this way—nor does it need to be. One key is good planning—keeping track of commitments, saying no to things we don't really need to do, knowing in advance what we have to spend—and sticking to it. And don't leave everything to the last minute!

But there is a deeper solution to having a good Christmas—and that is to rediscover its true meaning. At Christmas we celebrate the birth of Jesus Christ, who came down from heaven to save us from our sins. May you see His glory this Christmas season!

WISDOM FOR TODAY

During this Christmas season, Lord, help us to remove anything that serves to distract us from You. May our activities, attitudes, and acts of service all point others to the miracle of God coming to earth as a baby.

THE VICTOR

"Is anything too hard for the LORD? I will return to you at the appointed time next year and Sarah will have a son."
GENESIS 18:14

Can you blame Abraham and Sarah for doubting God's promise that within a year she would bear a son? Sarah had been childless all their married life, and now she was approaching the age of ninety. Could anything be more impossible? Humanly speaking, they were right; ninety-year-old women simply do not bear children.

But God gently reminded them that He was sovereign, and nothing was too hard for Him. And the following year the impossible happened: Isaac was born. God's promise to Abraham that he would become the father of a great nation (and the ancestor of Jesus Christ) could now be fulfilled.

Remember Abraham and Sarah the next time you encounter what seems to be an insurmountable problem. Nothing was too hard for God then—and nothing is too hard for Him today. If it were, why would we pray? But God is still sovereign over His creation, and He is still at work. That doesn't mean He always answers the way we wish He would—but never doubt His power, and never doubt His love.

WISDOM FOR TODAY

God has always been in the miracle-working business. There is no obstacle that He can't overcome for us, and there's nothing too difficult for Him to do. He still heals diseases, makes a way when there is no way, and changes human hearts.

THE GOD OF ALL COMFORT

Praise be to the God and Father of our Lord Jesus Christ, the Father of compassion and the God of all comfort, who comforts us in all our troubles, so that we can comfort those in any trouble.

2 CORINTHIANS 1:3–4

Does God honestly care about what is going on in our lives? When hard times hit or illness strikes, does He really care?

The answer is yes—a thousand times yes! When the apostle Paul wrote these words, he had just endured one of the hardest times in his life: "We were under great pressure, far beyond our ability to endure, so that we despaired even of life" (2 Corinthians 1:8). But in the midst of it God assured him of His compassion and presence, and in time God brought Paul through the trials he was experiencing and opened the door to new opportunities.

But why did God allow Paul to go through this experience? One reason is so he would be able to "comfort those in any trouble." Are you going through a difficult time? Thank God for His compassion, and then ask Him to teach you how to comfort others in their trials. Remember: God knows what it is to suffer, for His Son suffered on the cross for you.

WISDOM FOR TODAY

It's tempting to want to move on from difficult times as quickly as possible and never think of them again. Help us instead, Lord, to meditate on the ways You've delivered us and how we may be a source of hope to someone else.

LIVING IN HARMONY

Finally, all of you, live in harmony with one another; be sympathetic, love as brothers, be compassionate and humble . . . because to this you were called.

1 PETER 3:8–9

Have you ever asked yourself why some people aren't interested in becoming Christians? There are many reasons, of course, running the gamut from violent rebellion against God to ignorance of the Gospel.

But if you took a poll of people you and I pass every day on the street, many would say that the main reason they aren't attracted to the Christian faith—is the Christians they know. Some repel them by their self-righteousness; others show no love or compassion; still others show little concern for the world and its problems. Most of all, they'll point out, Christians can't seem to get along with each other. Why should we believe in Christ (they say) when He doesn't seem to make any difference in the lives of His followers?

Some of what they say isn't valid—but some of it is, and it should be a rebuke to those of us who claim to follow Christ. But our primary calling is to demonstrate to an unbelieving world the love and transforming power of Jesus Christ. Do others see Him in you?

WISDOM FOR TODAY

Lord, we want our love for You to be evident in all we say and do. Help us live and love in such a way that people see something different in us, and the testimony of obedient lives will draw others to You.

HE WILL BE CALLED WONDERFUL

He will be called Wonderful Counselor, Mighty God,
Everlasting Father, Prince of Peace.
ISAIAH 9:6

My dictionary defines *wonderful* as anything that is so unusual or magnificent that it causes wonder and amazement. What a description of Jesus! First, Jesus was wonderful in His preexistence. As the perfect man who was also God, He existed from all eternity. Only He is equally at home in heaven and on earth.

Jesus was wonderful in His birth. To right the wrongs of the world and redeem a fallen race, God did not send His heavenly angelic armies. He sent a tiny, tender, helpless Babe in the Person of His Son to accomplish this majestic purpose—born not of man but of the Holy Spirit.

Jesus was wonderful in His life. He mingled with sinners, yet His enemies could find not one single flaw in His character. His miracles and His teaching both testified to His divine authority.

Christ was also wonderful in His death. He died for others just as He had lived for others: To make our salvation possible. And this death led to the wonderful, glorious resurrection, opening for us the door to heaven and eternal life.

Jesus is wonderful indeed!

WISDOM FOR TODAY

The word *wonderful* seems so inadequate to describe You, Lord. We long for the day when we can fall at Your feet and praise You.

THE PROMISE OF REST

The LORD is my shepherd, I shall not be in want.
He makes me lie down in green pastures,
he leads me beside quiet waters, he restores my soul.

PSALM 23:1–3

No Psalm is better known or better loved than Psalm 23, which probably owes its origin (at least humanly speaking) to David's boyhood years as a shepherd. But has it become so familiar to us that we have forgotten its riches?

Look at the verses above. They tell us first of all that God is like a shepherd to us—guiding us, keeping us safe, protecting us from our enemies, giving us everything we need to sustain our lives. But they also hint at our tendency to wander and get in trouble, like the lost sheep in one of Jesus' parables (Luke 15:1–7). And so He "makes" us lie down in green pastures, and He "leads" us to quiet waters—things we might not do on our own.

What kind of "sheep" are you? Rebellious, prone to wander, resisting the gentle prodding of the Shepherd? Or gratefully submitting to His wisdom and His ways? Remember Jesus' words: "I am the good shepherd; I know my sheep and my sheep know me" (John 10:14).

WISDOM FOR TODAY

Left to our own devices, Father, we would wander off for sure. Help us stay close to You through daily prayer and Bible study so we recognize and respond to the call of the Shepherd.

JOY, HOPE, PATIENCE, AND PRAYER

Be joyful in hope, patient in affliction, faithful in prayer.
ROMANS 12:12

Discouragement and depression can come for many reasons. We all brush up against them—when we lose someone to death, for example, or experience a problem that overwhelms us. Depression may even come from chemical imbalances in our bodies; when that is the case, modern medicine often can help.

At the same time, when we feel discouraged or depressed we need to turn to God in prayer and commit the situation into His hands. This isn't a substitute for medical treatment if we need it; God ordained the physical laws that govern our bodies, and He can use the insights of medical science to bring healing. But ultimately our lives are in His hands, and when we face problems of any kind we need to turn to Him.

God wants us to be aware of His presence and His love during those often lonely roads. Knowing He is with us gives us hope—and from that hope, joy. We also find patience as we rest in His sovereign power and plan. And besides, where else can we turn but to Him?

Whatever you're dealing with, may you discover this truth in a new way: "The eternal God is your refuge, and underneath are the everlasting arms" (Deuteronomy 33:27).

WISDOM FOR TODAY

May we always allow times of hardship to draw us closer to You, Lord. Help us to be patient as You work to accomplish Your will even in our trials.

GOD IN THE FLESH

The Lord Himself will give you a sign: The virgin will be with child and will give birth to a son, and will call him Immanuel [which means God with us.]
ISAIAH 7:14

Jesus Christ lived only thirty-three years, yet He transformed civilization. And after two thousand years, countless millions worship Him.

Where did He come from? When He was born of the virgin Mary in a stable in Bethlehem, that was not His origin; that was His Incarnation—His coming in the flesh. The Bible teaches that He is God in human flesh, God Incarnate. Jesus—the eternal Son of God—never had a beginning; He will never have an end. He always was and He always will be.

When Jesus walked this earth, He made the blind to see, the deaf to hear, and the dumb to speak. He was the greatest teacher of all time, and He was also a man of compassion, love, and selflessness.

Yet consider the emphasis on His death. Three chapters in the book of Matthew, three in Mark, three in Luke, and six in John are devoted to the last twenty-four hours of Jesus' life. Why? Because Jesus was born to die as the final and perfect sacrifice for your sins and mine.

Praise Him this holy season!

WISDOM FOR TODAY

Let us never forget that the baby in the manger became the man on the cross. God, You came to earth knowing that You would suffer and die. We celebrate Your earthly birth and praise You that it made our rebirth possible.

THE CHRIST OF CHRISTMAS

Today in the town of David a Savior has been born to you; he is Christ the Lord.
LUKE 2:11

The famed movie director Cecil B. DeMille once told me that his film *The King of Kings*, made during the silent-movie era, was seen by an estimated 800 million people. I asked him why he didn't reproduce *The King of Kings* with sound and color. He replied, "I will never be able to do it, because if I gave Jesus a southern accent, the northerners would not think of Him as their Christ. If I gave Him a foreign accent, the Americans and the British would not think of Him as their Christ. As it is, people of all nations, from every race, creed, clan, can accept Him as their Christ."

Jesus came for us all—and today He can be your Christ. Today you and I can know the Christ of Christmas—who alone can wipe away our tears, lift our burdens, solve our problems, forgive our sins, and make us new. Your Christmas will be joyful indeed as you discover these truths!

One more thing: to whom will you introduce the Christ of Christmas?

WISDOM FOR TODAY

God sent His Son because of His immense love for the entire world. Jesus' death and resurrection make it possible to have access to the Father. Who in our lives today needs to hear the Good News?

MARY'S EXAMPLE

The angel said to her, "Rejoice, highly favored one, the Lord is with you;
blessed are you among women! . . . And behold, you will conceive in
your womb and bring forth a Son, and shall call His name Jesus."
LUKE 1:28, 31 NKJV

Mary was no more than a teenager when the angel Gabriel appeared before her with this astounding announcement. And her response offers us one of the most remarkable demonstrations of faith found in the Bible.

Mary was a virgin, engaged to a godly man by the name of Joseph, yet she was to be made pregnant supernaturally by the Holy Spirit. People would talk, shame would be attached to the pregnancy, and Joseph would probably leave her. But by faith Mary said to Gabriel, "I am the Lord's servant. May it be to me as you have said" (Luke 1:38).

Mary accepted God's will for her life, no matter what it might cost her. Following her example, I pray that God would give me grace and courage to be faithful to Him, no matter what price I may be called on to pay. May that be your prayer as well.

WISDOM FOR TODAY

We choose to humbly accept Your will for our lives, Father. We will trust You when You take us places we never intended to go and when You call us to do things we never thought we would do. Our lives are in Your hands.

THE INCARNATION

The Word was God . . . [and] the Word became flesh
and made his dwelling among us.
JOHN 1:1, 14

The word *Incarnation* comes from the Latin word *incarnatus*, meaning "to be made flesh." This great mystery of God's Incarnation—of God coming to earth in the Person of Jesus—is the message over which rationalists stumble, humanists are offended, and the world is bewildered. The unbelieving mind is confused by this truth, which runs counter to human wisdom.

The apostle Paul, reasoning with intellectual Greeks and Romans, said, "Beyond all question, the mystery of godliness is great: He appeared in a body, was vindicated by the Spirit, was seen by angels, was preached among the nations, was believed on in the world, was taken up in glory" (1 Timothy 3:16).

Sinful people are incapable of coming to God by their own efforts, so God in love and mercy descended to earth to save us. The creature could not go up to the Creator—so the Creator came down to redeem His creation. May the Holy Spirit of God confirm in your heart the wondrous mystery of the Incarnation.

WISDOM FOR TODAY

The Incarnation is a stumbling block to many, Lord, because they can't fathom that the God of the universe would humble Himself in such a way. Open the blinded eyes so they would see the truth of the Gospel.

God's Perfect Timing

When the time had fully come, God sent his Son, born of a woman.
GALATIANS 4:4

Someone once asked me why Jesus wasn't born many centuries earlier, in a less populated world and at a time when He might have had a much greater impact. That's an interesting thought, but Jesus was born when He was—neither sooner nor later—because God knew it was the best moment for Him to come.

Take, for instance, the fact that Jesus was born during the height of the Roman Empire. Unlike previous empires, the Romans built roads from one end of their vast territory to the other. These highways enabled the early Christians to spread the news about Jesus throughout the civilized world in only a few decades—something they never could have done if Jesus had come earlier.

Also, by then the human race had tried all kinds of religions and philosophies, yet none had satisfied the deepest longings of the human heart or taken away the burden of guilt. Many people were now open to His message of hope and new life.

Know that God's timing is always perfect. It was then—and it is today.

Wisdom for Today
God, You knew the exact time when Jesus would be born, and You have predetermined the precise moment of His return. Help us patiently wait and trust in Your perfect timing in all areas of our lives.

NO VACANCY?

There was no room for them in the inn.
LUKE 2:7

Before we denounce the unfriendly citizens of Bethlehem, we should admit that many people still refuse to have room for Him. Millions remember Jesus' birthday and speak His name in holiday greetings, yet they consistently close their hearts to Him, saying in effect, "There is no room in my soul for Christ."

We hear great cries for tolerance—but consider the bigotry toward Jesus. There is no room for His Word in our culture, where our children are without reverence for God or faith in the Bible. There is no room for our Lord's creed of purity and self-denial when the media sends forth a constant barrage of profanity and indecency and materialism. There is no room for the promise of His cross and His blood. The angel's statement, "He will save his people from their sins" (Matthew 1:21), is rejected by those who deny that the Child in the manger is our Emmanuel, God with us.

What will you do to make more room in your heart—and in your life—for Jesus?

WISDOM FOR TODAY

It's easy, Lord, to fill our lives with so many pleasures and pursuits that we unintentionally leave no room for You. Give us the discipline to purge things from our hearts, calendars, and lives that take up space that should belong to You.

A MESSAGE IN THE NIGHT

There were shepherds living out in the fields nearby,
keeping watch over their flocks at night.

LUKE 2:8

The first Christmas worship service was conducted not in a temple, a cathedral, or a synagogue, but in the great outdoors. The tidings of Christ's birth echoed in the skies as the angel of the Lord proclaimed the good news to lowly shepherds.

Do you think it strange that this glad word was not first given to the priests, the scholars, or the Pharisees? The reason is clear: God speaks to those who are prepared in their hearts to listen. Apparently these humble shepherds were prepared, and therefore able to discern the voice from heaven above the noisy din of earth's confusion.

It is also significant that this angelic message was delivered at night. It was night not only because the sun had gone down but because the world was shrouded in spiritual and moral gloom—just as it is today. Often when things are darkest, God makes Himself known.

Is it night for you this Christmas season? If so, may Jesus reveal Himself to you in a powerful and real way. Like the shepherds, prepare your heart to hear His message—one of God's love, forgiveness, and peace—because Christ has come.

WISDOM FOR TODAY
God, You came to shepherds who were faithfully doing what shepherds do. May we, likewise, be found faithfully working when You call.

WHEN GOD'S SON CAME TO EARTH

[The shepherds] hurried off and found Mary and Joseph,
and the baby, who was lying in the manger.
LUKE 2:16

It would have been logical to expect God to tear open the heavens and descend to earth in majesty and power on that first Christmas night in Bethlehem—but He didn't.

Instead, on that quiet night, a virgin mother laid her squalling newborn into a manger designed to feed cattle. The lowing cows, the sweet-smelling hay, and the dark sky illumined by a magnificent star provided the setting. Humble shepherds joined the carpenter-husband to witness the miracle and praise God for what He was doing. The most significant drama of the centuries was unfolding—the drama of salvation that would ultimately take this Child to the cross.

Truly God works in mysterious ways, His wonders to perform. The wheels of His mercy and justice move quietly and silently, but they do move. The birth of Jesus Christ—the Son of God, our Savior—went unnoticed by the vast majority of the world that first Christmas night, but no event in human history was more significant. May His birth—and all it means—not go unnoticed in our lives!

WISDOM FOR TODAY

Christmas is the season that we set aside to celebrate God coming to earth in human flesh. But the reality of that occurrence should have an impact in our lives all year long. May Your presence in our lives not go unnoticed by those around us.

WELCOMING THE CHRIST

Being divinely warned in a dream that they should not return to Herod,
they departed for their own country another way. . . . Then Herod, when
he saw that he was deceived by the wise men, was exceedingly angry.

MATTHEW 2:12, 16 NKJV

In his fear and raging jealousy, King Herod responded to the newborn Jesus with bloodthirsty hostility: "Destroy Him! Let Him die while He is still in His cradle!" This response grew and swelled, until one day many years later it became a mad mob's terrifying roar: "Take him away! Take him away! Crucify him!" (John 19:15).

In many hearts, this cry is still being shouted. The world rejects its Messiah. If He would remain a gentle and mild Jesus, that would be all right. Or if He remained a mystical dreamer, that would be all right. But a reigning Christ, an invading Christ, a revolutionary Christ, a life-changing Christ—that is unacceptable to millions of people. That is a menace to their way of life. It damages their self-determination and strikes at the roots of their stubborn independence.

During this Christmas season, however, may you welcome this reigning Christ, invading Christ, revolutionary Christ, life-changing Christ into your life anew.

WISDOM FOR TODAY

Lord, we believe that You are who You claim to be, and we welcome Your rule in our lives. We release any areas where we have attempted to maintain control and ask that You be Lord over all that we are and all that we do.

WHY DID HE COME?

God was reconciling the world to himself in Christ,
not counting men's sins against them.

2 CORINTHIANS 5:19

Christianity has its roots in the deep, firm soil of history. Jesus' Incarnation—God invading human history with His presence in the form of man—is on the record. Every time you write the date, you attest to the fact that God entered human history.

Jesus came into the world so we might know that God cares how we live, what we believe, and how we will die. Jesus came to demonstrate to us that we were made to have a personal relationship with God. He came to bridge the gap that separated us from our Creator.

Every time Jesus fed the hungry, He was saying, "I am the bread of life" (John 6:35). Every time He healed someone, He was saying, "It hurts Me to see you in pain." Every time He lifted the burden of sin, He was saying, "Your heavenly Father is grieved when you remove yourself from His grace."

Every miracle Jesus performed and every word He spoke remind us that He came to reconcile a lost world to our loving, compassionate God. Has this happened to you?

WISDOM FOR TODAY

Thank You, Father, that when sin entered the garden, You had a rescue plan already in place. No matter what we've done, reconciliation and forgiveness are possible because of Jesus' death on the cross.

GOOD NEWS!

If every one of [the things Jesus did] were written down, I suppose that even the whole world would not have room for the books that would be written.

JOHN 21:25

In light of these words of John, we should not be surprised that we have four accounts of Jesus' life in the Bible, for each of the four Gospels gives us details about our Lord that are not found in the others.

As they wrote under the inspiration of the Holy Spirit, Matthew, Mark, Luke, and John each gave us a distinctive portrait of Jesus. Matthew, for example, shows us Jesus as the Messianic King, sent by God to fulfill the Old Testament's prophecies about a Savior. That is why Matthew quotes from the Old Testament so much, for "this has all taken place that the writings of the prophets might be fulfilled" (Matthew 26:56).

Never forget: these four accounts of Jesus' life aren't merely interesting stories. Instead, they are accurate, historical accounts of the most important event in human history: the coming of God's Son into the world. Because He came, we can know what God is like. And because He came, we can be saved from our sins. This is Good News—which is exactly what the word *Gospel* means.

WISDOM FOR TODAY

Thank You, Lord, for the pages of Scripture that give us glimpses into Your time here on earth. May we seek to imitate what we learn of You from the Gospel accounts: Your compassion for hurting people, Your hatred of sin, and Your intimacy with the Father.

FIX YOUR EYES ON JESUS

"The Spirit of the LORD is upon Me, Because He has anointed Me to preach the gospel to the poor."
LUKE 4:18 NKJV

The Man who read these words from Isaiah 61 and made this claim is Jesus of Nazareth, the Compassionate Christ. As Isaiah had prophesied, Jesus made the blind to see, the crippled to walk, and the deaf to hear. We live in a world filled not only with physical suffering but problems like guilt, loneliness, emptiness, and fear. Jesus is interested in suffering people. If we are believers, we should be too.

Jesus is also the Crucified Christ. Good works won't get us to heaven. Only what Jesus did when He died in our place and shed His blood can open heaven's door for us.

In addition, Jesus is the Conquering Christ. He rose from the dead as the Conqueror of sin and death and hell. Because the Risen Jesus holds the keys of hell and death, we don't ever have to experience them for ourselves.

And finally, Jesus is the Coming Christ: someday He will return to establish His kingdom of peace and blessing.

May your faith and hope be in Christ—today and always!

WISDOM FOR TODAY
Everything about Your birth, death, resurrection, and return is good news for those who have put their faith in You, Lord.

OUR UNCHANGING GOD

"I the LORD do not change."
MALACHI 3:6

God is the same yesterday, today, and tomorrow. And because He is unchanging, He is utterly trustworthy and faithful.

God is unchanging in His holiness: "Holy, holy, holy is the LORD Almighty!" (Isaiah 6:3).

God is unchanging in His demand for holiness and integrity in our lives: "Consecrate yourselves and be holy, because I am holy" (Leviticus 11:44; 1 Peter 1:15–16).

God is unchanging in His judgment: He will judge all the earth, welcoming some into His eternal presence and sending others to eternal death (Matthew 7:22–23).

God is unchanging in His love: He sent His Son to die on the cross for us sinners. The Bible says, "God demonstrates his own love for us in this: While we were still sinners, Christ died for us" (Romans 5:8).

God's way of salvation has not changed. The same message—the message of Jesus' sinless life, His sacrificial death, Jesus' victorious resurrection—that has transformed lives in the past transforms lives today.

May our devotion to our unchanging God never waver but only grow stronger with each day as we walk with Him!

WISDOM FOR TODAY
There is comfort in knowing the character of God. He is not fickle, uncertain, or able to be manipulated. We trust Him to be who He has always been.

LOOKING BACK

One thing I do: Forgetting what is behind and straining toward
what is ahead, I press on toward the goal to win the prize for
which God has called me heavenward in Christ Jesus.
PHILIPPIANS 3:13–14

What are your thoughts as you look back over the last year? Was it a year of heartache and loss, tragedy and sorrow? Or happiness and joy, success and achievement? Or something in between? Do you close the book on this year with regret or with relief?

No matter what your answer is, I hope you will pause and prayerfully ask yourself two important questions. First, how do you think God looks on this past year in your life? Did it bring you any closer to Him? Did it expose any weaknesses or find you wandering from His way? Was He disappointed in your responses to its challenges?

Second, what lessons will you take from this year into the next? What did God teach you? What did He try to teach you? What needs to change—and how will it happen?

Don't be bound by the past and its failures; Paul's goal was to forget the past and press on in obedience to Christ. But don't forget its lessons either.

WISDOM FOR TODAY

We are grateful for the triumphs and the trials, Father, knowing that You were present in them all. May the new year bring us new opportunities to trust You more, grow our faith, and live out the Gospel.

ABOUT THE AUTHOR

Billy Graham, world-renowned preacher, evangelist, and author, delivered the gospel message to more people face-to-face than anyone in history and ministered on every continent of the world in more than 185 countries. Millions have read his inspirational classics, including *Angels, Peace with God, The Holy Spirit, Hope for the Troubled Heart, How to Be Born Again, The Journey, Nearing Home, Hope for Each Day,* and *The Reason for My Hope.*

MY DEVOTIONAL THOUGHTS